ALA PROGRAMMING GUIDES

5-Star
Programming and Services for Your 55+ Library Customers

American Library Association
Chicago
2003

Barbara T. Mates

While extensive effort has gone into ensuring the reliability of information appearing in this book, the publisher makes no warranty, express or implied, on the accuracy or reliability of the information, and does not assume and hereby disclaims any liability to any person for any loss or damage caused by errors or omissions in this publication.

Composition and design by ALA Editions in Janson Text and Formata using QuarkXPress 5.0 for the PC

Printed on 50-pound white offset, a pH-neutral stock, and bound in 10-point coated cover stock by McNaughton & Gunn

The paper used in this publication meets the minimum requirements of American National Standard for Information Sciences—Permanence of Paper for Printed Library Materials, ANSI Z39.48-1992.∞

Library of Congress Cataloging-in-Publication Data

Mates, Barbara T.
      5-star programming and services for your 55+ library customers / by Barbara T. Mates.
          p.   cm. — (ALA programming guides)
      Includes bibliographical references and index.
      ISBN 0-8389-0843-8
      1. Libraries and the aged—United States. 2. Adult services in public libraries—United
States. I. Title: Five star programming for your fifty-five plus library customers. II. Title.
III. Series.
Z711.92.A35 M38 2003
027.6′22—dc21   2002151504

Printed in the United States of America

07   06   05   04   03   5   4   3   2   1

*This book is dedicated to my mother, Ann Trask,
and my father, the late Tony Trask,
and to my husband, James.
Your love and caring are essential to my being.*

*This book is also offered in memory of
our lifelong friend, Gloria Sanson,
who took seriously ill
and died as this book was being written.
You are missed by us all!*

CONTENTS

FIGURES   *xi*

ACKNOWLEDGMENTS   *xiii*

INTRODUCTION   *1*

1   Who Are All These Older People and Where Do They Live?   7

The Fifty-Plus Population Is Financially "in Control"   *7*

The Fifty-Plus Population Believes in Advocacy   *8*

Leisure Time Is Important to the Fifty-Plusers   *8*

Aging Is Also about Diversity   *8*

The Senior Class of Baby Boomers (Ages Fifty-Five to Sixty)   *9*

Looking at the Population Aged Sixty to Seventy   *10*

Looking at the Population Aged Seventy to Eighty-Five   *11*

Looking at the Population Aged Eighty-Five and Older   *11*

Where Do They Live?   *12*

Which States Saw the Largest Increase in the Older Population?   *12*

Where Will We See Future Population Growth?   *13*

Using the Numbers for Planning Purposes   *13*

Conclusion   *13*

2   Special Needs within the Older Generation   *15*

Aging and Vision   *16*

Hearing Loss   *16*

Changes in Mobility and Dexterity   *16*

Cognitive Changes   *16*

A Word about Alcohol and Prescription Abuse   *17*

Creating a Usable Environment for Older Adults with Impairments   *17*
The Americans with Disabilities Act (ADA)   *17*
Seniors with Vision Impairments   *18*
Helping Overcome Hearing Loss in the Library   *21*
Appropriate Furnishings for Seniors with Impairments   *22*
Useful Items for Persons with Limited Dexterity and Mobility   *24*
Wheels in the Library   *25*
Libraries Helping Seniors at Home   *25*
Conclusion   *26*

3   Staff and Seniors   *27*

Respect Basic Human Needs   *27*
Practice Good Manners   *28*
Select a Leader and Pursue Ongoing Training   *28*
Establish Service Guidelines   *28*
Serving Older Patrons Who Are Blind or Have Low Vision   *29*
Hire Seniors as Staff   *32*
Conclusion   *33*

4   Programming for Seniors   *34*

Program Planning for Seniors Begins with Seniors   *34*
Finding the Seniors to Ask   *35*
Establishing a Senior Advisory Board   *35*
Partnering with Community Groups   *36*
Creating Partnerships for Seniors   *36*
The Successful Senior Program   *36*
Basic Rules for Program Planning   *36*
Types of Programs   *37*
Computer Training   *40*
Book Talks and Book Discussions   *40*
AARP 55 Alive   *41*
Older Adults Month   *41*
Conclusion   *41*

5   Older Adults and Reading   *43*

Special Media and Collection Development   *44*
Book Talks   *44*
Book Discussion Groups for Seniors   *44*
Book Discussion Groups for New Senior Readers   *47*
Conclusion   *48*

6 Outreach Library Programming *49*

Staff, Planning, Partners, and Volunteers Needed *50*
Library Services in Nursing Homes *50*
Books and Media by Van and Cart *54*
Library Services in Senior Centers *55*
Library Services in Senior Housing or Assisted-Living Facilities *55*
Library Services to the Homebound *56*
Library Service to Seniors Using Mobile Services *56*
Bringing Programming into the Senior Environment *57*
Extending the Senior Book Club to the Community and Vice Versa *60*
Computer Training *60*
Conclusion *61*

7 Computers and Seniors *63*

Profile of Seniors Currently Online *64*
Outfitting the Library's Computers for Senior Hands and Eyes *64*
A Comfortable Work Space for Seniors *66*
Software for Seniors—Screen Magnification Programs *66*
Software for Seniors—Screen Reading Programs *66*
Microsoft Programs *66*
Seniors as Learners—Providing the Right Training Tools *67*
Introducing the Computer to Seniors *67*
Instructing Seniors *68*
What to Teach *69*
Using the Library's Website as an Instructional Resource *71*
Conclusion *72*

8 Seniors and Accessible Websites *76*

Website Considerations for Seniors *76*
The Model Senior Website *77*
Building a Links Library for Seniors *81*
Focused Forums for Senior Surfers *81*
Conclusion *82*

9 Preparing and Distributing Marketing and Informational Materials for Senior Programs *83*

How Is Marketing to Seniors Different? *83*
Use the Print Media *84*
Content Should Be Easy to Read *84*

Consider Translating the Text for Non-English-Speaking Audiences   *84*

Format the Text   *86*

Test the Documents   *88*

Where Do You Distribute Promotional Materials?   *88*

Reach Seniors through Radio and Television   *90*

Reach Seniors Using Promotional Items   *90*

Reach Seniors through Word of Mouth   *90*

Conclusion   *91*

10   Funding Senior Programs   *92*

Foundations: A Good Source for Funding New Programs   *93*

The Basics of Successful Grant Proposals   *93*

Answer Questions Before They Are Asked   *93*

Proposal Elements   *94*

Why Grant Makers Give a Thumbs Up   *95*

Keep in Touch and Say Thank You   *95*

Local and Small Foundations   *95*

National Funding Organizations   *96*

Government Funds and Assistance   *96*

Theme Grants   *96*

Your Local Wal-Mart   *97*

Funding from Friends and Neighbors   *97*

Nonfinancial Contributions   *97*

Using the Web for Fund-Raising   *98*

Conclusion   *98*

AFTERWORD

Reaffirming the Need for Senior Services   *101*

APPENDIX 1

Resources   *105*

APPENDIX 2

Suggested Bookmarks for Seniors   *113*

APPENDIX 3

Proven Five-Star Senior Programming Initiatives   *121*

INDEX   *151*

FIGURES

I-1   What Do You Know about Aging?   *3*

1-1   World Events during the Formative Years of Various Senior Age Groups   *9*

1-2   Estimated Percent of Older (65+) Population Growth to 2030   *10*

1-3   Percent of Population Age 65 and Older by State   *12*

2-1   Is Your Library Senior-Friendly?   *18*

2-2   Example of Fluorescent Task Lamp with Magnifier   *19*

2-3   Broad-Tip Pen Makes Writing More Visible   *19*

2-4   Signature Guide Allows Low-Vision People to Sign on the Line   *20*

2-5   CCTV Enlarges Text from Book   *20*

2-6   Ideal Adaptive Workstation   *23*

2-7   Key Handles and Reachers Can Assist People with Certain Types of Physical Impairments   *25*

5-1   To Get You Started: A Year's Worth of Book Discussion Titles for Senior Groups   *47*

6-1   Statement of Goals   *52*

6-2   Library Policies and Procedures Statement   *53*

6-3   Adult Read-Aloud Resources   *59*

7-1   Alternate Key Tops   *65*

7-2   Selling the Concept of Computer Use to Seniors   *67*

7-3   Multnomah County Library Online Tutorial Main Page   *72*

7-4   Multnomah County Library Online Tutorial for the Computer Desktop   *73*

8-1   Font Choice Makes a Difference   *77*

8-2   Designing Functional and Friendly Senior Library Websites   *78*

8-3   Tips on Formatting Senior-Friendly Web Content   *80*

8-4   Website Evaluation Checklist   *81*

9-1   A Sample Flyer That Uses Senior-Friendly Design   *85*

9-2   Tips for Formatting Printed Materials for Seniors   *86*

9-3   Chicago Public Library Caregiving Institute Flyer   *87*

ACKNOWLEDGMENTS

Although there is only one author listed for this work, it is the product of many. I wish to express my appreciation to all those who shared programming ideas and service delivery methods with me for this work. I can honestly say that meeting you (albeit via the Internet for most) made the gathering of information sheer enjoyment. I regret that I cannot possibly convey the joy and pleasure each of you brings to the profession of providing library services to older adults. I hope your creativeness and dedication is indeed contagious.

I would like to take this opportunity to call attention to the "foremothers" of library service to older adults, Clara Lucioli, Fern Long, and Linda Eastman, as well as those who worked with them, and offer a respectful thank-you from those of us who tread in your footsteps. These Cleveland Public Library librarians had the insight to realize that an organization such as the Live Long and Like It Club was needed by seniors in the greater Cleveland area and worked to establish and maintain the club. The Live Long and Like It Club became a model for senior library programming for decades, the tenets still being viable.

I thank my friends and colleagues (old and new) who helped facilitate my finding information, making contacts, and often just listening. I trust you to know who you are. Please know your generosity of time and spirit are a never-ending source of strength.

A special thank-you to my husband, James, for the graphics and the proofreading.

A big thank-you to Marlene "Marilyn" Chamberlain, ALA editor. The importance of your humor, guidance, and understanding while working together on this book cannot be overstated. I am sure I incorrectly called you *Marilyn* as many times as I called you *Marlene*, yet you maintained your grace and professionalism and spoke with me in spite of my mental block.

To Eloise Kinney, copy editor, thank you for caring about this project and doing such a thorough job editing the book. I enjoyed our electronic conversations and feel I have made a new friend. It is always helpful to find someone who resides on the same wavelength as it makes the editing process so much easier.

To Mary Huchting, I really appreciated having the opportunity to work with you again. Your common sense and astute judgment put me at ease.

To Dianne M. Rooney and Angela Gwizdala, the layout of this book really impressed me. You made everything fit without looking overcrowded.

I also wish to thank all of the American citizens, especially the booksellers, publishers, librarians, lawyers, and legislators such as Congressmen Dennis Kucinich, D-Ohio, and the late Paul Wellstone, D-Minnesota, who are willing to swim against the current to make and keep public information public.

Introduction

The statistics on the aging are irrefutable. The need is undeniable.
The library response is inadequate.

—Sylvia Crooks and Lois Bewley,
University of British Columbia's School
of Library, Archival, and Informational Studies

When talking professionally about service to "underserved" populations, what population do we immediately think about? Perhaps persons with disabilities, the homeless, minority populations, or those who are living in poverty. But one of the largest of the underserved library populations is seniors, or older adults.

Older adults can have disabilities; older adults can be living in poverty or can be homeless, wealthy, middle class, African American, Caucasian, Asian, Latino, American Indian, Alaska Native, Native Hawaiian, biracial, lesbian, gay, bisexual, or transgender. Simply put, service to older adults is indeed a cross-cultural concern, as they are a part of almost every library community.

But few libraries are developing programming that encourages the seniors seen in the community's shopping malls or places of worship to become library users. The reasons for this are unclear. Some administrators state that there is not a need for specialized services (older adults can blend into adult programming), while others claim that seniors simply do not have any interest in libraries. Some of the concerns simply come from preconceived notions of what it means to age.

1

Society and Aging

Generally speaking, our society does not value the aging process. In her work *The Fountain of Age*, Betty Friedan speaks of the misconceptions society nurtures when we think about "growing older." Friedan states that we tend to see aging as a "declining process" rather than the "liberating process" it could be.[1] We think growing older relegates our future to "grandparenting" filled with old memories, then memory loss, aches and pains, incontinence, and eventually the nursing home. Friedan, however, champions the reality that this is simply ageism. Although physical or psychological needs might send some people down a bleak road, most of us can, and will, experience life to its fullest.

What Is Ageism?

Robert Butler, who was the first director of the National Institute on Aging, identified the term *ageism* in 1969.[2] He classified ageism as a type of bigotry similar to racism and sexism, defining it as "a process of systematic stereotyping and discrimination against people because they are old."[3] In 1990 Erdman Palmore, a noted authority on ageism, identified it as "any prejudice or discrimination against, or in favor of, any age group."[4]

Ageism, like any other prejudice, is perpetuated by society. Daily we are bombarded by negative aging images on the airwaves and in print media. Advertisements from pharmaceutical manufacturers try to sell us drugs that promise to banish the pain of arthritis that comes with "age." In a tone used for expressing condolences or speaking with young children, assisted-living facilities insinuate "mom" or "dad" will be safer in their complexes than left alone to their own devices. Manufacturers of hygiene products guarantee older adults that they will "stay dry" and that their dentures will stay in place, allowing them to play with their grandchildren without embarrassment. The truth of the matter is that most people age differently, and many will not ever need the aforementioned products.

Ageism also exists because of the widespread use of demeaning language and negative humor about old age. Although polite society avoids derogatory terms about race and gender, terms and colloquialisms to describe a person who is older find their way into conversations with a wink and a laugh. Some of these terms include *geezer*, *old fogy*, or the classic *dirty old man*.[5] Baby boomers are becoming quite comfortable using the term *senior moment* to cover for temporary memory lapses.

In addition to jokes and digs directed toward aging, institutions help perpetuate ageism. If given the choice between hiring someone older than fifty-five or someone who is younger, businesses tend to choose the latter. Businesses have also been known to relocate senior staff members to smaller offices or promote staff members who are fifty or under, as they feel the younger staff members have families to support and more useful years left.[6] Human resource departments frequently have seminars relating to sexual harassment, yet few talk about ageist viewpoints as grounds for discrimination suits.[7] Ageism results in a general complacency about inadequate social provision for vulnerable older people.

Are You or a Coworker an Ageist?

As hard as it is to accept, many of us harbor ageist concepts simply because we see and hear comments and really do not think about what is being portrayed by the statement. However, by stepping back and taking a real look at what it means to get older, most of us will learn that getting older really does mean getting better, and age is just a number. To see if you or other staff members are dwelling among those tending to believe the many myths and stereotypes about aging, take the quick quiz in figure I-1. Before you answer, take a few minutes to think about friends, parents, coworkers, and patrons who are older. The correct answers and explanations for the answers are also given. If there is evidence of ageism within the institution, then it must be addressed.

Ageist No More

Combating ageism is not an easy task. Fortunately, there are advocacy groups, positive thinkers, and role models who can help defeat the negativity. Trying to put a positive spin on aging are membership groups like AARP (formerly known as the American Association of Retired Persons), CARP (Canada's Association for the Fifty-Plus), and the Gray Panthers. Groups like these constantly strive to present older adults as the diverse group of people that they are, that is, a group who can and will continue to learn as they grow.

FIGURE I-1
What Do You Know about Aging?

Answer True or False to the Following Statements on Aging

1. Everyone eventually becomes senile.
   False: only 20 to 25 percent of people age eighty or older become senile.
2. Depression is a serious problem for seniors.
   True: loss of self-esteem, loneliness, and anxiety increase as we age.
3. The numbers of older people are growing worldwide.
   True: the United Nations has acknowledged concern that the entire world is becoming older and has established guidelines for interactions.
4. Families in the United States have a tendency to abandon their older members.
   False: 80 percent of all men and 60 percent of all women live in family settings, as opposed to skilled-care facilities.
5. Intelligence declines with age.
   False: in many instances, intelligence increases as we age.
6. As we age, we need to take more vitamins and minerals to stay healthy.
   False: although we should cut down on salt, sweets, and fats, there is no reason to consume extra vitamins if we eat a balanced diet.
7. Everyone's sight and hearing has a tendency to decline with age.
   False: some people will never need hearing aids or corrective eye surgery.
8. Personality changes with age.
   False: we continue to be who we want to be as we age.
9. Many older people are hurt in accidents that could have been prevented.
   True: ensure that there is good lighting, reduction of glare, even surfaces, and nonskid flooring in all environments.
10. Older adult drivers have a tendency to have more accidents than their younger counterparts.
    False: older adults have fewer accidents.
11. Older adults are the fastest-growing group of computer users.
    True: although seniors constitute the smallest portion of the population using computers, their numbers are quickly growing.
12. Older adults as learners require more time to learn tasks and need more opportunity to practice new skills.
    True: instructions need to be broken into units of information. Older adults have a better chance of retaining the information if they can practice new skills immediately upon learning them.
13. Seniors have a difficult time eliminating irrelevant information.
    True: many seniors tend to think intuitively rather than linearly as they age.
14. Most seniors do not have much disposable income.
    False: people over age fifty account for 80 percent of the wealth of financial institutions.
15. Seniors tend to be generous, loving, caring, and kind.
    True and false: some people will possess these traits, but others will be narrow-minded, grouchy, and mean, same as in nearly every age group.

The information above was gleaned from or formulated using the following resources: Erdman Palmore, *The Facts of Aging* (New York: Springer, 1998); Joining Generations: An Intergenerational Programme of the McGill Centre for Studies in Aging Education Task Force, available at <http://www.healthandage.net/html/min/joining_gene/content/page4_1.htm>; Special Committee on Aging, "What Is Your Aging I.Q.?" (quiz prepared by the National Institute on Aging) in *Lifelong Learning for an Aging Society* (Washington, D.C.: Government Printing Office, 1991) and available at <http://www.crab.rutgers.edu/~deppen/agingIQ.htm>; and Plus Publications, 50 Plus Facts, available at <http://www.pluspubs.com/plus%20publications/50_plus_facts. htm>.

Senior-focused membership groups want the world to know that seniors can and do learn new tasks, such as surfing the Internet or surfing the Pacific Ocean. Diversity of the generations is always stressed, which involves pointing out the fact that some seniors will need special accommodations to "surf," and some will not.

The vitality and spirit of seniors, such as widely recognized people like John Glenn, Paul Newman, and Sophia Loren, as well as those who reside in the library's community, need to be promoted. Positive aging stresses that it is never too late to learn and that lifelong learning makes for a long life. What better place for seniors to learn than at the library?

Libraries Can Help Fight Aging and Alzheimer's Disease

David Demko, professor of gerontology and proponent of the enlightened approach to aging, maintains that "Seventy-five percent of human aging can be self-regulated. . . . Human beings need to keep physically and mentally active, setting goals, and work to keep their self-esteem high."[8]

Demko's beliefs are proven, in part, by a groundbreaking study conducted by Robert Friedland, a neurologist at Case Western Reserve University School of Medicine, in Cleveland, Ohio.[9] The study used a questionnaire addressing twenty-six lifetime "nonoccupational activities," such as playing a musical instrument, playing challenging board games, or learning a new language. The questionnaire was given to persons in their early seventies who had Alzheimer's disease (or their caregivers) and those who did not. The test results indicated that those who devoted time to intellectual activities from early adulthood through mid-adulthood had less of a chance of contracting Alzheimer's disease. Amir Soas, who coinvestigated this study, advises baby boomers who want to lower their chances of contacting Alzheimer's to "Read, read, read. Do crossword puzzles. Learn a foreign language or a new hobby."[10]

The library is the perfect place to pursue these interests.

Library Associations' Guidelines for Services to Older Adults

The American Library Association (ALA), the Canadian Library Association (CLA), and the International Federation of Library Associations and Institutions (IFLA), as well as many other library associations throughout the world, recognize the need to identify the idea of library services to older adults as a specialized concept. Sections and groups meet regularly to discuss ways in which services to older adults can be expanded.

Both the ALA and the CLA have succinct, clearly written guidelines that encourage a basic commitment to serving older adults. The ALA guidelines state, "It is essential for the leaders and policy makers of the library to understand that service for older adults is not a fad; that the need and demand for library services will only increase . . . and nothing short of a total moral and financial commitment to library services

for older adults will meet the needs and demands of the present and future older library user."[11] This, however, is not the road most libraries are taking.

Although most public libraries have such specialized positions as "Youth Services Coordinator," few libraries support a "Senior Services Coordinator." This is not to say that "Adult Services Coordinators" or "Outreach Coordinators" do not relegate segments of their agendas to services for older adults. Indeed, some coordinators achieve great results. By and large, however, there is a real void in the coordination of services to older adults.

Why Are There Special Needs and Demands for Older Adults?

If we are to think of older adults simply as adults who are older, why then are we talking about focusing our attention on specialized services for them? The reality is that each generation has its own commonalities that living through the same time brings.

The Commonality of Retirement

In the introduction of the CLA's guidelines, readers are reminded that although "older adults are not a homogenous population that can be easily categorized . . . and that within the broad category of 'older adults' lie several generations with different life experiences and different sets of experience . . . there are special circumstances that most older people share that service providers must take into account."[12]

The Commonality of a Shared History and Memories

E. J. Josey and Claudia Gollop, in their work "Improving Library Services to the Older Multicultural Community," wrote of the "challenge to develop quality library and information programs for a growing multicultural aging population . . . as in many instances, members of a multicultural population may not have had the opportunity to use public libraries and information services during their younger years, because of segregation and racism in certain parts of the country."[13] Josey and Gollop indicated that this group of older adults might feel that their lack of sophistication and their low literacy may cause them to think that they "do not belong in libraries."[14] The feeling of not belonging may be shared for other minority groups, such as Hispanic American seniors, Native Americans, and Americans who were naturalized in their youth but never learned to speak English well. Josey and Gollop's conclusion was that special efforts must be made to assure this group that the public library is open to them.

There are also examples of shared experiences that are not relegated to race but occur by simply living through the same events in time. Ask several generations what the original "Woodstock" is. Baby boomers will answer, "It was a time of music, free love, and fun." The baby boomers' parents will answer, "It was a disgusting, drug-filled orgy and a blight on morality." The baby boomers' children will more than likely identify Woodstock as the bird in the Peanuts comic strip.

It is the comfort of shared memories and emotions that helps some people learn more effectively and comfortably. Although some older adults may relish the thought of learning computer usage with their grandchildren, many find comfort in learning new tasks with their peers.

The Need for Library and Information Services for Older Adults—The 1995 White House Conference on Aging

The U.S. National Commission on Libraries and Information Science, the ALA, and the National Library Service for the Blind and Physically Handicapped of the Library of Congress sponsored a conference in February 1995 to determine what priorities and policies concerning the library and information needs for older adults should be addressed at the 1995 White House Conference on Aging, when it convened in May 1995. More than 200 persons participated, including lay citizens, library users, and librarians, who developed twenty-four policy recommendations. Conferees voted to determine which of the policy recommendations should be the five highest priorities when presented to the conference. The top-five recommendations, in priority ranking, follow:

1. *Older Adults and Federal Legislative Policy.* Any act that has an information component must include explicit identification of libraries as access points and agencies of implementation.

2. *Older Adults and Disabilities.* Libraries should be made accessible to older adults with disabilities by creating barrier-free access to buildings and continuing progress with online catalogs; providing a comfortable, user-friendly environment; and offering sensitivity training for staff members.

3. *Older Adults and Research, Education, and Training.* Federal, state, and local research initiatives should require multiagency collaboration.

4. *Older Adults and Lifelong Learning, Arts, and Humanities.* Programs for older Americans should be recognized as a critical component of the national, state, and local educational infrastructure, and their importance for the quality of intellectual and civic life is to be reflected in educational policies and funding at the national, state, and local levels.

5. *Libraries, Older Adults, and Technology.* In pending telecommunications reform legislation, preferential rates should be provided to libraries and similar institutions.[15]

The common thread of the recommendations centered around the themes of cooperation, adequate funding, and the establishment of library and information services to address the specialized information needs of the older adults who have little formal education or are disabled, cultural minorities, veterans, caregivers, rural elderly, or women. By comparing the priorities made with library services currently available for older adults, it can be seen that the recommendations were not adequately addressed.

One Senior's Challenge to Libraries

Some libraries, inspired by the preconference, developed programming for older adults but let them falter as funding cuts were made or something more pressing appeared on the horizon. Harold Ott, a then seventy-seven-year-old library user from Yeadon Public Library, testified at the preconference and set forth a challenge to libraries:

> Because [we] grow older, we do not become less interested in the world around us. Older people

are still alive, still growing, and still learning. For many of us libraries are the place where everything began. . . . It was a place where all was possible. The library is still a place we go to learn, to dream, and to imagine. . . . And now, with computers and the Internet, the opportunities and potentials for older adults are limitless . . . I hope libraries will meet the challenge.[16]

Five-Star Programming and Services was written to encourage libraries to take up the challenge set forward by Ott. Although some libraries throughout the world are conducting wonderful programming initiatives for seniors (*see* appendix 3 for some five-star programs), there is still much to be done. We need to start now to make the library environment accessible, educational, entertaining, and inviting. We need to make our services available to those who no longer are able to visit the library. We need to make our libraries places where we want to be, because, as Mary Jo Lynch, director of the ALA Office for Research and Statistics, discovered, between 2010 and 2014, 21 percent of all librarians will reach the age of sixty-five.[17]

NOTES

1. Betty Friedan, *The Fountain of Age* (New York: Simon & Schuster, 1993).
2. ModuleAgeism, Berkeley University Class Notes, available at <http://socrates.berkeley.edu/~aging/ModuleAgeism.html>.
3. Ibid.
4. Erdman Palmore, *Ageism: Negative and Positive* (New York: Springer, 1990).
5. ModuleAgeism.
6. Age Discrimination: A Pervasive and Damaging Influence [WWW home page of Administration on Aging], available at <http://www.aoa.gov/factsheets/ageism.html>.
7. ModuleAgeism.
8. Douglas Kalajian, "Five New Ways to Think about Aging," *Palm Beach Post*, June 21, 2001. Posted on the LifeExtension Foundation website, available at <http://www.lef.org/newsarchive/aging/june_2001.html>.
9. The research of Dr. Robert Friedland and Dr. Amir Soas, available at <http://www.aha.org/whatsnew/Dr_Friedland_Soas.htm.>
10. Ibid.
11. Library Services to Older Adults Guidelines, Library Services to an Aging Population Committee of the Management and User Services Section of the Reference and User Services Association of the American Library Association, available at <http://www.ala.org/rusa/stnd_older.html>.
12. Canadian Library Association Interest Group on Services for Older People and approved by the CLA Executive Council, November 24, 2000.
13. E. J. Josey and Claudia Gollop, "Improving Library Services to the Older Multicultural Community" (paper presented at the 1995 White House Conference on Aging, Washington, D.C., May 1995).
14. Ibid.
15. U.S. National Commission on Libraries and Information Science, *Toward the 1995 White House Conference on Aging: Priorities and Policies for Library and Information Services for Older Adults* (Washington, D.C., 1995).
16. Ibid., 44.
17. Mary Jo Lynch, "Reaching Sixty-Five: Lots of Librarians Will Be There Soon," *American Libraries* (March 2002): 56.

1

Who Are All These Older People and Where Do They Live?

We are in the midst of the most extraordinary evolutionary event of all time: the mass aging of our society.

—Ken Dychtwald, Age Wave

Today's older adults form a population that demands attention. Their sheer numbers, and their ability to influence the driving forces around them, cannot be ignored. In the year 2000, 2 million persons celebrated their sixty-fifth birthdays, but this number is expected to increase by 34 percent over the next two decades, which means by the year 2030, the older population will number about 70 million.[1] The U.S. Census Bureau states that, although there are only 70,000 centenarians living in the United States today, that number will jump to at least 834,000 by 2050 (a midrange estimate).[2]

Although each generation has unique challenges, one can look at the population that is currently fifty years of age or older and be impressed with the impact they have in so many facets of society.

The Fifty-Plus Population Is Financially "in Control"

When researchers combine generations of people older than fifty to determine market power, this group possesses some startling results! Men and women who are age fifty or older account for

more than $2 trillion in income;

80 percent of personal wealth in financial institutions;

50 percent of all discretionary spending power—2.5 times the average per capita; and

high home ownership. Of those who are fifty years of age or older, 79 percent own their own homes, of which approximately 67 percent are mortgage free.[3]

Marketing gurus are stressing the fact that corporations that want to remain solvent over the next fifty years will have to redirect their advertising dollars to the older population.

Libraries should also heed this advice. Aside from the fact that serving seniors is the right thing to do, if your library is supported through any type of taxes, it behooves the library to reacquaint itself with this group of people. The baby boomers are sure to ask "What's in it for me?" before they approve additional funding levies.

The Fifty-Plus Population Believes in Advocacy

Generally speaking, the senior population is one that believes that there is power in numbers and, therefore, in membership advocacy organizations. Currently, the most powerful membership organizations in the world are AARP (formerly called the American Association of Retired Persons, founded in 1958) and its affiliate, CARP (Canada's Association for the Fifty-Plus). Together, they boast 34.5 million members!

Senior advocacy groups such as the Older Women's League (OWL), the Alliance for Retired Americans, and the Gray Panthers are frequently consulted when information about older adults is needed. In addition to offering members camaraderie and support, these groups serve as an educational and entertainment forum for their members. Additionally, members of these groups are watchdogs for issues affecting the well-being of seniors at all government levels.

Well-organized advocacy groups have chapters in most states and have the potential to help or hinder legislative initiatives, including those that affect libraries. AARP and the Gray Panthers use "telephone trees" (phone lists of like-minded associates) as "power tools." When one of the groups' watchdogs

spots an initiative that could possibly hurt those over fifty years of age, they activate telephone trees in each state or district affected. Volunteers call the sponsor's office to voice their opinions and encourage members on their lists to make the same calls. Though members are divided in political affiliations, they will unite into a power bloc when their well-being is threatened.

Leisure Time Is Important to the Fifty-Plusers

Another common interest among older adults is their use of leisure time. Spending time with family is one leisure-time activity seniors enjoy; however, there are more. In fact, today's adults who are age sixty or older

represent 80 percent of all luxury travel, spending 74 percent more on a typical vacation than eighteen- to forty-nine-year-olds;

are avid gardeners;

spend approximately six hours a week reading;

exercise. Sixteen million fifty-plus adults exercise at least three times per week. Within the last decade, the number of adults sixty-five or older joining health clubs increased 700 percent;

are the fastest growing group of computer users; and

are the largest group of people who volunteer their services for the purpose of "helping others."[4]

Aging Is Also about Diversity

To effectively serve all seniors, library staff should recognize the various subgroups that will have different outlooks on life because their formative years span different portions of the twentieth century. Although people who are fifty-five, seventy-five, and ninety-five can all be recognized as older adults, they will not necessarily respond to the same types of programming and may not have the same needs. Figure 1-1 illustrates that the formative events of the oldest and the youngest seniors do not overlap.

Ethnic diversity issues should also be acknowledged. The U.S. Administration on Aging (AoA), for example, notes that seniors who are African American,

FIGURE 1-1

World Events during the Formative Years of Various Senior Age Groups

Date	Event	Formative Years for Age Group			
		55–60	60–70	70–85	85+
1910	WW I				X
1920	Roaring Twenties				X
	Lindbergh Flight			X	X
1930	Great Depression			X	X
1940	WW II		X	X	
1950	Korean War	X	X	X	
	McCarthy Era	X	X		
1960	*Sputnik*	X	X		
	Vietnam War	X	X		
1970	Moon Landings	X			
1980	Personal Computers				

Formative years assumed to be from ages ten to twenty-five.

overall, have more preventable health concerns that are not being addressed than others in the community who are the same age, resulting in a shortened life expectancy.[5] This is primarily because of a lack of culturally sensitive community-based initiatives.

Likewise, the AoA notes that there are many languages, cultures, and religions in the Hispanic senior community.[6] Many older Hispanic American adults are immigrants with limited English-language skills who worked in low-paying jobs that did not provide retirement benefits. This results in 24 percent of Hispanics living below the poverty level—double the rate of older white, non-Hispanic seniors.

Because the media tends to portray lesbian, gay, bisexual, and transgendered (LGBT) people as young, proud, and defiant, society as a whole does not realize that there are between 1.75 and 3.50 million seniors who are also LGBT.[7] Many of the oldest of the old are reluctant to discuss their sexual orientation with their families, friends, and health-care professionals for fear of discrimination and estrangement. This group of individuals may have trouble coping, lapsing into depression when their partners die, in part because of the inability to find peer support.

The AoA also recognizes the differences of the American Indian, Alaska Native, and Native Hawaiian peoples.[8] These groups of elders did not have the same access to nutrition education as others in their cohort and have a tendency to suffer from depression,

alcohol abuse and dependence, diabetes, and oral health problems. There is a need for community-wide health education, as well as screenings, for these groups of seniors. Figure 1-2 illustrates how some of these minority groups will have significant growth in their number of seniors in the next thirty years.

It is important to realize that these cultures, as well as those seniors who emigrated from Europe or from Asia or the Pacific islands, will be part of the various aging classes. There will also be seniors who only read Chinese as well as World War II refugees who still can only speak enough English to get by.[9] Being aware of the ethnic diversity of the library's service area will help ensure that the library can act responsibly toward its seniors.

The Senior Class of Baby Boomers (Ages Fifty-Five to Sixty)

The world experienced an "explosion" of births during the time period immediately following World War II that was so great that sociologists coined the phrase "baby boom." Those born during the years 1946 through 1964 are generally considered baby boomers. Researchers and writers consider the senior class of the baby boom generation to be part of today's senior population, causing long-range planners to realize that the world is indeed aging in a big

FIGURE 1-2

Estimated Percent of Older (65+) Population Growth to 2030

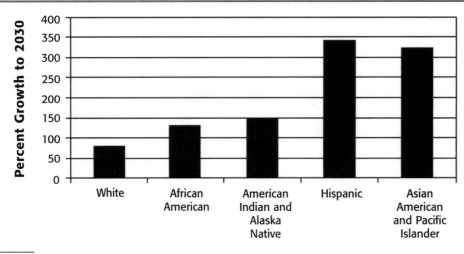

Source: U.S. Administration on Aging, The Many Faces of Aging: American Indian, Alaska Native, and Hawaiian Native Program

way. Statisticians have estimated that one baby boomer turns fifty every seven seconds.[10]

Baby boomers are the first U.S. generation, as a whole, to be well educated and given the most opportunity for success. This generation was the first generation to grow up watching television as well as participating in air-raid drills. They listened to the Beatles, Bob Dylan, and Peter, Paul, and Mary. As teenagers they witnessed the assassinations of the Kennedys and Martin Luther King Jr. They saw the Civil Rights Amendment passed and man walk on the moon for the first time. This generation had some of its members sent to fight and die in Vietnam, while others demonstrated their indignation to the chants of "Hell no, we won't go" and "Make love, not war." It was a generation that saw some of its members openly use drugs, be promiscuous, and "live together" without a formal marriage decree. This is the generation that was urged to "stay forever young."

Boomers are now part of the sandwich generation and part of the corporate world. Many of them are caregivers for grandchildren, nieces, and nephews as well as assisting their parents and grandparents. This layering of generations is primarily a result of youth giving birth before they themselves are able to care for the children and the fact that people are living longer, allowing more generations to exist simultaneously.

One thing to be aware of is that boomers have a selfish tendency when it comes to donating their time.

Researchers predict that boomers will have to be coaxed into volunteering by being offered incentives such as discounts within the service community, frequent flyer miles, or the promise of like services if needed at a future date.[11] The tendency to not volunteer could harm several important senior volunteer programs in the United States.

The library service needs of this complex group might require learning how to "parent" in today's world, planning for a financially successful retirement, or understanding how to help their mothers or grandfathers learn how to use a computer. Some baby boomers who are stressed might find a library's book discussion group or poetry group a useful escape hatch. Other boomers only want the library to provide the latest materials available.

Looking at the Population Aged Sixty to Seventy

This is the generation who saw the birth of "rock and roll" as they swooned over Chuck Berry, Elvis Presley, and Jerry Lee Lewis. Following the lead of Fats Domino, they started the dance known as the "twist," scandalizing their parents. This is the generation that drove muscle cars as they laid rubber on the strip. Their nemesis was Joseph McCarthy, and they worried about the Korean War and *Sputnik*.

Members of this generation are generally healthy and energetic and mostly new to the concept of retirement. Wanting their finances to be secure and wanting their retirement years to be healthy are important concerns.

Many members of this generation may not have been introduced to computers and the World Wide Web (WWW). Some members of this generation are also feeling the stresses of the "sandwich" concept of caregiving. It is not so unusual for younger members of this generation to be raising older grandchildren and assisting their parents. Developing computer skills would help members of this group gather information that could help them to successfully navigate the new roads they have to travel. Additionally, presentations on coping skills, health care, and finances might be appreciated.

Looking at the Population Aged Seventy to Eighty-Five

This generation knows what personal sacrifice and hardship are all about. The people who are age seventy to eighty-five were children or young adults during the Great Depression and fought in World War II. They saw women play professional baseball, work in defense factories, and accept material shortages.

This generation "heard" silent pictures talk and jitterbugged to the big-band sounds of Louis Armstrong and Tommy Dorsey. This generation saw the birth of the commercial airline industry. This is the first generation to purchase television sets and automatic washers and dryers. This is the generation that worked hard, saved their money, and made the world a better place.

Most people of this generation left work before computers became an important office tool. This is especially true of the female members of the generation. This generation believed in the concept of the nuclear family, before the term was coined, and many women's "careers" were spent as homemakers. Thus, there are many women who have never touched a computer keyboard.

The number of members in this generation is actually growing as modern medicine successfully treats ailments such as heart disease and strokes. Because women have a tendency to live longer than men, there are significantly more women in this cohort than men. This group should be courted as library advocates, as they will show up at the polls to vote and are a very powerful component of volunteer programs.

In spite of the hardships this generation successfully faced, they like to reminisce about their youth and their struggles. For many, a good afternoon is spending time talking about the formation of labor unions, which lifted them from poverty, or talking about being in foxholes, hiding from enemy forces. For others, learning how to use a computer to enable them to link up with their grandchildren on a regular basis would be the greatest thing since the invention of sliced bread.

Looking at the Population Aged Eighty-Five and Older

Those members of U.S. society who are age eighty-five and older form the most rapidly growing cohort of all of the older generations.[12]

These people, like the generation before them, lived through the Great Depression and fought in World War II. They saw refrigerators, telephones, and automobiles become part of daily life. This was the generation that fought for minimum wages and helped establish child labor laws. Their music was that of Jelly Roll Morton and Rudy Valle.

Many of this generation are first-generation Americans (or Canadians), their parents having immigrated to North America in the early 1900s. They had to work hard to make ends meet. Most members of this group toiled in mills and mines and still value a dollar and hard work.

Many African Americans of this generation are the grandchildren of slaves. They have heard personal narratives of cruelty and injustice. They too worked hard to feed and clothe their families. Members of this generation, who migrated to the North, were the first of their race to earn decent pay for a day's work.

As a whole, this group of seniors wants programs and services that respect their accomplishments while helping them remain a part of the mainstream. They will always appreciate a cup of coffee at programs and will come dressed in their best clothes. Generally speaking, this group can be relied on to vote for tax levies and help the library whenever and wherever needed.

Where Do They Live?

People have a tendency to think that most older people live in warmer-weather states such as Florida, Texas, and California. This is only partially correct. The automobile factories and steel mills of Michigan, Pennsylvania, and Ohio lured many immigrants at the turn of the century. These states continued to offer veterans job opportunities as they returned from war. Many of those simply stayed in these states raising their families.

The turn of the century saw more than 50 percent of the U.S. population over the age of sixty-five living in nine states: California, Florida, New York, Texas, Pennsylvania, Ohio, Illinois, Michigan, and New Jersey. Census data also reported that those over the age of sixty-five accounted for more than 14 percent of the populations in nine states: Florida, Pennsylvania, West Virginia, Iowa, North Dakota, Rhode Island, Maine, South Dakota, and Arkansas.[13] The list given in figure 1-3 indicates how the age sixty-five and older population is distributed among the states.

Which States Saw the Largest Increase in the Older Population?

It is important to know which states have the most seniors living within its boundaries, yet it is also important to know which states have the fastest-growing senior populations. This growth is partially spurred by older adults relocating once they retire. Some of these states are the same as those with the highest senior population, but there are a few surprises.

The 2000 census revealed that fourteen states witnessed a 20 percent population increase for persons over the age of sixty-five. These states were Nevada, Alaska, Arizona, New Mexico, Hawaii, Utah, Colorado, Delaware, South Carolina, Wyoming, Texas, North Carolina, Idaho, and Georgia.[14]

Although ageists have a tendency to think that seniors live in one big building, they are part of every community. Most do, however, live in metropolitan areas (75 percent) with half living in suburban areas and one-quarter in central cities.[15]

FIGURE 1-3
Percent of Population Age 65 and Older by State

5-6%	7-8%	9-10%	11-12%	13-14%	15-16%	17+%
Alaska	Utah	California Colorado Georgia Texas	Washington, D.C. Idaho Illinois Indiana Kentucky Louisiana Maryland Michigan Minnesota Mississippi Nevada New Hampshire New Mexico New York North Carolina Oregon South Carolina Tennessee Vermont Virginia Washington Wyoming	Alabama Arizona Arkansas Connecticut Delaware Hawaii Iowa Kansas Maine Massachusetts Missouri Montana Nebraska New Jersey North Dakota Ohio Oklahoma Rhode Island South Dakota Wisconsin	Pennsylvania West Virginia	Florida

Source: Administration on Aging, based on July 1, 2001, U.S. Census Bureau estimates

Where Will We See Future Population Growth?

Much to the frustration of long-range planners, "demography is not destiny."[16] There are projections and indicators as to which states are expected to see a surge in the population over the next few decades, but these are not certainties. One of the unknowns is the baby boomer generation. Some feel they will migrate; some say they will stay put; still others say they will keep on the road. The only demographic people feel safe making a prediction about is for the people who are eighty-five or older. Persons over the age of eighty-five tend not to move out of state, meaning if your state has a high population of folks who are fast approaching the age of eighty-five or who are eighty-five or older, they are likely to stay.

Use the Numbers for Planning Purposes

Statistics and demographics are easy to locate, will at least give staff a look at the current age of your community, and project what the number may be in the years ahead. These numbers will be needed when explaining why there is a need for increased senior services as well as when grants for programming are sought. Most of the statistics that staff will need can be found on the U.S. Census website, with analysis summaries on the AARP, CARP, and the AoA websites.[17]

Although library staff should be mindful of the projections, they should also be in contact with local chambers of commerce, growth associations, and real estate agents. These organizations keep a close watch on who is moving out of and who is moving into a locality.

It also helps to be aware of new assisted-living facilities being built in the area as well as observing shoppers in supermarkets and department stores on "senior appreciation days" to see if there is an increase in this population. The library's neighborhood health-care facilities and local pharmacies should also be able to share basic information such as whether they are registering more people for senior prescription discounts or processing fewer Medicare applications. Sometimes just being a good neighbor will alert you to population changes.

Conclusion

It is important to understand that although there are differences between the various generations, there are also similarities. Each generation will have its own catchwords and memories, but the generations will mutually be joined on important issues that affect each and every one of them, such as low-cost prescriptions and health care. Likewise, as a group, older adults may not be aware of today's pop culture and laugh aloud when they find out that the Goo Goo Dolls and Barenaked Ladies are male singers.

However, one of the most apparent and important links between the older adult generations is that they are all looking for purpose and expect to be acknowledged and respected. Libraries that afford them this recognition will see an increase in the usage of the library by older adults as well as support and commitment from the community as a whole.

NOTES

1. Administration on Aging, A Profile of Older Americans: 2001, available at <http://www.aoa.dhhs.gov/aoa/stats/profile/2001/1.html>.
2. Fred Warshofsky, "The Methuselah Factor," *Modern Maturity* (November-December 1999). Available at <http://www.aarp.org/mmaturity/nov_dec99/Methuselah.html>.
3. Plus Publications, 50 Plus Facts, available at <http://www.pluspubs.com/plus%20publications/50_plus_facts.htm>.
4. Facts from Plus Publications, available at <http://www.pluspubs.com/plus%20publications/50_plus_facts.htm>; and Shirley B. Rouse and Barbara Clawson, "Motives and Incentives of Older Adult Volunteers," *Journal of Extension* 30, no. 3 (fall 1992), electronic journal, available at <http://www.joe.org/joe/1992fall/index.html>.
5. U.S. Administration on Aging, The Many Faces of Aging: Serving Our African American Elders, available at <http://www.aoa.gov>.
6. U.S. Administration on Aging, The Many Faces of Aging: Serving Our Hispanic American Elders, available at <http://www.aoa.gov>.
7. U.S. Administration on Aging, The Many Faces of Aging: Lesbian, Gay, Bisexual, and Transgendered Older Persons, available at <http://www.aoa.gov>.
8. U.S. Administration on Aging, The Many Faces of Aging: American Indian, Alaska Native, and Hawaiian Native Program, available at <http://www.aoa.gov>.

9. The Many Faces of Aging series was a campaign to promote Older Americans Month in May 2001. Media kits were prepared in various languages such as Chinese and Spanish and can serve as an example for launching a diversified campaign. Available at <http://www.aoa.gov>.

10. BabyBoomerHeadquarters.com, The Boomer Numbers, available at <http://www.BBHQ.com>.

11. Corporation for National Service, Dawn Lindblom, New Age of Volunteerism: Baby Boomers and the New Age of Volunteerism, available at <http://www.etr.org/nsrc/pdfs/fellows/lindblom.pdf>.

12. Administration on Aging, A Profile of Older Americans: 2001, available at <http://www.aoa.dhhs.gov/aoa/stats/profile/2001/1.html>.

13. Warshofsky, "The Methuselah Factor."

14. Ibid.

15. Ibid.

16. Yves Carriere, From Baby Boom to Senior Surge, Expression 13-2, available at <http://www.hc-sc.gc.ca/seniors-aines/pubs/expression/13-2/exp13-2e.html>.

17. Online Statistical Data on Aging, available at <http://www.aoa.gov/aoa/STATS/statlink.html>, provides links to a multitude of resources relating to aging, such as aged minorities, aged by disability, and aged by state, and includes projections. The U.S. Census, available at <http://www.census.gov/>, enables users to sort by age, grandparents' status, economic status, and more. *See* appendix 1 for AARP, CARP, and AoA websites.

2
Special Needs within the Older Generation

Most people say that as you get old, you have to give up things.
I think you get old because you give up things.

—Senator Theodore Francis Green

Although it has been stated that humans age differently, we all face physical and psychological changes at approximately the same time. Overall, the older members of our society are disproportionately affected by sensory impairments.[1] For some, vision and hearing start to diminish; others are affected by arthritis and find that they are not quite as agile as they were in their youth.

Fortunately, medical science has provided medications and procedures to remedy many of the inconveniences that age brings. Also, necessity encouraged the invention of many devices that allow most people who are experiencing physical changes to continue to fully experience life. Although the library is not about to assume the role of physician, it can adapt and extend its environment to accommodate the needs of seniors. This might require purchasing assistive materials, rearranging the physical plant, or rethinking the library's service delivery methods.

This overview of potential changes in human beings should give library staff an idea of some of the physical changes seniors may be experiencing as well as offer libraries potential solutions to help overcome potential service barriers. Staff should be aware that the physical changes that occur with aging are not experienced by all members of the population. Also, when changes do occur, they may not be experienced to the same degree. Therefore, a suggested accommodation that works for one senior may not work for another.

It is also helpful to be aware that all persons do not accept their newly acquired limitations with the same outlook. Some may welcome accommodations, while others will succumb to loss.[2] Some seniors do not admit they are experiencing physical limitations and struggle to interact effectively with their friends, neighbors, and loved ones.

Whatever the physical or mental state of a senior, library staff should know that they can make as much difference in the life of a senior as they can in the life of a child. Their understanding and willingness to work to develop meaningful library experiences for seniors may serve to stave off feelings of uselessness and help seniors to acquire new goals and dreams.

Aging and Vision

Even though there are many seniors with visual impairments or blindness, remember that the degree of vision loss varies from person to person, and it is not unusual to meet a senior with twenty-twenty vision. Changes in vision are the result of anatomical changes that occur as the eye ages. Noticeable uncorrectable vision loss increases beyond the age of sixty.[3] These changes in vision may be caused by such diseases as glaucoma, macular degeneration (the leading cause of vision loss among Americans age sixty or older), cataracts, diabetic retinopathy, and presbyopia (the loss of accommodation, or focusing power).

Other conditions affect the eyes as we age. These conditions include the reduction in depth perception, floaters, and dry eyes. Most of these conditions can be accommodated through increased lighting, heightened color contrast, reduction of glare, and medical intervention.

Hearing Loss

Hearing loss is by far the most common impairment among the older population and affects more men than women. Hearing impairments affect one-third of all those over seventy and 50 percent of those over eighty-five, yet older adults are less likely to have hearing evaluations and to use hearing aids than they are to have visual examinations and wear glasses.[4]

The amount and type of hearing impairment varies from person to person. Some individuals simply miss hearing a few sounds or words; others may hear the words mumbled, even though the speaker is speaking normally. Some of the common types of hearing impairments include tinnitus (ringing), conductive hearing loss, sensorineural hearing loss (caused by illnesses such as tumors, poor blood circulation, high blood pressure, stroke, and even certain prescription drugs), and presbycusis (the most common impairment, which is a slow, progressive loss of hearing, affecting the inner ear).

The loss of hearing is one of the most difficult impairments for many seniors to accept and resolve. Some older adults who have a hearing loss may become withdrawn and appear confused, unresponsive, or uncooperative simply because they cannot hear and are too embarrassed to discuss their disability. Patience and inclusive strategies can best serve to prevent some seniors from becoming depressed.

Changes in Mobility and Dexterity

Arthritis is a problem for many older adults and often brings involuntary "oohs" and "ouches" when the pain begins. In fact, pain caused by diseases that affect movement are responsible for more than 7 million doctor visits every year. For many, lifting objects, such as a typical book, is difficult. For others, walking down a long walkway or lifting their feet over a rug may be impossible. Some conditions affect mobility or dexterity or both and make some tasks difficult to execute but do not cause pain; these include osteoarthritis, rheumatoid arthritis, stroke (some strokes leave people with cognitive impairments), and Parkinson's disease (it strikes the central nervous system and may cause rigidity in the muscles, tremors, slowness of movements, and poor balance).

Seniors also have a higher incidence of falling and breaking hips, legs, or arms than the rest of the population. These falls usually have some type of contributing factor, such as a visual impairment.

What these physical changes mean is that some seniors may need to use a wheelchair or scooter when they come to the library. Some seniors who have physical disabilities may not even be able to get to your library; you may have to take the library to them.

Cognitive Changes

Of all the myths of aging that abound, the one that scares us almost as much as being blinded is that aging may make us addled. The good news is that the older brain is extremely resilient and far more productive than scientists had originally thought. In fact, this is one area of aging where we might actually get better as we get older.

Marilyn Albert, neuropsychologist and star of the PBS series *The Secret Life of the Brain*, states, "Our brains have an innate capacity for change no matter how old we are."[5] Tests show that language skills, IQ, abstract thinking, and verbal expression all hold steady in the aging brain except when attacked by disease.[6] The one disease that does attack the brain is Alzheimer's disease, a progressive, degenerative disease that robs people of their memory, thinking ability, and individuality. Only 1 percent of the population at age sixty-five has Alzheimer's, but the chance of contracting it doubles every five years thereafter. The risk of contracting Alzheimer's is lower among populations with higher levels of education.

Perhaps Denise Park, a research scientist at the Center on Aging and Cognition at the University of Michigan, sums it up best: "As we age, we get better at mulling over situations, reflecting on them, and drawing upon our life experiences to arrive at decisions."[7] The one caveat, however, is that the brain does have to cope with limited storage space. New information or lessons must compete for space with old memories, which may mean that the brain is slower at manipulating information (i.e., seeing something, remembering it, and acting on it). Researchers believe that eventually there will be a way to chemically "expand" the storage part of the brain. But until that happens, exercise, both physical and mental, can keep us sharp.

A Word about Alcohol and Prescription Abuse

Some seniors have problems that may appear to be caused by aging but are actually caused by the misuse of prescription drugs or alcohol or both. Alcohol abuse tends to be attributed to loneliness, depression, or past history. Many of the prescription abuses are not intentional but caused by seniors forgetting that the medication was already taken or subscribing to the theory that if "one pill is good, two must be better." Some of the symptoms include shaky hands, forgetfulness, belligerence, and an unsteady gait when walking.[8] Staff should refer to the library's policies relating to substance abuse when working with seniors who may be under the influence of chemicals.

Creating a Usable Environment for Older Adults with Impairments

As previously stated, for almost every human frailty or disability, scientists, engineers, and therapists have designed an accommodation that will allow individuals to maintain their place in society. When the concept of Universal Design—designing products, environments, and communications for the "widest possible array of users"—becomes embedded in the work ethic of architects and designers, accommodations will have to be considered.[9] Although it may appear that developing an access solution plan for persons who have visual or hearing impairments may be difficult, it is not. More often than not, common sense and sage advice will guide staff to a reasonable solution.

Ensuring that the library is a safe and accessible environment for older patrons who have impairments does not require a large budget. Assuming that the building complies with the mandates of the Americans with Disabilities Act (ADA) of 1990, often all that is needed is some astute redecorating and a few minor purchases. The library should appoint a senior advisory board and consult the board before selecting items for purchase. Sometimes what we think will be useful for seniors will actually cause them more problems.

The Americans with Disabilities Act (ADA)

It has been more than a decade since the Americans with Disabilities Act (ADA) was ratified, and as a consequence, some of its mandates have begun to be forgotten or overlooked. Although the library's building may be new, staff should not assume that ADA mandates have been met. This situation can arise because someone didn't double-check calculations, thought the design presented a better "look" for the area, or tried to save construction costs.

The library's ADA coordinator and his or her staff should do a building and ground "walk" and "wheel" to ensure that the designer has heeded the requirements. Time is not always kind to structures and buildings. Areas that once were adequate may have become worn with age or modified to a point at which they no longer comply.

A checklist for accessible facility design for seniors (formulated using the spirit of the ADA) is provided in figure 2-1; however, the entire ADA document may be found on the ADA website.[10] Additionally, the

FIGURE 2-1

Is Your Library Senior-Friendly?

✓ Sidewalks are smooth, safe, and in good repair.

✓ There are handrails on both sides of the stairways.

✓ Doors are wide enough for a person using a wheelchair or scooter to enter.

✓ There is space to maneuver while opening or closing the door.

✓ The floor is surface safe, without loose doormats.

✓ There are relatively few changes in the floor level, and those are clearly marked.

✓ Switches, doorknobs, and faucets in lavatories are easy to operate.

✓ A person using a wheelchair can access the public telephone and drinking fountain.

✓ Glare is not a problem.

✓ Task lighting has been added.

✓ An adjustable computer station has been added.

✓ Sturdy, nontipping chairs have been added.

✓ A large monitor (at least fifteen inches), adaptive software, and large-print key tops have been installed.

✓ Mouse alternatives have been added.

✓ An electronic magnifier (CCTV) has been installed.

✓ Items such as pocket talkers, signature guides, chunky pens, handheld magnifiers, reachers, and so forth have been purchased.

✓ Meeting rooms are accessible and provide an atmosphere conducive to people with hearing impairments.

✓ The library's website meets accessibility guidelines.

✓ The library has a senior services staff person or an advisory committee on senior services.

And most importantly—

✓ Staff have had sensitivity training on working with older adults.

✓ Older adults have had input into the planning sessions for library services for seniors.

National Library of Canada has published a very informative and useful barrier-free design book for libraries, which includes a checklist. Although specific measurements may apply to Canadian mandates, the checklist can be used as a template for other libraries.[11] Buildings that adhere to the spirit of the ADA are safe and more usable for all library patrons.

Seniors with Vision Impairments

Seniors with vision impairments can benefit from thoughtful and inexpensive additions to the library setting such as task lighting, glare reduction devices, and magnifiers. Such aids as Closed Circuit Television Video displays (CCTVs) and special format collections can also make a big difference to low-vision patrons.

Establish Good Lighting

The need for proper lighting cannot be emphasized enough. In their guidelines for service to older adults, both the American Library Association (ALA) and the Canadian Library Association (CLA) stress the need for adequate lighting in libraries to allow seniors to read or navigate in a room. When we reach the age of thirty, we need more light than we did when we were fifteen, and this need grows as we age.[12] By the time we reach the age of eighty, we will require ten times more light than we did when we were twenty-five. Interior designers often incorrectly assume that "high wattage" is the only answer for persons with visual impairments. In fact, lighting that is too bright can actually cause more difficulties for this group of people because of glare. It is suggested that optimal lighting conditions include more than one light in a room, a light source directed onto the reading or other material, and higher wattage lightbulbs.[13]

Get Rid of the Glare!

It is necessary to eliminate or reduce glare and shadows. Glare is caused by bright light reflecting from shiny surfaces or when the visual impairment causes light entering the eye to "bounce around" rather than to focus. The most common shiny surfaces include highly polished floors, highly enameled floors and walls, and highly polished metal countertops. Additionally, glass walls or partitions can create havoc for people with low vision (also for people with cognitive impairments or people who are just in a hurry and not paying attention), as they cannot see the edges of the glass and may walk into them. It is important that libraries do not allow designers to create glare obstacles within the library.

The American Foundation for the Blind (AFB) and the AARP (formerly known as the American Association of Retired Persons) offer some useful lighting tips:

In reading areas provide fluorescent task lamps.

Dust and replace burned-out lightbulbs regularly.

For window coverings, use adjustable blinds or drapes to allow for the natural adjustment of light.

For windows where there is a lot of glare, apply a window coating such as 3M Scotchtint Sun Control Films or Solar Gard.

Take advantage of color contrasts. For instance, in rest rooms install door handles that contrast with the door and switch plates that can be differentiated from the wall treatment.

Lighting in staircases should allow easy navigation and eliminate shadows.[14]

James Mueller, in his book *The Workplace Workbook 2.0*, recommends that backlighting should be avoided and that one-third of the lighting come from task-lighting level, at not less than 30 degrees to the line of sight.[15] Figure 2-2 shows an example of a task-lighting lamp with a magnifier. Mueller also recommends lighting on LCD displays, which is contrary to what is usually seen at computer workstations.

FIGURE 2-2
Example of Fluorescent Task Lamp with Magnifier

Offer Helpful Low-Vision Aids

In addition to good lighting, some items can make visual disability manageable. These items for the most part are inexpensive (under $50), easily acquired, and should be added to the library's supply list:

- Broad-tip pens (figure 2-3 illustrates the use of such a pen)
- Signature guides, which help low-vision people sign in the correct place (*see* figure 2-4)
- Yellow acetate sheet print enhancer—a piece of film that is laid over paper that is too white or bright to help cut glare
- Large-print and tactile games
- Handheld magnifiers

HANDHELD MAGNIFIERS

Handheld magnifiers come in a wide range of magnification and quality of lenses. A selection of magnifiers should be purchased in the two- to eight-power magnification range for patron use. As corrective-lenses wearers know, one lens prescription does not fit all. Also, many eyeglass wearers know that sometimes it takes more than one try to find the right prescription. This trial and error extends to magnifiers. Many seniors would appreciate experimenting with the magnifiers in their home environment over a period of a few weeks. A selection of magnifiers could be added to the collection for circulation to patrons.

FIGURE 2-3
Broad-Tip Pen Makes Writing More Visible

AMERICAN LIBRARY
ASSOCIATION

AMERICAN LIBRARY
ASSOCIATION

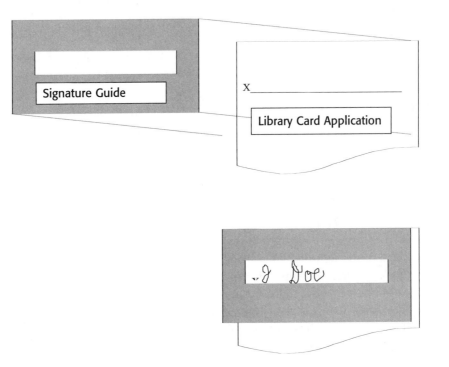

If your library is able to find funds that allow for the promotional giveaways, or offer door prizes at programs, all of the above items would be useful and a good way to introduce reluctant patrons to the virtue of helpful accessories.

Use Closed Circuit Television Video Displays (CCTVs)

Closed Circuit Television Video displays (CCTVs) are not a new technology, yet they remain one of the most important items to include in a library setting for people with vision-enhancement needs. CCTVs are user-friendly and help patrons to fully exploit their vision. If the library can only buy one piece of equipment, this should be it.

Items that patrons wish to be magnified are placed on a platform, over which is mounted a video camera. The image from the camera is displayed in the desired magnification to allow the objects to be viewed, as shown in figure 2-5. Virtually anything

FIGURE 2-5
CCTV Enlarges Text from Book

small enough to be placed on the platform can be magnified. This includes items such as personal correspondence, photographs, collectibles, prescription bottles, newspapers, and so forth. Full-color units also allow the user to adjust the color of display, which helps people compensate for loss of color perception. Moreover, the viewing table is sturdy enough to allow patrons to write checks or notes, allowing them to view their script on the monitor as they write.

The prices of CCTVs vary as to the size and features included, ranging from $1,800 to $3,500. Digital technology entered the CCTV marketplace in 2002. Betacom Technologies (Canada) offers a product with a lowered price while increasing the quality and ease of use. The competition between CCTV suppliers should be advantageous to their customers.

Maintain Special Format Collections

Readers with diminishing vision usually wish to use their remaining vision to access the printed word. The larger and bolder print found in large-print books assist them in accomplishing this task. Where once large-print books were out of reach for many libraries, most large-print publishers have purchase plans that make them obtainable.

Longer commutes have spurred the growth of the audio book industry. As a result of this growth, there are more producers and a wider selection of titles, both on tape and compact disc. More competition also translates to lower prices and an issue date that usually coincides with the print edition. This trend allows libraries to build audio collections that can supplement their print collections.

Libraries can also supplement their special format collections with the help of their Regional Library for the Blind and Physically Handicapped, a cooperating entity of the National Library Service for the Blind and Physically Handicapped (NLS), a division of the Library of Congress. All states and territories of the United States have access to the service; however, media holdings do vary. Some regional libraries offer Braille, large-print, and cassette services (archives of discs are available), while others may only offer cassettes.[16] Libraries willing to purchase a Braille embosser or refreshable Braille display may provide their patrons with access to approximately 4,400 digitalized books via the NLS's Web-Braille initiative.[17] In Canada, citizens are offered similar services

through the Canadian National Institute for the Blind (CNIB).[18]

Helping Overcome Hearing Loss in the Library

The days of a quiet, tranquil library are for the most part long gone. It is not unusual to simultaneously hear children laughing, computers chiming, and librarians conducting rather loud reference interviews. This popular scenario can create havoc for those with hearing loss. The greater the background noise, the more difficulty individuals will have in understanding speech. The library can make a few adjustments within its environment to help seniors with hearing impairments. A few tips follow:

Minimize sounds coming from air or heating units by baffling sound away from study areas.

Minimize glare. Glare inhibits people who are hearing impaired or deaf from receiving visual cues, further limiting their ability to communicate effectively.

Use sound-absorbing materials in areas where seniors might gather.

Arrange a seating area away from areas that tend to have a high noise level. The seating should allow patrons to face each other as they speak.

Use accessible signage to communicate important information.

Ensure that adaptive computer software, which provides visual cues to audible screen events, is installed. Check out Jaws and SeeBeep and similar software.

Purchase an individual listening system as well as FM listening systems for meeting rooms.

Install a telecommunication device for the deaf (TDD) machine at the library's service desk.

Personal Listening Devices

Personal listening devices are easy to use and are usually nonthreatening to seniors. They help to tune out background noises for persons while amplifying the intended communication. The speaker places the unit's speaker near his or her mouth while the listener slips on a set of specially designed headphones. The range from listener to speaker can be as far as ten feet. Units are in the $125 to $150 price range and require minimal training to use. These devices can be useful tools at the circulation desk or while conducting the reference interview.

FM Hearing Assistance Systems

If the library plans to conduct programming for groups, it should consider investing in an FM listening system. Like the personal listening devices, the FM sound system blocks out the background noise and reverberation found in group gatherings. A transmitter sends the sounds to headsets worn by those with hearing impairments. Most systems come with four receiver headsets. These devices vary in price from $700 to $1,000, depending on the quality of the unit and the distance the signal needs to travel.

Telecommunication Devices for the Deaf (TDDs) or Teletypewriters (TTYs) and Relay Services

Unless a senior has been deaf, severely hearing impaired, or speech impaired from a younger age, he or she will probably not be familiar with or use telecommunication devices for the deaf (TDDs) or teletypewriter (TTY) machines. These types of devices work like an instant messaging system and e-mail. Conversation is typed and sent back and forth between recipients.

Seniors who have become speech impaired for reasons such as stroke or laryngectomy can benefit from the device. The library can offer these persons an opportunity to explore the devices in a nonrehabilitative setting.

This device can be used as an in-person communication device as well. Staff and persons who have difficulties communicating aurally or orally may simply type and read the conversations.

Libraries without a TDD or a TTY device should be aware of the relay services, mandated by the ADA. These services enable people with access to TDDs or TTYs to communicate with people and organizations that do not own them. The conversation is facilitated by a relay operator, who reads what the TDD or TTY user is typing and voices the message to the hearing recipient over a standard phone and conveys the response back to the TDD or TTY user. This relay continues until both parties are finished communicating.[19] The library (or any other institution) can also avail itself of the service if it wishes to contact a patron with a TDD or TTY unit.

Appropriate Furnishings for Seniors with Impairments

Libraries can choose from a variety of furnishings to make seniors more comfortable and libraries more user-friendly. Appropriate seating as well as desks and workstations are available.

Seating

All patrons should be able to sit on chairs that they know will allow them to get up with confidence. Therefore, it is useful to chose armchairs that are sturdy and do not swivel. Arms allow patrons with low vision to have a reference point as to where the actual seat is in relation to their bodies. Sturdy armchairs also are helpful for people with physical limitations, as the sturdiness allows them to transfer their weight for longer amounts of time as they seat and unseat themselves (weaker chairs start to wobble when extended downward pressure is placed upon them). Good seating should have full backrests and stable bases. Staff should be aware of "rising assist" cushions for persons who have trouble sitting. The cushions, aptly named, help a person rise out of the chair with greater ease.[20]

Color and fabric should also be considered. The AFB recommends that when selecting new upholstery, choose one that has texture, as texture provides tactile clues for identification. It is also helpful to avoid shades of purple, as some people lose the ability to see these shades when they reach their eighties.

Functional furniture can look modern while being senior-friendly. Resist falling under the spell of an architect who tries to convince you otherwise. Seniors prefer a sedate and stable chair so as not to risk tilting the chair when sitting or getting up.

Desks and Workstations

The ADA mandates for desks and workstations can serve as guidelines for selecting most library furniture that will be useful to seniors. Figure 2-6 displays the many elements of an ideal adaptive workstation (*see* also chapter 7, "Computers and Seniors," for more information on software, an alternative mouse, and the computer itself). When setting up workstations, keep these important criteria in mind:

Simplicity, stability, and reliability

Affordability. Peruse the Internet or your local office supply store. Many European furniture designers have long been aware of the need for accessible and universal design.

Appearance should blend in with other library furnishings

Shopping for furniture described as simple, reliable, and inexpensive requires some forethought and common sense. Consider bringing some seniors along to "test-drive" the furnishings for the library. What feels comfortable for a staff member of twenty-five may seem like a torture device to a senior of seventy-five.

FIGURE 2-6
Ideal Adaptive Workstation

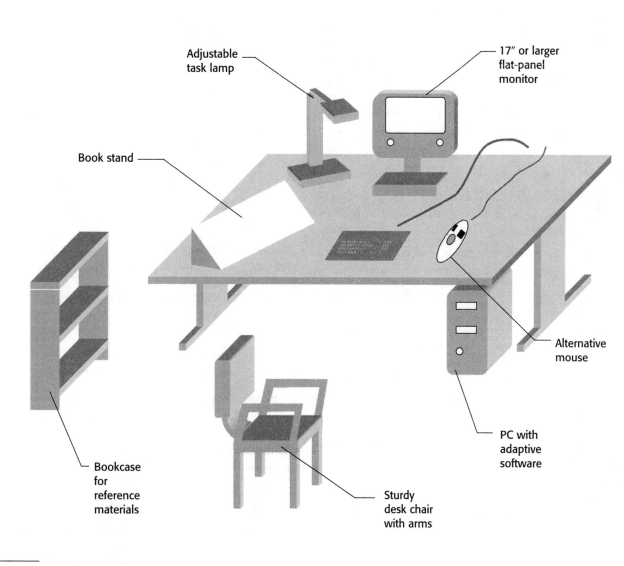

Artwork designed by James Mates

Useful Items for Persons with Limited Dexterity and Mobility

Arthritis and rheumatism cause some older adults to lose their dexterity, range of motion, and the ability to lift objects or push heavy doors. This may also translate to the inability to manipulate switches, push buttons, turn door handles, grip standard writing instruments, or manipulate computer mice. There are simple and inexpensive solutions to many of these obstacles.

Lavatory Handles, Keys, and Switch Plates

If the library's lavatories have doorknobs, it would be useful to substitute door levers, which allow the patron to simply push downward on the lever rather than grasping a knob and twisting it. Lever handles provide a flat surface that opens the door easily with the touch of closed fist, elbow, or finger. Depending on the quality of the lever set you purchase, expect to pay between $25 to $50 per set. The AARP offers the following tips for selecting and installing the levers:

Choose a handle that curves back toward the door to prevent snagging clothes and other items.

Choose a handle that is at least five inches long, as it gives greater leverage for people with limited movement.

The lever handles should be installed no higher than forty-four inches from the floor.

Remember to install them on both sides of the door.

If the door is to be locked, choose a freewheeling or clutch-type lever handle as they are designed to give way—but still remain locked—when any amount of pressure is applied.[21]

Should your lavatory door require the patron to use a key to enter, purchase a key handle for the key as shown in figure 2-7. The key handle allows the individual to insert the key into the lock by him- or herself.

If the facility still has a standard flip switch for the lighting, consider replacing it with a rocker switch. The rocker switch requires less directed movement than the flip switch.

These accommodations, although designed for those with physical impairments, will also be appreciated by caregivers of young children. Holding a child's hand while carrying bags can be quite "disabling." Levers will allow patrons to use the back of a hand or a finger to manipulate the door.

Handrails

Patrons should have safe access to the entire library. If your facility has stairways or long passageways with handrails, check to see if they are user-friendly. Handrails are designed to help people avoid falling while making them feel secure. They are helpful to have even if there is only one step. The AARP offers the following guidelines. Handrails should

allow the user to grip the rail between the thumbs and fingers;

support 250 pounds at any point;

be rounded, as this shape fits the contours of the human hand better than any other design;

be no more than 1 1/2 inches in diameter. The most comfortable diameter is 1 1/4 inches;

be installed on both sides of the stairway to allow users to take advantage of their strong sides; and

be mounted approximately 1 1/2 inches away from the wall to allow adequate grasping space for knuckles and fingers.[22]

Although these items would be added for seniors, note that they will aid all users and the staff. There are days when all of us need the security of a handrail, and who doesn't appreciate an easier-to-open door?

Gadgets That Help Those with Physical Impairments

As the world ages, new catalogs that come under the guise of "health" themes are arriving in mailboxes. Open them up and you'll find therein products that had formerly been relegated to catalogs focusing on disability or aging aids. Listed below are some items that may be useful to older adults:

Arch Assist Palm Support—Arch Assist offers support to the palm and promotes a natural arched hand position to reduce pressure on the transverse carpal ligament when typing.

Pik Stik Reacher and EZ Reacher—Reachers, as shown in figure 2-7, help individuals grab

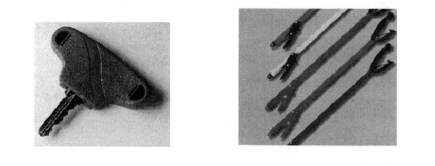

items that are too high or too low without bending, stretching, or straining. These devices extend one's reach by 2 1/2 feet.

Easy Grip Pens—Wide, soft barreled writing instruments do not require users to grip them as tightly as their standard counterparts, easing tension on arthritic fingers.

Book Stands—Researchers, as well as seniors, will appreciate being able to read books without having to hold them. Book stands hold reading material open and at the correct angle for strain-free reading or studying.

Page Turners—Some seniors and some persons with disabilities do not have the sensitivity and dexterity required to turn a single page and would find using a book stand with an automatic page turner, similar to the Book Butler, useful.

"Shopping" Baskets—Users may appreciate small "shopping" carts that can travel over carpeting and floors with a basket for the books, CDs, and DVDs they wish to borrow.

No doubt as items are added to the library's collection, patrons will suggest that the library consider purchasing other items that they only heard about. Many patrons would prefer to try the items before buying, and the library represents an environment without any "disability or rehabilitation" stereotype attached to it. The more comfortable and useful the library becomes for seniors, the more seniors will linger and learn. Staff will find that some of the products listed may be useful to them as well as the general public.

Wheels in the Library

Seeing people scoot through grocery and department stores is becoming commonplace. Commercial entities have concluded that the longer a consumer stays in a store, the more potential there is for purchasing merchandise. Libraries should use the same reasoning and provide scooters or wheelchairs for seniors who have difficulty walking long distances or for extended periods of time.

Although many of the people who avail themselves of scooters or wheelchairs have their own devices, knowing a wheelchair or scooter is available for use at the library is useful. It is cumbersome and time-consuming to load and unload them from vehicles. Note that many patrons who use scooters are mobile and have the ability to walk from the parking lot and into the library.

Whether the library chooses to purchase a scooter or a wheelchair will depend on the library's size and budget. Scooters range from $1,800 to $2,000, while standard wheelchairs are priced at under $500. Those libraries with larger budgets or larger senior populations may consider purchasing both. Some people with low vision will probably be more comfortable using a wheelchair, while those who travel independently will prefer a scooter.

Libraries Helping Seniors at Home

It was previously mentioned that the library should consider loaning accessibility devices to seniors. The King County Library (Washington) and Lee County Library (Florida) Systems, as well as other libraries, have had successful loan projects in place for several years, and others, for example, the Medina County District Library (Ohio), loan magnifiers. The King County Library and the Lee County Library Systems loan items such as small magnifiers, pens, signature guides, easy-to-grip utensils, book stands, and assisted-listening devices. The amount and type of equipment will be dictated by the library's budget, donations of devices, and the makeup of the senior community. In 2002 Lee County received a grant that allowed them to loan CCTVs to patrons in their service area.

Conclusion

As age steals away some of our stamina and some of our senses, science, ingenuity, and common sense enable us to embrace life and learning at our fullest potential. Being aware of the needs of the generations and providing accommodations that are within the library's budget will help older persons continue to prosper and work as a community.

NOTES

1. M. Desai et al., "Trends in Vision and Hearing among Older Adults," *Aging Trends*, no. 2 (March 2001): 1–8.
2. Ibid.
3. American Foundation for the Blind, Normal Changes in the Aging Eye, available at <http://www.afb.org/info_document_view.asp?documentid=203>.
4. Desai et al., "Trends," 5. Between the ages of seventy and seventy-four, 29 percent of the Caucasian population was identified as having a hearing loss, compared to 14 percent of the African American population; at age eighty-five and older, 53 percent of the Caucasian population had a hearing loss, compared to 32 percent of the African American population.
5. Richard Restak, All in Your Head, *AARP Modern Maturity*, available at <http://www.modernmaturity.org/departments/2002/health/0105_health_a.html>.
6. Ibid.
7. Ibid.
8. Hazelden Foundation, How to Talk to an Older Person Who Has a Problem with Alcohol or Medications, available at <http://www.hazelden.org/newsletter_detail.dbm?id=174>.
9. According to their website, "Universal Design is a worldwide movement based on the concept that all products, environments, and communications should be designed to consider the needs of the widest possible array of users." Universal Design uses the concept that if a person with a disability can use the design,

then it will work well for everyone. More on this subject is available at <http://www.adaptenv.org/universal/index.php>.
10. Full documentation can be found on the ADA website at <http://www.access-board.gov/>.
11. Wendy Scott, *The Accessible Canadian Library II: A Resource Tool for Libraries Serving Persons with Disabilities* (Ottawa, Ontario, Canada: Her Majesty the Queen in Right of Canada, as represented by the National Library of Canada, 1996).
12. AARP, Electrical and Lighting Modification Devices: Lighting, available at <http://www.aarp.org/universalhome/electrical/lighting.html>.
13. American Foundation for the Blind.
14. The American Foundation for the Blind Information Center, Creating a Comfortable Environment for Older Individuals Who Are Visually Impaired, available at <http://afb.org/info_document_view.asp?documentid=1417> and AARP.
15. James Mueller, *The Workplace Workbook 2.0: An Illustrated Guide to Workplace Accommodation and Technology* (Washington, D.C.: Dole Foundation, 1992).
16. To locate a library in your area, consult the NLS's directory, available at <http://www.loc.gov/nls>.
17. A Braille embosser is a device that reproduces Braille cells onto paper and can be purchased for as little as $2,000. A refreshable Braille display is a device that allows patrons to read what is displayed on the screen by feeling cells with their fingertips. The strip with pin actuators, which form and reform the words, is installed in front of the keyboard. The refreshable displays are expensive ($5,000) and very sensitive. To learn more or register for Web Braille, *see* the NLS website, available at <http://www.loc.gov/nls/reference/factsheets/webbraille.html>.
18. Contact the CNIB library: <http://www.cnib.ca/library>.
19. Northeast Technical Assistance Center, "Tipsheet: How to Use Telecommunications Relay Service," available at <http://www.netac.rit.edu/publications/tipsheet/relaya.html>.
20. Susan E. Cirillo and Robert E. Danford, eds., "Library Buildings, Equipment, and the ADA, Compliance Issues and Solutions," in *Proceedings of the LAMA Buildings and Equipment Section Preconference, June 24–25, 1993, New Orleans* (Chicago: American Library Assn., 1996).
21. AARP. Doors and Doorway Modification Devices: Lever Handles, available at <http://www.aarp.org/universalhome/doors/handles.html>.
22. AARP. Doors and Doorway Modification Devices: Handrails, available at <http://www.aarp.org/universalhome/doors/handrails.html>.

3
Staff and Seniors

*Reaching out to senior hands, hearts, and minds will further strengthen
the sense of belonging and mutual respect that always benefits communities.*

—Allan Rock,
Minister of Industry

Although many of today's practicing librarians are only a few birthdays away from becoming senior citizens, many of the library's support staff are not. Some teenagers have not ever spoken at length with an older adult, and some members of Generation X may have fallen prey to the stereotypes presented by the media. Additionally, staff members who are thirty years of age or younger grew up using a computer; they have difficulty conceiving that there was a time when typewriters were the chief workplace tool. Therefore, heightened awareness of seniors' needs and staff sensitivity training are musts. It is helpful to make staff aware of the potential of older adults as well as sensitize them to their needs. The entire staff need to accept the concept that it is important to provide seniors with library services, or programs will not work. Seniors will sense signs of indifference or patronization and will not return in the future.

Respect Basic Human Needs

Staff should be aware that human beings have needs throughout their lifetimes. These needs do not stop when the calendar changes our age from fifty-four to fifty-five or seventy-nine to eighty. Although many of our needs stay the same as we age, the *degree* of need may vary. The following are just some of the basic needs of older adults:

- To be loved and praised regardless of age
- To be needed and respected despite limitations
- To be given credit for what you know
- To be given choices and allowed to make mistakes
- To be productive, to be effective, to have goals
- Companionship
- Security and consistency
- Privacy
- Beauty
- Intellectual stimulation
- Meaningful recreation[1]

These concepts are actually the nucleus of both the written and unwritten mission and vision statements of many libraries; however, there is a tendency to fulfill the mission and visions by focusing on youth. Once staff understand that fulfillment of some of the basic needs of seniors is obtainable within the library's structure, they will share the enthusiasm of many librarians whose focus is service to seniors and act as advocates for increased programming.

Practice Good Manners

As with all patron-staff interfaces, politeness, promptness of service, and attention to the interview is essential, and these good manners should be a service priority. This is especially important when working with some of the oldest group of seniors. Many seniors think that having a good job is a privilege, and they expect quality service each and every time they visit. They may perceive inattention as a slight and may think that they are being shunned or cast aside. This is not meant to imply that staff should render additional service at the expense of other patrons. Respect and tolerance will go a long way in bridging the generations.

Select a Leader and Pursue Ongoing Training

One member of the staff should be chosen to serve as the internal senior services coordinator. This ensures that the concept of extending services to seniors will

not fall through the cracks. This person would be able to act as liaison with community aging groups, coordinate senior activities and services, and keep abreast of subject areas such as aging legislation and computer use by seniors. In doing so, staff and public are made aware of issues, trends, and needs of the senior community. The designated senior services coordinator may also be able to participate in professional organizations, select appropriate service materials, and develop senior services training modules. Larger facilities may require that a small committee be established, wherein members are assigned specific tasks, such as "Senior Cyber Links Coordinator" or "Senior Outreach Programs Development Coordinator."

The senior services coordinator can also serve to help coordinate in-service staff training as necessary to make services to seniors a part of the library's overall training. Staff and volunteers need to be aware of the visible and hidden conditions that may be affecting some older adults and how the library may accommodate their needs. In conjunction with the training sessions, issues such as confidentiality, equitable service, and access should be discussed. It is also helpful to have older adults or representatives from senior groups participate in the training sessions.

Establish Service Guidelines

Many public libraries maintain service guidelines to specific target groups, such as youth or disadvantaged persons. Few, however, have service guidelines for seniors. A good start is to use the American Library Association (ALA) and Canadian Library Association (CLA) guidelines and modify them to suit the language of the library's vision and mission statements. Public service staff should receive specific training in how to serve older patrons. The tips listed below can be used as a template:

Staff should not use patronizing, condescending, or childish expressions or tones when talking with or about seniors.

Public service staff should allow extra time to complete all library transactions.

Staff should use open-ended questions to elicit information.

Skillful communication techniques should be used, which include repeating key points in various ways and avoiding the use of "catch phrases," professional lingo, or acronyms.

Staff should show (not just tell) the patron how to do a task.

Staff should avoid multitasking when working with a senior, allowing their focus to be on the senior library patron.

Staff should make listening a priority.[2]

As previously stated, seniors are a diverse, minority group—service is not "one size fits all." Some seniors expect personalized service that addresses their needs, which will be varied.[3] The following discussion of working with seniors with various types of impairments is offered to remind each staff member to think about the person he or she is working with rather than lump all seniors into one group, with one approach.

Serving Older Patrons Who Are Blind or Have Low Vision

Recognize that a significant number of older persons will have a visual impairment; however, do not assume that all seniors will have visual impairments. If people lose their vision later in life, they may not learn cane travel and may not have a white cane. The person with a visual impairment is not always easy to recognize; be alert for patrons who are holding print items close to their eyes, walking up close to signs or spines, or have their faces a few inches away from computer monitors. Take the following steps if you become aware that the patron has a visual impairment:

Go up to the individual and introduce yourself and your location immediately.

Remember to always speak to the individuals directly, not to the person who may have brought them.

When conducting the reference interview, find out what they want and in what format.

When describing where something is located, use specific terms and resist pointing out directions.

Unless the person has a hearing impairment, keep your voice in an easy, conversational tone. Put your welcoming smile on; it will show in your voice. It is not necessary to raise your voice or speak slowly.

When a patron must sign a document, use a signature card or place the upper-left-hand corner of an index card at the exact place the signature is to begin, and the patron will be able to touch and follow the top edge of the card and use it as a guide.[4]

Serving Older Patrons Who Are Deaf or Hearing Impaired

Recognize that many older adults have hearing impairments, and many do not use hearing aides (older seniors resist this accommodation more strongly than any other life-altering event). Therefore, staff may not get any cue from the older adult that the patron's hearing is impaired. A few signs to look for are that the person is looking at your mouth all the time (done to visually catch conversational cues), the person may not answer staff when queried, or the person may give an inappropriate answer. Persons with hearing loss may speak unusually loudly or softly and experience anger caused by increased paranoia.[5] If you realize you are talking with a hearing-impaired senior, remember these tips:

Whenever possible, face the hard-of-hearing person directly and on the same level. Do not stand at an angle or in bright light. If the person is accompanied by someone who can hear, continue to talk to the patron who needs the service.

Suggest moving to a quieter location if the area where the conversation is taking place is a noisy or distracting one. The area should be well lit and free from glare.

Allow patrons to "read" natural, unexaggerated facial gestures.

Remove gum, lozenges, or candy from your mouth before speaking

Keep hands, glasses, pencils, and other objects away from your mouth when talking.

When asked to repeat something, try to rephrase it rather than repeat it verbatim. The patron may be able to hear certain tones better than others. A good example is: a patron's fine is a quarter, but they may not be able to hear the "qua" sound; staff may try telling them they owe twenty-five cents.

Do not speak loudly or overarticulate. Raising your voice usually does not work and is often seen as aggressive by the patron with the impairment.

Try not to approach the patron from behind.

Be patient, tolerant, and as open as possible. Older adults who become hearing impaired or deaf later in life simply do not have the skills needed to solely rely on visual cues.

If oral conversation reaches an impasse, consider using a word-processing program as a conversation tool. Staff and the patron can simply type their questions and responses, as they read each other's comments. A simple pad and pencil can be used in the same way.

Be familiar with the TDD/TTY devices and the state's mandatory relay services.[6]

Sarah Hamrick, director of Information Services, Gallaudet University Library, stresses that it is essential that hearing-impaired or deaf patrons and staff understand each other. She suggests repeating statements, if necessary, and writing down important words in your responses to ensure the reference interview is accurate.[7]

Remember to announce the availability of special accommodations for the deaf and hard-of-hearing in print. Staff can introduce the devices in a positive, nondemeaning manner by simply asking older adults to try the device and give staff their opinion as to its value. Helping the library decide if a product works or is useful is a task many would be willing to do without feeling intimidated.

Serving Older Patrons with Speech Communication Impairments

Some older adults have difficulty speaking in a manner in which they can be understood. This can come from having a stroke or other illnesses that damage the vocal cords. The inability to speak clearly can be the effect of diseases such as cerebral palsy, multiple sclerosis, or Lou Gehrig's disease. Some speech difficulties can also be attributed to stuttering or poorly fitting (or absence of) dentures. Whatever the cause, the answer usually demands patience and understanding. The following methods will encourage a more effective conversation with someone who is having difficulty talking:

Staff should encourage the patron to take his or her time.

Staff should not exhibit body language that indicates that they have other tasks to do. Let patrons complete their own sentences.

Staff should rephrase the patron's answer to ensure that they understand the patron correctly.

Staff should ask questions in a manner that only requires short answers or a nod or shake of the head.

If the speech is totally incoherent, staff should ask the patron if it would be easier to communicate in writing.[8]

Serving patrons who have difficulty communicating orally requires patience and often a keen ear. Remember, not being able to express oneself can be a frustrating experience for individuals who are mentally sharp.

Serving Older Patrons with Agility and Mobility Impairments

As people age, they find there is a decline in their flexibility, strength, speed of completing tasks, fine motor control, and hand-eye coordination. The fallout of this decline means that affected patrons may have trouble filling in check-off boxes, both on paper and on the computer, and may have trouble manipulating a computer mouse or switches.

Staff should be aware that they may not always have blatant visual cues to identify seniors who have physical disabilities. Although some senior patrons will use a cane, walker, or wheelchair, many patrons will not. Some patrons may walk a little slower, but some will walk briskly, as their disability may be confined to their upper body (i.e., hands, arms, neck). There are some general tips to keep in mind when it has been identified that the senior you are working with does have a physical disability:

When talking to someone in a wheelchair, crouch down or sit so that you can make eye contact. This will relieve the patron's physical stress of constantly looking up.

If the patron is using a mobility aid, offer to conduct the reference interview at a nearby table where you both may sit.

Offer, but do not insist, to retrieve library service items for the patron. Offer to place items on an accessible table or desk rather than hand them to the patron directly.

Ensure that items such as book trucks, step stools, or toys are not in the aisles.

When a senior has a physical disability that may hamper his or her ability to sign documents, ask what can be done to make the task simpler.[9]

Staff should be aware that some of the diseases that cause physical disabilities, such as arthritis, rheumatism, and osteoporosis, can also incur pain. This pain may make the patron less patient with the staff. Staff should be advised that patience and understanding will help with most interactions. However, staff do not have to tolerate verbal abuse or respond to inappropriate language. Staff should always refer to the library's policy guide in these situations.

Serving Older Patrons with Changes in Cognitive Function—Social or Emotional

Changes in cognitive function, including memory, reasoning, and abstract thinking, affect a very small percentage of younger seniors, although the percentage does rise with age.[10] Some thought processing may take longer, and there may be a need to have directions explained differently, but, overall, most seniors' brains stay sharp.

Some seniors experience social changes that are caused by loss of income, loss of social networks through retirement or death, society's "isolating" attitude toward seniors, and a lack of transportation to participate in recreational activities.[11] These factors work to make ambulatory seniors housebound, keeping them from being a part of the community and the library.

Some seniors also experience emotional changes as they age. These changes are brought on by loneliness, isolation, tension, work, anxiety about becoming dependent on others, and fears about safety, security, and loss of access to activities they enjoyed when younger.[12] Seniors experiencing these changes may need to be convinced that there is a place for them in the library and that the library is there to offer them recreational and educational opportunities. They will have to be drawn out of their cocoons. Some tips for working with seniors experiencing cognitive, emotional, and social changes follow:

Be ready to explain tasks in a different manner, avoiding colloquialisms, jargon, and slang.

Place emphasis on personal contact to draw people out of their world and into the library's.

Increase outreach efforts to senior gathering places such as churches and senior centers.

The library staff will find many people in nursing homes not coping well with the emotional changes, cognitive changes, and social changes they live with. Some of the residents may feel abandoned and disoriented. Staff whose jobs include outreach to seniors in nursing homes should be aware that it may be necessary to give a sense of time and place in addition to providing library services. They should be aware that many residents of nursing homes are still sharp and can be reached.

Serving Older Patrons with Low Literacy and Language Skills

Staff should remember that both the United States and Canada saw great immigration during the twentieth century. Additionally, the United States and Canada suffered a severe economic depression that caused many of today's older seniors to quit school and seek employment. This means that some seniors may never have learned to absorb written communications effectively. They may have coped by emphasizing oral communications, developing strong memory skills, or relying on relatives. These compensatory actions may no longer be available to the oldest seniors. Therefore, when formulating written instructions, informational brochures, or documents, write in a style that is not demeaning yet is accessible to those who have not finished high school. Plain language and sensitive choice of wording can help eliminate communication barriers and help reach the entire senior pool.

Be aware that some seniors may be comfortable with reading materials written in their native language (e.g., Russian, Chinese, Polish, French, Italian, Slovenian, German, Greek, etc.). Although it may not be possible to have all documents translated into diverse languages, it may be possible to do a few. Libraries can seek translators among their staff and share language skills with each other or seek to partner with various organizations in the community.

The following are some general tips for staff to

keep in mind when working with seniors with low literacy rates and educational attainment:

Use simple language and sentence structure.

Consider having the library's basic documents translated into the native language of the seniors in your service area. Staff or religious organizations can help to determine what languages are necessary as well as help with the translations.[13]

When building a large-print collection, consider adding high-interest, low-vocabulary materials.

Do not rely on printed materials as the library's sole marketing tool for reaching seniors. If seniors cannot read the printed document, they will not get the word that the library is offering services for them.

Much of what is considered good public service practice comes back to practicing patience and understanding. Staff should understand that a senior's inability to understand written communications does not make him or her stupid or less likely to use the library's services.

Serving Older Patrons with Cultural and Ethnic Needs

Library staff should remember that all seniors were not afforded the same liberties and access to information as we experience today. For instance, African American seniors who lived in certain areas of the country were not allowed access to all public libraries in their communities. Many were relegated to use substandard libraries. Some of these seniors still may have to be convinced that senior library programs include them.

European immigrants also faced discrimination in the workplace and in the larger industrial communities. These immigrants were often called disparaging names but found solace and educational opportunity within the public library. Libraries became a gathering place where immigrants could learn English and have access to publications in their native languages. Some of these seniors may appreciate a return to the time when libraries offered programming just for them. Some libraries, such as the Brooklyn Public Library (New York), have programming that encourages communications both in the senior's native language and in English.

Some tips when working with seniors with diverse cultural and ethnic needs follow:

Be aware that some seniors were not treated fairly when they were young and may not believe that the library's programs are inclusive.

Respect ethnic diversity and build senior collections and programming to reflect differences and sameness.

Seek to highlight all of the seniors' ethnic backgrounds at some point during the year.

Retain a deposit collection of books in seniors' native languages.

Provide basic information in native languages.

Being aware of and focusing on ways to cater to the ethnic diversity of the library's seniors will ensure that all are thought of in a special way. Staff and patrons can grow and learn from each other's struggles and triumphs.

Hire Seniors as Staff

In some cultures, it is not unusual to find several generations living together under the same roof. However, in Western culture, families are scattered. Except for holiday visits, the generations rarely touch. Holidays and vacations may accommodate brief exchanges of love, fulfilling family "obligations," yet there is not enough time to fully realize the challenges and wonders of growing older. For these reasons, and many more, it is helpful to have seniors on staff either in a volunteer capacity or as paid staff.

Senior staff members can be the bridge needed to reach the target community as well as being "in-house product evaluators." If thinking about a new color scheme for documents, the senior staff would be there to tell if the color scheme is accessible for them. When developing programming, they could be solicited as to good times for programs, types of programs, speakers, and locations for programs. Some active seniors may also offer ideas for soliciting new patrons.

The greatest gain of having seniors on staff is the interplay among the generations. It offers a wonderful opportunity for younger staff members to learn that the seniors' parents hated rock-and-roll as much as their parents hated heavy metal. It is good for them to learn that older adults also lost at love or went through financially hard times. It is enriching for them to learn of political, social, and military battles fought and won. It makes staff embrace additional services for seniors.

Conclusion

Many of today's seniors fought long and hard to partake in many of life's daily activities, including access to information, and some are still fighting. Additionally, there are seniors who did not face discrimination who are now finding themselves fighting the stereotypes and prejudices associated with aging in an effort to retain their rightful place within the community. The library should not be one their battlegrounds.

It is not enough to simply retrofit the library's physical plant and purchase devices that will help seniors more effectively access information and services; seniors must feel welcome. Seniors, like most people, can tell when they are the recipients of insincere deference. Libraries whose staff have had awareness training, who partner with senior organizations, and recruit seniors as volunteers or paid staff will realize that seniors are just like them, just a little older, and just maybe a little wiser. Seniors will find that their needs are taken seriously and that the library is on "their side."

NOTES

1. Texas Agricultural Extension Service, Texas A&M University System, Human Relationships and Practical Psychology in Working with Older Adults, available at <http://fcs.tamu.edu/aging/basic_ human_needs.htm>.
2. Minister of Public Works and Government Services Canada, *Communicating with Seniors: Advice, Techniques, and Tips* (Ottawa, Ontario, Canada: Health Canada, 1999), available at <http://www.hc-sc. gc.ca/seniors-aines/pubs/communicating/comsen_ e.pdf>.
3. Lynette Hawkins, Seniors Want Great Service Too, ON Business Library, available at <http://www. novatrain.com/articles_html/LynetteHawkins_597. html>.
4. Outreach and Special Services Division, Ohio Library Council, *Serving the Blind or Visually Impaired Library Patron* (Columbus: Ohio Library Council, 1997). Pamphlet.
5. The Hearing and Speech Center, Communicating with Senior Citizens, lecture notes, available at <http: //www.hearingcenter.com/services/sencom.html>.
6. Outreach and Special Services Division, Ohio Library Council, *Serving the Deaf and Hearing Impaired Library Patron* (Columbus: Ohio Library Council, 1997). Pamphlet.
7. Sarah Hamrick, e-mail to author, March 2002.
8. Terri Goldstein, Succeeding Together: People with Disabilities in the Workplace, chapter 11, *Speech Disabilities*, available at <http://www.csun.edu/~ sp20558/dis/emcontents.html>.
9. Outreach and Special Services Division, Ohio Library Council, *Serving the Physically Disabled Library Patron* (Columbus: Ohio Library Council, 1997). Pamphlet.
10. Minister of Public Works, *Communicating*.
11. Ibid.
12. Ibid.
13. Do not rely on the free Web translators. The library should work with community organizations to get the translation done correctly, preferably by a bilingual staff member proficient in English and the chosen language. The person should also know something about the library as well as the community to which the message is being delivered. The translator should be given a chance to look at the document and the option of passing on the translation task if he or she cannot accomplish the translation in a timely manner. For further information on translating text into foreign languages, *see* Center for Medicare Education, Translating Materials for Non-English Speaking Audiences, available at <http://www.medicareed.org/ pdfs/papers61.pdf>.

4
Programming for Seniors

I am still learning.
—Michelangelo, at ninety

Programming for seniors is not a new concept. In fact, in 1946 the Cleveland Public Library began a unique educational program for seniors called the Live Long and Like It Club. The club's intent was to focus on educational topics including travel, health, retirement, and world government but expanded its agenda to include often held book discussions, poetry readings, and recitals. The club, with a membership of 500, represented a cross section of the Cleveland community. Although some members barely made ends meet, others arrived in chauffeur-driven automobiles. It is said that members "tramped through blizzards and ninety-degree heat to attend the semimonthly or weekly meetings."[1] The group adopted as their motto the encouraging words of Michelangelo, who, at age ninety, said, "I am still learning."[2]

Program Planning for Seniors Begins with Seniors

The number-one rule when developing programming for older adults is that the programming plan reflect the seniors' rights to "dignity, purpose, self-esteem, fairness, equity, and compassion, as well as reflect upon the core community values."[3] Effective senior programming and management should have a clear focus on continuous evaluation, flexibility, and input from seniors. Establishing senior program-

34

ming is a two-way street, as seniors want to contribute to the library community's well-being. Seniors want to be able to pass on their skills and knowledge in exchange when learning new tasks.[4] Successful programming for seniors requires that they take the lead in defining needs, finding solutions, and guiding program content and format. Library staff, however, can guide them to the resources currently available and the resources that could be available.

Finding the Seniors to Ask

A good way to find seniors to help plan senior programming in the library is to look to the seniors who are already coming to the library. Other good resources include the local chapters of the AARP (formerly known as the American Association of Retired Persons), the Gray Panthers, your state's governing body responsible for aging issues, and the Area Agency on Aging.

When you begin to ask seniors what types of services and programs they want the library to provide, follow these tips:

Ask seniors what they want as library activities. Be prepared to tell them general plausible programming types.

Request seniors currently using the library to ask their friends who do not use it what types of programs would encourage them to visit the library.

Ask seniors what time would be convenient to get together for programs.

Ask seniors to select a library location that is accessible via public transportation.

Visit grocery and department stores on "senior appreciation days" and take a quick survey of seniors.

Establish and maintain contacts with groups that work with seniors. Request that they ask their colleagues and clients what type of programming will bring seniors into the library.

Collecting a cross section of seniors' thoughts, ideas, and suggestions for the library's senior programming efforts will ensure that library staff are on the same wavelength with the senior community. This will prevent the misspending of funds and effort on programs no one wants. Be ready to accept the fact that there may not be a consensus, and you won't please everyone all the time.

Establishing a Senior Advisory Board

Seniors should be the catalyst for senior programs. An active advisory board allows regular input into the library's long- and short-term planning. When forming the advisory board, involve people with different skills and strengths, diverse professional expertise, community involvement, various levels of educational attainment, and ethnic origins. Do not hesitate to include seniors from places such as senior centers, assisted-living facilities, and nursing homes. Transportation is likely to be a problem for persons living in nursing homes, but they could join the meetings via phone.

A workable advisory committee has no fewer than five persons and no more than twelve. As members of the committee are selected, remember that the library's representative is the person who is in charge of the group and must always be mindful of the interests of the library.

The members of the board should be given specific responsibilities and bylaws established. The actions of the board should be to

develop a clear vision and achievable objectives,

plan for long-term programming and sustainability,

determine the resources required and whether the board can help acquire them,

help plan and present library-related education and entertainment programs,

suggest community resources that can contribute to senior services and help build a mutually supportive relationship with the library,

help anticipate needs and troubleshoot potential problems,

clarify what a successful senior program is expected to be and agree on ways to measure the success,

develop a communications plan to promote the library's programming and to sell the project to potential program underwriters or new partners,

search out corporate and nontraditional funders, and

develop a method to maintain excitement during the time lag between the planning stage and the implementation of the programming.[5]

Senior advisory boards also help assure library administrators that they are involving the target community in both the planning and maintenance processes. Additionally, the community partnerships that are established in this way can help to raise the library's profile within some governmental bodies. Demonstrating the library's ability to involve other agencies and citizens is extremely useful when the library seeks additional funding from its primary and secondary fiscal agents.

Partnering with Community Groups

Partnerships bring the benefit of "economy of scale" by sharing both responsibility and funding requirements. When planning programs for seniors, involve other members of the community whenever possible. Partnerships take time to establish and maintain but are useful for innovative resource sharing, marketing, and funding. They also help reinforce credibility in the eyes of the public, which translates into a "believability" that is necessary to motivate a change in behavior.[6] Additionally, partnering with other organizations brings greater resources to the table, which helps when applying for large community grants.

Organizations such as the library's local Area Agency on Aging, American Red Cross, YMCA or YWCA, and community hospitals always stand ready to help develop and sustain programs for seniors. Civic groups such as the Jay-Cees, Kiwanis, and Lions Clubs are also partner possibilities, as their membership includes seniors. Do not forget to include the business community when seeking partners; it is to their benefit to promote improved programming for seniors.

To find partnering possibilities, observe the establishments where older adults frequent and use this knowledge to approach potential partners. For instance, some department and grocery stores frequently have "senior appreciation days." These merchants are keenly aware of the value of senior patronage and may be willing to work with the library on projects involving seniors.

Creating Partnerships for Seniors

Partnerships can either be formal or informal, but partners should always maintain clear communication and have well-defined roles. Establishing a clearly defined time line ensures that partners will always be on the same page, heading toward the same goal. Tasks such as writing, printing, reporting, organizing, purchasing, and leading the team should be assigned. Libraries should not relinquish leadership if the program idea is theirs and is definitely library oriented, even if a partner attempts to send it in another direction.

The Successful Senior Program

Successful senior programs are those that the seniors lead and participate in with the support of the entire library staff, who wish to make senior programming a success. Additionally, successful senior programs

support the library's mission and vision statements, as well as the library's long- and short-term goals;

act as important library marketing tools, because they can be promoted in the media; and

are noticed by the voters, media, politicians, and community leaders, all of whom are assets when funding issues are concerned.

It is important that programming efforts capture the wisdom of seniors, promote the theme of seniors being contributors to society, and recognize the seniors' potential to learn and grow.

Basic Rules for Program Planning

After identifying the general goals and objectives of specific programs and assigning staff to execute the program, general library programming guidelines should be followed. However, consider these additional items when developing programs for seniors:

Identify and prepare book lists, bookmarks, and brochures in large print. Flyers announcing the program should invite patrons to contact the library in the event that they have special needs.

Ensure accessibility to the program site for all seniors.

The meeting room should be accessible to people with varying degrees of mobility; the meeting room chairs should be comfortable.

Arrange the room to ensure that everyone can see or hear and understand the presentation.

If there is more than one speaker, be sure all speakers introduce themselves, as persons with low vision or who are blind cannot read name tags or nameplates.

It is helpful to announce the locations of washrooms, water fountains, and emergency exits, giving specific directions. If refreshments are being served, announce the location and the choices.

Schedule a few minutes for staff to close the program, perhaps summarizing key points of the presentation.

Develop simple and focused evaluation forms. Shorter forms, in large print, will have a better chance of being filled out.[7]

Library staff who are currently promoting senior programs have discovered that many older adults like to make an "early day of it" and prefer afternoon programs. However, some older adults may not have a way to get to the library, unless someone drives them. So, it may behoove the library to schedule senior programs in the afternoon but also develop intergenerational evening programming.

Types of Programs

The possibilities of senior programming are endless. Programs should strive to promote the library's collections and services. Efforts should be made to reach both people who are library users and nonusers. Ideas can be generated by local events, current events, holidays, planning events with senior centers, the senior advisory committee, and calendars with offbeat holidays such as National Pie Eating Day.

There are programs that are pure entertainment, programs that teach new skills, programs that help patrons find (or renew) a hobby, programs that help with daily life skills, and programs that educate.

Entertainment Programs

Some seniors will prefer programs that only require them to "sit back and relax." This type of program might include movie screenings or musical performances.

If the library is planning a series of musical events, a theme should be chosen that could give the series continuity. Possible themes include the following:

"A Musical Salute to World War I" (World War II, the Korean War Year)

"The Birth of Bluegrass" (Rock and Roll, Motown)

"Music of the Gershwin Brothers" (Rogers and Hammerstein, the Beatles)

If the library's budget is small, it may be necessary to locate talent who will play gratis or for only a small fee. Music schools often have lists of students seeking venues at which to perform before a live audience, and many secondary schools have "showcase" bands or orchestras willing to play at community events. It may also be useful to check out coffeehouses and bookstores that feature live entertainment, because the acts that perform at such locations are often playing for exposure rather than large fees.

Film series are also a possibility when considering entertainment programming. Creating a successful and meaningful series does take planning. It is important to identify a theme of the series, as opposed to going through a catalog at random to select a group of movies. Possible themes include the following:

"These Guys Can Still Act!" Movies featuring actors such as Paul Newman, Robert Redford, James Garner, and Sean Connery

"The Evolution of African American Film." Movies that demonstrate the growth of African American filmmaking, from the early stereotyped blaxploitation titles to the artistry of Spike Lee

"Celebrating Our Diversity." Films from seniors' ancestral homes

"The Hunks and Glamour Girls of the 1940s and 1950s"

It is important to investigate rental fees, copyright agreements, and other rules the film supplier may have and the responsibilities of the renting or borrowing agent.[8] Most film companies charge a fee for public showings of their movies, even if admissions are not charged.

Educational Programming

Some seniors like programs that help them enhance skills, improve self-care, expose them to individuals with similar interests, and stimulate thinking. Others seek out information about their ancestors and embark on genealogical quests or learn how to control stress and maintain a healthy diet. Possible topics for educational senior programs include the following:

Investing in stocks and bonds

Income tax preparation. The IRS, in cooperation with the AARP, can provide your library with staff who will prepare seniors' income tax returns free of charge.

Using the computer or the Internet

Reading insurance forms and submitting claims

Health topics, including nutrition

World events and people

Facts about the community

How to hone driving skills

Starting a small business. What to look for when considering a franchise

Photography

Grandparenting skills. There is a significant growth in the demographic of grandparents raising their grandchildren.

Writing memoirs or poetry

When AARP conducted a survey to determine how and why people over age fifty learn about new things, 90 percent responded that they want to keep up with what's going on in the world, for personal growth, and for the simple joy of learning something new. They also wanted to learn in a relaxed setting and not pay a great amount of money for the education, making libraries the perfect venue.[9]

Speakers on many educational topics can be found by consulting with your local high schools, colleges, community agencies, corporations, or retailers. For instance, banks have financial planners who would be able to present a discussion on the subject of bonds, a real estate agent would be able to talk about the advantages and disadvantages of purchasing a condominium, your local hospital could provide a speaker on the subject of high blood pressure or children's nutrition, and park services personnel could present a talk on conservation or nature.

Refining Skills and Rediscovering Hobbies

The AARP survey also found that adults age fifty and older are most interested in learning about subjects that would improve the quality of their leisure time.[10] This included learning more about a favorite hobby or pastime. For example, some older adults are interested in learning more about sports, as many of them follow the home team or still actively participate in sports. Other older adults like participating in nature programs and hearing about the hobbies of their youth. Themes in these areas could include the following:

"Cooking for a Smaller Nest"

"Evaluating Old Stamp Collections" (Coin Collections)

"How to Determine if Stored Items Are Trash or Treasure"

"Creating Memory Books"

"Doll Collecting." Patrons can be invited to bring their childhood dolls to the library for "tea" as a specialist talks about collectible dolls.

"Model Railroading." A model train expert may be willing to appraise patrons' trains as he talks about the history of railroading.

Call on the library's neighbors to present programs that will help seniors refine their skills and find or rediscover hobbies. The local florist may be willing to present a program on flower arranging, while an antique shop may be willing to talk about a topic such as spotting fakes.

If your library is in a college town, the local college might have a public speaker's bureau well versed in a variety of interesting subjects. Do not hesitate to pick up the phone or log on to the Internet to find out what's out there. Most of all, do not forget to ask the senior community to find out what speakers might be dwelling therein.

Intergenerational Programs

Five-Star Programming and Services focuses on library services for seniors, but it would be shortsighted not to include the pluses of intergenerational programming. The programming can either be planned as intergenerational from the inception or simply evolve.

Although not billed as a senior program, a program on gridiron legends would be intergenerational, as would one discussing Nick-at-Night Programming. Other "nonplanned" intergenerational topics could include subjects such as pet care, local history, and historical topics.

Planned intergenerational programming involving teens and seniors can be successfully orchestrated using the computer workstation. For example, a government grant to a 4-H Technology Corps successfully validated the theory that youth can indeed work with seniors who are new to computer technology. The test group developed a step-by-step guide for other corps members to use to teach seniors how to access the Medicare website.[11]

The library can also consider recruiting members of the Senior Corp or Foster Grandparents to help with youth activities such as reading clubs. The seniors can learn the language of the youth, and the youth can share the wisdom that the seniors naturally transmit.

Reminiscing

All people anticipate future events and think back through their past experiences. Reminiscence, or life review, is one of the primary tools for carving out who we are and what our existence means.[12] Researchers have found that reminiscence may become a tool for adapting to one's environment and can become a coping mechanism. Reminiscing with another person or group can help individuals achieve a sense of humanity and self-worth.[13]

Successful reminiscing programs use the senses of sight, smell, sound, and touch to trigger memories. Items such as old photographs, movie posters, sheet music, and advertising jingles are often used to start discussions of years gone by. Aromas such as alfalfa, fresh air, popcorn, watermelon, and fried chicken often trigger memories of seniors' youth by bringing to mind endless summer days and nights. Aromas such as motor oil, rubber, and diesel fuel may remind a senior of his or her parent's car or truck, or perhaps the family's first new car. Touching a piece of chalk may encourage discussions of a game of hopscotch or writing lessons on the chalkboard in school.

Most seniors like being able to reminisce and talk about the good times, and bad, which gave meaning to their being.[14] Once people start remembering and discussing these memories, they will find that there are others with similar memories. Shared experiences help to lay the groundwork for forming new friendships, even at the later stages in life.

ENCOURAGING REMINISCING

Howard Thorshiem and Bruce Roberts, noted authorities in the field of reminiscing, maintain that facilitators need to perform three tasks when leading successful reminiscing programs:

- Help people talk about what is meaningful to them.
- Help people actively listen with respect.
- Help people gain a sense of trust in the reminiscing experience.

Thorshiem and Roberts further state that the secret to great reminiscing programs is performing all of the aforementioned tasks at approximately the same time.[15] Reminiscence facilitators need to be aware that they may have to rephrase or repeat comments to enable the entire group to understand what is being said.

REMINISCING TIPS

Reminiscing may focus around a specific time in the past or around such life experiences and events as birthdays, living on a farm, having children, toys, games, music, historical events, hobbies, and holidays. Once a reminiscing topic is chosen, remember the following tips:

Provide a comfortable, warm, well-lit room with a minimum of extraneous noise.

Limit groups to five or six members to allow everyone a chance to "remember," but do not exclude more participants if the interest is there.

Ask relevant questions at natural pauses in the story.

Ensure there is time for each person to express him- or herself.

Respect sensitive or uncomfortable areas or topics.

Encourage participation; never push it.

Provide props or ask participants to bring in items they would like to talk about.

Assist confused individuals (who may repeat themselves) by leading them to their goal of telling their entire remembering story.[16]

Some libraries have ongoing reminiscence programs both in the library and at senior centers or nursing homes. Staff members have indicated that they grow through hearing about the seniors' lives and value the sharing of the group.

FINDING THE REMINISCENCE SPARK

For those who do not have the time or staff to determine reminiscence topics, there are a few tools that can help. BiFolkal is the leader in packaging "ready-to-go" programs.[17] The program kit includes everything one needs to hold a session, without having to seek any additional resources. For those with smaller budgets, BiFolkal also maintains "mini-kits" that are still excellent remembering tools. For those libraries without any budget to purchase reminiscence resources, a look through the BiFolkal catalog or website will serve to give staff a multitude of ideas. BiFolkal's newsletter also helps staff to remember upcoming holidays and events while providing some useful ideas.

ElderSong is another resource that can be used in reminiscing programs. The organization sells themed tapes and books that encourage the remembering of those events.[18] The tapes encourage discussions on themes ranging from "Remembering 1951" to simple sing-alongs. Two popular magazines, *Good Old Days* and *Reminisce*, can provide many topics to talk about.[19] *Reminisce* provides what they call "touchstones" by inviting readers to send in their memories on certain topics, such as handkerchiefs.

The Stoke-on-Trent (United Kingdom) Libraries have developed reminiscence boxes that are lent to patrons. The library's boxes contain photos, familiar objects, and toys to look at and hold. Box themes range from "Fashion" and "Famous Local People" to "The Forties" and "Courtship and Marriage."[20]

Other ideas for reminiscence programs can be found on several websites that provide teachers with discussion guides to use with their classes. The Public Broadcasting Service (PBS) and the Library of Congress websites are two of the richest sites to use for this purpose.[21]

Attics, basements, and resale shops are also treasure troves for finding "something" to talk about, as are ideas from the participants themselves. If conducting a reminiscence program at a nursing home, ask staff if the participants have photographs they can share. If so, residents and staff of both the library and nursing home can "show-and-tell" stories about those pictures. Be prepared for tears and smiles as people remember their past. In addition to helping people link with one another by finding common ground, reminiscence activities have even been known to bring people with advanced cases of Alzheimer's momentarily back to reality.

STORYTELLING AND COLLECTING

Storytelling is a form of reminiscence. With families spread across North America, as well as being pulled in so many directions with activities, one of the cultural aspects that becomes lost is storytelling. Grandchildren will no longer hear about the time guests at the Zdybalski wedding were only served a loaf of rye bread for lunch, how a grandfather was killed in a coal-mining cave-in, or how the library's neighborhood used to look. These are stories that should be told and shared; they are important to the cultural fiber of nations. If a person does not share the stories with others, they are gone forever.

The library should consider hosting storytelling and collecting sessions. These can be recorded for posterity and shared with future generations. Cathy Spagnoli is a master storyteller and collector who knows how to get stories from people's memories into a format that can be preserved.[22]

Spagnoli suggests that staff use broad themes such as religious events, injustices, embarrassing times, love and marriage, lost fortunes, first times, victories, friendships, survival, pets, migration, schooling, sports, family lore, or getting in trouble. A great project would be to collect neighborhood stories into a booklet to celebrate the library's anniversary or be sold as a fund-raiser for other senior programming needs.

Computer Training

When an Internet inquiry is made using key search words such as "activities and seniors" or "seniors and trends," the greatest number of hits returned focuses on seniors and computers or the Internet. Seniors' use of the Internet is growing and is a popular topical request of many. The library can be of assistance in helping older adults cross the formidable digital divide.

Book Talks and Book Discussions

No library programming discussion can be complete without a discussion of book talks and book discussion groups. Knowledge of books is still what we in the library profession are known for, and many patrons still expect us to be able to recommend a good book to them. Others thirst for a chance to share their pleasure or dismay at reading titles and eagerly seek a book discussion group. Both of these programs work well as senior programs and are portable, which means they can be taken off-site.

AARP 55 Alive

Some libraries host a preplanned program developed and run by AARP, called 55 Alive. The program was designed to help drivers who are age fifty and older improve their driving skills. Graduates of the course may be eligible to receive a state-mandated, multiyear discount on their auto insurance premiums. The classes are taught and administered by a nationwide network of AARP-trained volunteers.[23]

Older Adults Month

In the United States, May has been designated Older Adults Month. This can serve as a vehicle to kick off an array of senior programs, to announce a new service for seniors, to highlight the accomplishments and abilities of seniors, and to say to seniors, "Thank you!" The month of the celebration may vary from country to country, but the theme of recognizing seniors as builders of today's world (and tomorrow's) is universal.

In 2001 Alberta, Canada, held its Fifteenth Annual Senior Citizens Week. In so doing, a planning events booklet, which offered many unique and fun suggestions for celebrating seniors, was compiled.[24] Many of its ideas are easily transferable to the library venue:

Compile a book of biographies of long-time library patrons. This book could preserve the history of the library's earliest users.

Display the artworks of seniors. This can include painters, potters, weavers, and needle artists. At the opening reception, artists can be invited to talk about their craft.

Celebrate the disappearing arts. These arts can include soap making, whittling, and darning.

Organize a fair whereby agencies that have information for seniors can set up shop to share their information.

Set up book displays featuring senior achievers.

Organize a kite-building workshop, and, where location permits, let the seniors attach a hope, a dream, or a memory to its tail and let it fly.

Organize a senior fashion show (for men and women). Encourage a local barber and beautician to provide hairstyling tips and a makeup artist to offer makeup tips for mature skin. Be sure to include models who are using wheelchairs, walkers, and canes as well as those who walk unassisted. The models should be a microcosm of the senior population.

Organize a specialty fashion and footwear show. This show would focus on fashions designed for arthritic hands and for those with severely limited mobility.

Whatever the library decides, be sure seniors know about the event or events. Phone trees should be activated and the media alerted. Tote bags and other promotional items should be developed and distributed. The personal touch is always important, so remind public service staff to place flyers in books of known seniors and tell them that they hope they can attend the event and bring a friend as well. Additionally, politicians and government agencies should be alerted and invited to attend and contribute toward the event.

Conclusion

Programming for seniors is fun and rewarding and serves to make the library a community resource for both the seniors and their families. There are many programs that do not require a great deal of planning or resources, just commitment from the library to make them happen. For the more complex programs, community organizations and commercial enterprises can help the library receive funds as well as bring creativity and diversity to the types of programs offered.

Whatever the type of program, library staff should always remember to include seniors and senior care providers in the planning. The ultimate goal of the program should be to make the library and its outreach services the place for seniors to be educated, entertained, and enlightened.

NOTES

1. C. H. Cramer, *Open Shelves and Open Minds: A History of the Cleveland Public Library* (Cleveland: Case Western Reserve Univ., 1972).

2. Ibid.

3. Health Canada, Experience in Action: Community Programming for Healthy Aging: Core Values in Seniors' Programs, Fact sheet 1, available at <http://www.hc-sc.ga.ca/seniors-aines/pubs/factshts/fs1e.htm>.

4. Ibid.

5. Anne M. Ring, *Read Easy: Large Print Libraries for Older Adults: Planning Guide, Operations Manual, Sample Forms* (Seattle, Wash.: CAREsource Program Development, 1991).

6. Home2Ocean website, Benefits of Partnerships, available at <http://www.home2ocean.org/workbook/section2/page65.html>.

7. RUSA-SUPS Services to Adults Committee, *Adult Programming: A Manual for Libraries*, RUSA Occasional Papers, no. 21 (Chicago: Reference and User Services Association, American Library Assn., 1997), 5–6; Health Canada, *Communicating with Seniors: Advice, Techniques and Tips* (Ottawa, Ontario, Canada: Minister of Public Works and Government Services Canada, 1999), 1b.

8. RUSA-SUPS Services to Adults Committee, *Adult Programming*, 13–14.

9. AARP Survey on Lifelong Learning, Executive Summary, conducted for AARP by Harris Interactive, available at <http://research.aarp.org/general/lifelong_1.html>.

10. Ibid.

11. Health Care Financing Administration website, Teens Teaching Internet Skills Video Promotes 4-H Internet Training for Seniors on Medicare, available at <http://www.nnh.org/ttis/ttisinfo.htm>.

12. Texas Agricultural Extension Service, Texas A&M University System, Reminiscence: An Important Task for Older Adults, available at <http://fcs.tamu.edu/aging/reminiscence.htm>.

13. Ibid.

14. Health Canada, Experience in Action: Community Programming for Healthy Aging: Core Values in Seniors' Programs, Fact sheet 6, available at <http://www.hc-sc.ga.ca/seniors-aines/pubs/factshts/fs1e.htm>.

15. Howard Thorsheim and Bruce Roberts, *I Remember When: Activity Ideas to Help People Reminisce* (Forest Knolls, Calif.: Elder Books, 2000).

16. Texas Agricultural Extension Service.

17. BiFolkal may be reached at 609 Williamson St., Madison, WI 53703; 800-568-5357; or <http://www.bifolkal.org>.

18. ElderSong publications may be found at <http://www.eldersong.com>. The site also offers ideas on music programs and humor and provides a birthday calendar of the famous.

19. *Reminisce* subscription information is available at <http://www.reimanpub.com>. *Good Old Days* information is available at <http://www.goodolddays Magazine.com>. This magazine also can serve as a resource for music collections of yesteryear as many advertisements pertain to memories of another time. The Age Exchange also offers a wide range of books that explore the memories of a variety of ethnic peoples. Available at <http://age-exchange.org.uk>.

20. Available at <http://www.stoke.gov.uk/council/libraries/services/reminiscence.html>.

21. The PBS website is available at <http://www.pbs.org>, and Library of Congress's American Memory website is available at <http://memory.loc.gov/ammem>.

22. Cathy Spagnoli hosts a website at <http://www.cathyspagnoli.com> that includes even more suggestions for telling and collecting stories. Storytelling for seniors is also discussed in chapter 6.

23. Libraries wishing to host an AARP 55 Alive workshop can fill out a form at <http://www.aarp.org/55alive>.

24. Recognizing Alberta's Seniors—Contributing to the Future is available at <http://www.seniors.gov.ab.ca/services_resources/advisory_council/seniors_week/planningevents.pdf>.

5
Older Adults and Reading

Iron rusts from disuse, stagnant water loses its purity . . .
even so does inaction sap the vigors of the mind.

—Leonardo da Vinci (1452–1519),
The Notebooks

Long before there were free education and free lending libraries, reading was often a social activity. Factory workers often had books read to them to relieve the tedium of work, after which there were spontaneous discussions about the book.[1] The tradition of reading aloud, which allowed everyone to enjoy the printed word, carried over to the worker's household. Talking about what was read was an important part of their day, their life, and their culture.

The culture of the twentieth century was one that valued reading and the written word. It was, therefore, natural to see libraries hosting book discussion groups. Successful library-sponsored programs, including those targeted at the senior population, have a long history of centering around the "book." Librarians wisely hypothesized that when there wasn't a way to attend school, self-education through reading was a way out of the ghetto. During the Great Depression and the post–World War II years, reading groups flourished. In 1947 the Cleveland Public Library had more than fifty Great Books reading groups, with 2,000 members.[2] It seems reasonable to believe that the youth of 1947 would still want to read and discuss books.

Special Media and Collection Development

All reading groups should choose titles that are available in a format all members of the community can read, but it is essential for senior groups to ensure titles that will be discussed are available in large print, recorded format, and Braille. Libraries can also supplement their special media materials by borrowing. As previously discussed, it is helpful when there is a basic collection of books in formats that seniors with declining vision can access.

Large Print and Recorded Media

The publishing industry as a whole has recognized the growing need for large-print and recorded materials. Over the last few years the number of companies producing multiformatted books has risen, and as a consequence, the selection of books has grown, allowing prices to remain stable.[3]

When purchasing audio titles to use with book clubs, buy the unabridged edition. Unfortunately, those doing the abridgement aren't always good judges as to what may be important to readers and what may be analyzed and discussed in a book discussion group. It would be unfair for a person to be excluded from discussing a point because the text wasn't there to "read" in the format they used.

Although it's a time-consuming task, another option for securing some of the classics in large print is to download titles found on public domain literature websites and reformat them into large print or Braille. The text can be taken in a word-processing document, the type enlarged, and the book newly formatted and printed. Care should be taken to provide a wider left margin, allowing staff to punch out holes for a three-ring binder. Many of the titles on these websites are the classics, and classics always make for good book discussions.[4]

Braille

Generally speaking, people who become blind later in life do not learn to read Braille, but this does not mean that libraries should neglect this medium. People who learned Braille at an early age will want to continue to read Braille throughout their lives. Some may rely on it more, if their hearing becomes diminished.

Unlike recorded and large-print book publishers, there are only a limited number of producers of Braille. Most Braille is costly to purchase and con-sumes a lot of shelf space. There are a few exceptions, as some benevolent groups produce health guides or religious materials in Braille, free of charge (or on a cost-recovery basis). It is also possible to borrow titles from one of the Braille lending libraries, which are part of the National Library Service for the Blind and Physically Handicapped (NLS) network.[5] The NLS maintains a multitude of titles (modern and classic) that would make for good reading and discussion.

Special Media Books, Free for the Borrowing

Remember that libraries that do not have a budget for recorded books, or those that want to offer more titles, can still provide readers with a browsing collection of recorded books. The NLS network of cooperating libraries throughout the United States and its territories can provide books on cassette.[6] Some of these libraries also loan large-print books and descriptive videos to patrons and libraries in their service areas. A similar service is orchestrated by the Canadian National Institute for the Blind, Library for the Blind. The Canadian service also offers their patrons access to a multitude of electronic texts, made possible by savvy partnerships.[7]

The United States and Canada are not the only countries that provide loans of materials in special media. Countries such as the United Kingdom, Australia, New Zealand, Holland, Sweden, the Netherlands, Russia, France, Germany, and Japan all have lending libraries. This could be useful if there are members in the reading group who have language needs in addition to access needs. Loan procedures and collection media formats vary, but generally, most libraries will only loan titles to NLS cooperating members.[8] Most network libraries will work with public libraries to offer needed titles for patrons through interlibrary loans.

Book Talks

Book talking is a tool used by most public service librarians throughout their workday. The public still relies on library staff to give them the insider's track on the latest and the greatest books that are being published. Admittedly, there are book reviews and reviewers everywhere, but the librarian is still the person who knows about the really good books.

Book talks are used with the senior population much as they are with the general population. They are used to tantalize and inspire patrons to read books they are not aware of or unsure if they want to read. They are also used by seniors to keep them up-to-date with new titles, new authors, and new ideas.

Nora Jane Natke, a professional book talker and proprietor of Hooked on Books, Ltd., has been working with senior populations in Florida for a number of years. She has provided book-talk programming at libraries, assisted-living facilities, senior complexes, and charitable groups. She has found the experience stimulating, as seniors are encouraged "to read and share their love of books." Natke offers the following tips for presenting effective book talks for seniors:

Schedule the book talks at a time that will appeal to most seniors. The themes of "Breakfast and Books," "After Lunch with Books," and "Early Evening and Books" often work.

Know your audience. Be aware of patrons who may have vision, hearing, or other physical-access disabilities. Ensure the talks are held in an accessible venue.

When planning book talks, try to center the talks around themes, for example, "Great People in Fact or Fiction," "Thriller-Chillers," "Italian American Stories," "African American Stories," and "Gandhi, Mandela, and King," or authors such as Ayn Rand, Chaim Potok, and M. K. Rawlings.

Never talk about a book you didn't read and like.

Presenters should plan to spend five to ten minutes on each title.

Always introduce yourself, your library, your service, and any special services offered by the library of which the participants may be unaware.

Distribute a list of books that will be discussed.

Display print or recorded books in a manner that will encourage participants to browse.

When giving the talk, refer to the theme of the book talk, that is, what is the "link" that binds the books together?[9]

Distribute "See You Soon" bookmarks or flyers with the dates of future book talks clearly indicated at the end of each talk.

If doing book talks off-site, distribute library business cards or flyers to make participants and their families aware that the library is coming to them.

Although it may not be necessary to seek an evaluation from each book-talk presentation, it might be useful to occasionally assess the talks to determine if the presentations are on target with seniors' needs.[10]

The purpose of book talks are to encourage reading, yet some participants might attend book talks for companionship or to keep current with what is being read by others. A good book talk will allow the senior participants to conduct a cursory conversation with acquaintances. A good talk will also help seniors feel they are part of the mainstream.

Book Discussion Groups for Seniors

Why a reading group for seniors, rather than encouraging them to become a part of the adult reading group? Some of the oldest of the older adults are slightly stigmatized when in a group that is comprised of youth, who seem to speak another language. Many will embrace their own group because they know there will be people in this group who, like them, may have visual or hearing impairments. Seniors will feel comfortable talking about what the book means to them when they know that others will get their meaning.

In addition to library-hosted book discussion groups, there are many senior-hosted "online" book discussion groups on the World Wide Web (WWW).[11] Many of the titles have been discussed by hundreds of seniors and could be used with the library's senior book group.

Starting the Group

Once the library decides to start a book discussion group, it is necessary to organize. It is important to consider seniors who are currently patrons as well as those seniors who have not visited the library for some time. The goal of the book discussion group should be to share literature while making (or retaining) old friends.

As with most book clubs, club members and staff will have to determine how often to meet, how titles will be selected, and who will lead the discussions.

Additional suggestions for starting and maintaining the senior book discussion group follow:

1. Survey current patrons to determine a time and a place for the group to meet. Keep a list of those patrons who said they are interested in joining a book club to enable staff to notify them of details when formulated. Schedule all dates for the defined time period.

2. Advertise the formation of the book club at places such as senior and recreation centers, community websites and bulletin boards, bookstores, coffeehouses, and the library's bulletin board. Be sure that the typeface used to announce the club is easy to read.

3. Send formal invitations to those on your mailing list as well as any community partners that the library may have.

4. Start all meetings on time. Use the first meeting as a planning session. Get to know the group by asking the participants for titles of their favorite books.

5. Determine how many and what type of special media books might be needed on an ongoing basis. It's acceptable to ask members which version of a book they would like. Determine if you will need any type of listening aids for persons with hearing impairments.

6. It is sometimes helpful to distribute a listing of typical discussion questions, suggesting readers read the book in hopes of finding answers to them.

7. When discussing the book, be sure to encourage all members to contribute while discouraging others from monopolizing the discussion.

8. A quick telephone call or postcard reminding seniors of the next meeting is always appreciated and many times needed.

Additionally, the room chosen should be free of white noise and distractions. Staff should also be careful about the number of people admitted into the group. Too large of a group dissuades some people from offering an opinion and encourages "clock watching."

For those just getting started with hosting a book discussion group, the following information will help with decisions about the questions to ask and the titles to choose.

TYPICAL DISCUSSION QUESTIONS

Most of the standard questions that apply to book discussion groups will work for seniors. Questions should be phrased to avoid the use of jargon and slang. The person posing the questions should speak as loudly as possible.

Librarians, when asked for a few standard book discussion questions, offered those below, with the caveat to pay attention to the intellectual comprehension ability of the group and the content of the book. If it is observed that participants do not understand topics such as theme, imagery, and characterization, staff might want to spend a few sessions talking about these topics, using an online senior course entitled "How Literature Works" as their guide.[12] Good starting questions include the following:

- Did you like the book?
- What was the theme? Were there multiple themes?
- Did you like all of the characters? If no, which didn't you like and why?
- If this movie was cast in the 1950s (or 1960s, 1970s, etc.), who would play what parts?
- Why did the author write this book? What do you think the author wanted you to learn?
- What did you think of the plot development? Was it believable?
- Did the author paint the time period accurately?
- What type of tone does the author use? Is it humorous, prophetic, ominous, optimistic, pessimistic, preachy, or threatening?
- Do you see this work being set in another country or another time?
- How did you feel at certain key times during the plotline? Were there moments when you felt mad, sad, or glad?
- What did you think about the ending?

With some groups it may be necessary to throw all the questions away and just talk about why the members liked or disliked the book.

POSSIBLE BOOK DISCUSSION TITLES

Should the book club decide to let the librarian choose all the titles, staff may be concerned that their individual reading tastes might not make for a varied and mind-expanding experience. Choosing titles to read outside of familiar topics will not be a problem as publishers now post book discussion guides on their websites.

Jim Pletz, director of Adult Services and Americans with Disabilities Act (ADA) Compliance for the Chicago Public Library (aka Czar of Book Clubs of Chicago), offers a few tips for choosing book discussion titles:

Choose books that do not have a lot of heavy sex or profanity. But be cautious to use this as a guideline rather than as a hard-and-fast rule.

Choose books that are reflective in nature, requiring seniors to call upon past experiences.

Choose books that have an obvious touchstone.

Choose books that reflect back upon life's experiences or books with quirky characters.[13]

Staff can also log on to aforementioned senior-focused websites to note what titles are being discussed and which are receiving insightful input from the participants. Staff might also check the websites of libraries that host senior book talks to see what readers in a different city or state are reading. Librarians could also consider teaming up with one of these libraries to allow the members of their reading group the opportunity to exchange thoughts about a book with seniors at another library. This could be done through e-mail, chat rooms, videotape, or letters. This would expand both the seniors' and librarians' reading experiences and allow them to meet new friends and colleagues as well.

Figure 5-1 offers some initial title ideas. These titles were used successfully by senior book discussion groups at the Chicago Public Library, Cleveland Public Library, SeniorNet, Vacaville Public Library (California), and Almaden Branch Library (San Jose, California).

Book Discussion Groups for New Senior Readers

If there are seniors in the library's service area with low literacy skills, or new older adult readers, staff should consider forming a book discussion group for them as well. There are books written for the express purpose of encouraging new readers to get hooked on books. A literacy volunteer who worked with new teen readers and senior readers shared the story of how her group read and discussed an easy-to-read short novel. The novel (a literacy program creation) opened at a funeral home, with a widow crying over the coffin of her late husband. As the plot transpired, the group learned that the widow was actually laughing so hard that she was crying. The group became so entranced with the twist that all of the members signed up for library cards and became regular library users. This is a story that can be repeated with ease, by connecting with your local literacy league.

FIGURE 5-1
To Get You Started: A Year's Worth of Book Discussion Titles for Senior Groups

Alexander, Michael *Beowulf: A Verse Translation*

Byatt, A. S. *Possession: A Romance*

Fitch, Janet *White Oleander: A Novel*

Guterson, David *East of the Mountain*

Hannah, Kristin *On Mystic Lake*

Harris, Joanne *Chocolat: A Novel*

Ishiguro, Kazuo *When We Were Orphans*

Lee, Harper *To Kill a Mockingbird*

Lewis, Sinclair *Elmer Gantry*

Mah, Adeline Yen *Falling Leaves*

McCourt, Frank *Angela's Ashes*

Milford, Nancy *Savage Beauty: The Life of Edna St. Vincent Millay*

Naipaul, V. S. *A House for Mr. Biswas*

Nordhoff, Charles, and James Norman Hall *Mutiny on the Bounty*

Sobel, Dava *Galileo's Daughter: A Historical Memoir of Science, Faith, and Love*

Stegner, Wallace *Angle of Repose*

Tolkien, J. R. R. *The Fellowship of the Ring: Being the First Part of the Lord of the Rings*

Vidal, Gore *Golden Age*

Conclusion

Senior book discussion groups can be a lot of fun and at the same time offer patrons and staff a chance to grow intellectually and socially. Suzanne Rostamizadeh, manager, Almaden Branch Library, San Jose, California, sums up the reason for establishing book discussion groups for seniors: "The seniors get an opportunity to share good reads, new authors, interact with each other, form bonds with each other . . . [and] the library gets increased circulation, additional library supporters, and a presence in the community as the book discussion members talk to other seniors about their experiences." Rostamizadeh added that she feels that she gets the same perks from the book club as the seniors.[14] This sentiment is shared by many librarians who host book discussion groups.

NOTES

1. Beth Luey, Starting a Reading Group: Reading in Company, Arizona Center for the Book, available at <http://aspin.asu.edu/azcb/readgrp.html>. In certain countries, such as Cuba, professional readers are employed by cigar factories to keep the workers entertained as they hand roll cigars.

2. C. H. Cramer, Open Shelves and Open Minds: A History of the Cleveland Public Library (Cleveland: Case Western Reserve Univ., 1972). The Great Books Foundation conducted leadership training programs, from which a number of discussion groups emerged on what many considered to be a "high literacy" level.

3. Bowker, Complete Directory of Large Print Books and Serials (New Providence, N.J.: Bowker, annual).

4. Project Gutenberg, available at <http://gutenberg.net/>, allows the easy download and printing of numerous public domain texts. Braille translating software and an embosser are needed to translate text to Braille format.

5. Patrons and institutions who qualify for the service may download and print one copy of titles, magazines, sports schedules, and Braille music through the NLS website. To learn more about the Web Braille service, or to register your patrons, go to <http://www.loc.gov/nls/web.blnd>.

6. All residents of the United States and its territories who cannot use standard print material because of a physical disability are eligible for this free service. To locate the regional library in your state, see <http://www.loc.gov/nls>. Recorded media from the NLS can only be played on a four-track cassette player, which plays the tapes at the speed of 15/16 ips. This is done to ensure only eligible readers will use the books and to conserve tape. All four sides of the tape are used, meaning a full tape will play six hours.

7. The Canadian National Institute for the Blind, Library for the Blind, available at <http://www.cnib.ca/library>.

8. An international directory of information on various special media lending libraries is Misako Nomura and Mayu Yamada, eds., International Directory of Libraries for the Blind, 4th ed. (Munich: K. G. Saur Verlag, 2000). Also available at <http://ifla.jsrpd.jp/default.htm>.

9. Natke presented a book talk to several women's groups in Florida using the theme "Superior Women" and books that demonstrated how women are superior at different points in their lives. Some of the titles and traits included were David's Harp (Chaim Potok) and Clan of the Cave Bear (Jean M. Auel), demonstrating a young woman's fiber and grit; and Out on a Limb (Shirley McClaine) and Terms of Endearment (Larry McMurtry), talking about the mature woman. Natke also selected books that talked about the "whole of a woman's life."

10. Nora Jane Natke, "Book Talking Seniors" (presented at the Northeast Florida Library Information Network [NEFLIN] Headquarters, Orange Park, Fla., August 10, 2000).

11. Two of the more popular book discussion groups are hosted by the AARP at <http://www.aarp.org> and SeniorNet at <http://www.seniornet.org>.

12. Tools for Readers: How Literature Works I offers a four-week course and is found on the SeniorNet website at <http://www.seniornet.org> (Books and Literature, Round Table Discussions). The discussion is led by an authority in literature and walks participants through three short stories.

13. Jim Pletz, e-mail to author, April 2002.

14. The Web page of the Almaden Branch of the San Jose Library is <http://www.sjpl.ca.us/branches/ab/default.htm>. The group has been in existence for two years and meets once a month. The group began with a core membership of five members and has doubled in size. The group chooses books a year ahead of time to enable all members to read a book when it is available through the system. The book club is marketed through the monthly senior newspaper. The monthly title is mentioned in the library's resource column in the neighborhood newspaper.

6
Outreach Library Programming

We take library services and entertainment to nursing homes and senior centers to show that library services are for all patrons . . . *this program leaves me feeling I have benefited more than those we serve.*

—Wanda McWhirter-Heaton,
Senior Outreach Coordinator,
Beauregard Parish Library, DeRidder, Louisiana

Although most seniors are able-bodied and can get to the library, some cannot. The reasons are varied. Some may reside in nursing homes, others may not have transportation to the library, and still others feel threatened by changing neighborhoods and prefer to stay home whenever possible. Although some of these people may no longer want library services, others may and simply are not given the opportunity to do so. The library can make a significant difference by moving library services out of the physical library and into the areas where these groups of senior citizens reside to provide library services for all seniors.

Providing outreach services is not a new concept. Using a generous bequest, the Cleveland Public Library started professionally structured library service to the homebound in 1940, with other library systems following suit.[1] Although certainly valued by those who receive it, outreach services seem to come in and out of vogue. Libraries with a strong outreach services department will have an administration that sees library services to seniors as part of the library's mission and develops programming to include this population. Communities that have strong outreach programs find that the library's efforts make a difference and appreciate the fact that the library cares about the senior citizens as much as they do the youth.

Staff, Planning, Partners, and Volunteers Needed

Outreach services require staff, planning, the forging of partnerships within the community, and, in most cases, a strong, reliable volunteer force. The proportion of these needs will vary from library to library and community to community.

Most libraries will initially need planning time for the programs because in-house programming efforts cannot always be duplicated outside the library. Staff will also need time to establish initial contacts with the facilities at which the library wishes to offer services. Time will also be needed to train staff and volunteers about the etiquette and skills needed to "take the library to the people." If extra staff are not hired to perform outreach duties, creative scheduling will have to be done to ensure that the library is covered during the times staff are away from the main facility.

Community partnerships and a volunteer core will also be needed as both may be required to contribute time and money during economic downturns. Outreach library services require many one-on-one interactions between library staff and patrons. The more hands the library has reaching out to the isolated senior community, the greater the chance that seniors will be touched by the library. For libraries with large service areas and small staffs, volunteers are invaluable. Volunteers can make the difference between seniors being served and seniors being served effectively. However, volunteers must be selectively chosen, trained, and encouraged to remain volunteers.

In an article entitled "Public Library Service to the Homebound," Candice Brown, then coordinator of Library Homebound and Volunteer Services for Aurora Public Library in Aurora, Colorado, stated she relies very heavily on volunteers for homebound visits.[2] Brown stated that although the program always needs volunteers, volunteers are carefully screened and never accepted right away. She stated that after the initial interview, she urges potential volunteers to go home and think about the commitment. She stated that this is an important process that is not to be taken lightly, inasmuch as the volunteers are paired with the homebound patron and relationships are developed. It would be hurtful to the patrons if volunteers are accepted during brief bursts of altruism or if volunteers are simply trying to pass away the time until something else comes along.

Persons recruited for volunteer programs that take them into people's homes should receive the same screening process as library staff. Fingerprinting and background checks should be done because the volunteers may be working with some of society's most vulnerable members.

Community partners can help not only with financial donations and the donation of goods and services, but also by encouraging their staff to help with library programs. Although the actual costs of most programs (beyond paid staff) are not significant, the factor of transportation must be considered. In most cases, outreach services involve the use of vehicles, and vehicles do need to be fueled, serviced, insured, and maintained to stay roadworthy. Business managers who are charged with balancing the library's budget might see outreach as an expensive venture as the per capita service cost is high compared to in-house services.

Library Services in Nursing Homes

For many, the thought of visiting nursing homes to provide library services is not relished. To some people, nursing homes bring to mind images of pain, suffering, loneliness, sadness, and dementia. In some instances, this is the true snapshot of life for the residents. The United States does not allocate enough funds to ensure that there is sufficient personnel to meet both the physical and intellectual needs of nursing home residents. Frequently, when budget cuts are made, activity personnel are the first to be downsized. This translates to lack of meaningful activities for the residents. Libraries can help fill this recreational and educational gap.

Nursing Home Residents

Contrary to popular opinion, nursing home seniors are a diverse group. It is a mistake to assume that the residents of any particular home will have anything more in common than their mailing address. Some residents will be

mobile and alert. These residents have a strong grasp of who and where they are;

wheelchair users and alert;

stroke patients. Patients who are in nursing homes because of a stroke may be there for rehabilitation purposes. Some may not be able to speak clearly but are mentally sharp. Others may have paralysis on one side and have some weakness. Distributing book holders along with books or providing them with books on tape will help keep them sharp;

memory impaired and mobile. Some patients will not display any form of physical impairment, but may have some form of dementia. It is possible for staff to reach some of them through their personal fogs with the use of stories, poems, games, reminiscing, or song;

blind or visually or hearing impaired;

dentally impaired. Some residents who are unable to care for dentures often must go without them. This may mean some will have difficulty speaking and others may be reluctant to do so because they feel embarrassed.[3]

Whatever the reasons persons have for being residents of a nursing home, they are a group that has experienced some degree of impairment or loss. They need the services a nursing home offers, such as medical care, rehabilitation, food, shelter, companionship, recreation, and socialization.

Staff Preparation

Some library staff will not have a problem with hopping into a vehicle and driving to the local nursing home to present library programs, but others may resist the idea. There are a variety of reasons why a staff member may have trouble with on-site nursing home programs.

Some may not be able to cope with the conditions they see, while others prefer simply not to see such conditions. Staff should be encouraged to look beyond physical appearances and surroundings and think of these residents as "interesting individuals who have experienced much in life [and] have a unique personality which is not dependent upon appearance."[4] Staff who are especially affected by residents who may appear to be confused or disorientated should be advised that some of these people could be reached by simply "reaching out, touching the person and looking them in their eyes."[5]

Other staff members may not want to visit nursing homes because they think they will be seeing their own future and are fearful of it. The more that staff learn about nursing home residents and realize that nursing homes can be better places with the library's input, the more these attitudes should change.[6]

Should staff continue to feel uncomfortable about presenting programs in nursing homes, do not force them to go. Both the residents and the staff at the nursing home will sense the discomfort and will feel responsible, adding an unnecessary emotional burden. Consider allowing staff who express interest in visiting to do so even if it means the shifting of job responsibilities.

Making the Initial Contact

It is always important for the library's outreach administrator to establish contact with the nursing home community liaison and tour the home before any library service commitment is made. Successful nursing home liaisons tend to be made when working with the marketing director or social services department. These staff realize the importance of a library partnership for their residents, and the partnership will be a useful selling point.

Library staff should not overcommit when making the initial appointment. Rather, the liaison should start out on a general tone, such as, "The library is exploring the possibility of expanding its services." Library staff should come prepared with questions to ask nursing home staff, a potential service plan, and reasons why they feel the library can add to the quality of life for the residents. Figure 6-1 offers staff an outline that can be adapted to suit the library's needs. This outline should be personalized with the library's name, address and phone number, and contact person and should invite the nursing home staff to call with questions.

The questions asked by library staff should be pertinent to the services the library wishes to provide. For instance, should the library wish to present formal programs, staff could ask if the nursing home personnel would assist with getting residents to the meeting room. If the library wishes to offer some type of book-cart service to the home, staff might want to ask if nursing home personnel could help them get the cart in and out of the library's vehicle and into the home. The following standard operating questions should be asked:

FIGURE 6-1
Statement of Goals

_____

Facility name: _____   **Date:** _____

Our library resources, including staff and volunteer efforts, are dedicated to pursuing and achieving the following goals:

1. To serve our older readers [residents or patients] by providing information, education, and recreation.
2. To create opportunities for choice and independent activity on the part of those we serve.
3. To use books and related programs for reaching and stimulating persons with differing interests and abilities.
4. To provide both direct and indirect support to other facility services and departments, including [activities department; community outreach; nursing care and care planning; family support].
5. To assist us in meeting our regulatory and contractual obligations, including promotion of resident rights and enhancement of the quality of life of those we serve.
6. To contribute to our reputation for innovative service and quality care, thereby assisting in meeting marketing, volunteer support, community service, and development goals.

Library Name   _____

Address   _____

Contact Person/Phone/E-mail   _____

_____

Copyright CAREsource, 800-448-5213; reproduced with permission.

_____

What role does the nursing home see the library playing for its residents?

What type of support is the nursing home willing to provide the library? This could be in the form of reimbursing the library for fuel or any supplies. It could also be in the form of marketing and publicity ventures.

Would the nursing home's liability insurance extend to library staff?

Who should library staff report to when they arrive at the nursing home?

What time(s) and day(s) would be best for library staff to visit? Frequency of visits, as well as days and times of visits, should always be mutually agreed upon.

Are ancillary equipment and services available?

Does the nursing facility have a room in which library materials can safely be deposited?

Can the nursing home provide a staff member or volunteer to assist library staff?

Is the nursing home willing to provide any type of sensitivity training for library staff?

Does the nursing home have a written policy for nonstaff members to follow?

Libraries that currently provide nursing home services have mixed feelings about establishing a formal service contract with the nursing home. Those in favor of a formal contract feel that the library's interests are being protected. Those that don't favor a contract think that the library is better able to terminate the service should funding or staff be cut or the nursing home itself not live up to its promises. The decision to use a contract should be made by the administration of the library based on the library's needs in relation to those of the nursing home.

A compromise to a formal contract may be developed using suggestions outlined in figure 6-2, a sample library policies and procedures statement that can be given to the nursing home administrator. The library may ask that this statement of library concerns be posted in a common area and distributed to all personnel. The library may also ask that the nursing home administrator review the policies with the staff and draft a letter to the library administrator acknowledging receipt and distribution of the library's policies and procedures.

FIGURE 6-2
Library Policies and Procedures Statement

Library Name

POLICIES AND PROCEDURES
(last reviewed and approved: _____, 20__)

1. *Purpose*
   Our sole reason for existing is to serve our patrons. Library resources and programs are available to all [insert description, e.g., residents of _____]. Readers [residents] are also encouraged to bring visiting friends and family to socialize, participate in discussion groups and book clubs, and use the library's collection of books, tapes, and materials.

2. *Hours of Operation*
   [Insert hours during which the library will be open for use.]

3. *Activity Programs*
   [Describe supplemental activity programs such as a book club, discussion groups, continuing education seminars, slide shows, workshops, and classes. Include some programs at a regular time and place and other special programs as announced.]

4. *Staff*
   [List library staff, including librarian, regular library assistants, and key volunteers; include work numbers, if appropriate.]

5. *Information Service*
   As your library, one of our missions is to answer your questions. If we can help you answer a question or pursue a personal interest with the use of our library collection, we will.

6. *Computer Access*
   [Here describe any computer capability your library has to the extent it is available for reader (resident) use.]

7. *Book Checkout and Return*
   [State how long books and tapes may be checked out for and the fact that they should be returned on time unless renewed.] There will be no fines for late materials; replacement of lost or damaged books is at the librarian's discretion.

8. *Library Advisory Committee*
   The library advisory committee's responsibility is to consult with the librarian concerning library operations and service to readers. Your input and participation are welcome.

   Remember, all library services are free of charge to all readers in the facility. Readership and participation in library-sponsored programs are recommended for all. Bring a friend. Meet a friend.

Nursing Home Visiting Skills

Library staff should follow some guidelines when going into nursing homes to present programs and to provide library services. Perhaps the most important one to remember is that you are actually entering the patron's habitat, not a public building. With all the bustling and shared areas that are indigenous to nursing homes, the privacy factor is often overlooked. For instance, if staff are delivering books to patrons in their rooms, a brief knock on the door is a courtesy that should be extended to the resident. If the resident is unable to respond, announce yourself before entering the room.[7]

Staff members already possess many of the skills needed to present programs in nursing homes, namely, a positive and respectful attitude to those they serve. Although there may be a temptation to take a caregiver's attitude toward those who appear to have retreated to their childhood, staff should retain their professionalism both in attitude and in deed. Some other tips follow:

Call the residents by name. Patient's names are usually posted on the door.

Always avoid condescending terms of address such as "sweetie." It is just as important to conduct a reference interview with the resident as you would any other patron.

Be prepared to listen. If time is tight, close the conversation by explaining that you have to go, but you would like to hear that story some other time.

Give the nursing home patron as many choices as possible, in reading, listening, and programming selections.

Be patient. It will take more time to interact with some of the residents who have disabilities.

Do not make promises that you cannot keep. If you cannot guarantee the new book on the library's next visit, do not say you will bring it next time.

Speak clearly and in an unpretentious manner.[8]

One other bit of advice is to touch the patient. Many of the outreach personnel contacted when writing *Five-Star Programming and Services* attested to the need to "reach out and touch someone." However, should the library's legal or other counsel caution against such practices, heed their advice.

Books and Media by Van and Cart

Some seniors who are unable to get up and out really appreciate having books, magazines, and music brought to them as a browsing collection. This means that they should always be allowed to choose items for themselves. Although it is commendable for staff to tuck a few books away that they know a resident will like, the resident should also be presented with a cart from which he or she can choose a few more titles.

The King County Library System, in Washington, provides book-cart service to numerous nursing homes in its service area. Jean Bowman, assistant managing librarian for the Traveling Library Center, explained that the library is able to do this using specially ordered vans. Bowman explained that the fleet consists of two large vans equipped with hydraulic lifts that carry two staff members and five to six carts of books and one minivan equipped with a hydraulic lift that carries one staff member and three carts of books. The carts are then secured by cargo belts. Staff try to ensure the top shelves are full and fairly tight when in the van to keep books from spilling. The carts are easily unloaded at the nursing home by the staff or volunteers using the hydraulic lift. Residents are able to choose their reading or listening needs from a wider range of offerings.[9]

The King County Library System is also able to use its mobile units to help circulate inexpensive adaptive devices. The Center for Technology and Disability at the University of Washington purchased a number of adaptive devices such as magnifiers, pocket talkers, reachers, phone amplifiers, book holders, and so forth for the library to distribute to the community. The Center for Technology and Disability thought it would be natural to partner with the traveling program inasmuch as "public libraries serve as information hubs in the communities and as such are uniquely positioned to play an active role in helping people to learn about adaptive devices."[10]

Libraries should be mindful of the quality and selection of items they offer outreach patrons even though there is the risk of items not being returned. Libraries may wish to establish a gift fund or budget line for the purpose of maintaining a collection of materials that they can take pride in. Include the following selections:

• Best-sellers. Large-print format would be helpful.

- Books and magazines whose focus is nostalgia or reminiscence
- Large-print books and magazines
- Recorded books. Note: always bring a few applications for the National Library Service for the Blind and Physically Handicapped's (NLS) program when visiting nursing homes.
- Paperbacks with larger-sized print
- Cassettes or compact discs
- Nonfiction titles on subjects such as sports and biographies and travelogues
- Classics
- Books that are richly illustrated

It is also useful to loan patrons such items as book holders, lap tables, or magnifying glasses. These items are not usually provided by the nursing home, and many patrons are not aware they exist or do not have the means to purchase them.

In most cases, traditional checkout methods are impractical when distributing books from a book truck. Libraries can devise their own method to handle this procedure, but it is suggested that staff place a slip of paper in each item before going on the road, listing its title and identification number. These slips can then be easily taken out of the book when handed to a resident, allowing the staff member to write down who was given the book, the date, and the nursing home location. When staff members return to the library, this information can be entered into the computer's database. To simplify the transactions, the items can be charged out to the agency. Unless neglect on the part of the agency is observed, replacement prices of items lost by patrons should be waived.

Library Services in Senior Centers

In many communities, the Multipurpose Senior Centers (MSCs) are often the "in place" for older adults and are playing a new role in helping older Americans and their families cope with the new millennium.[11] The centers are often supported by tax dollars or federal and state agencies. It is not unusual for the local senior center to sponsor nutrition programs, health programs, recreation programs, and information programs. Some centers also extend their services to adult day care.

Most senior centers do not have large discretionary budgets, and programming ventures must be self-supporting. The staff of the senior centers should be eager to work with public entities, such as the library, that can bring intellectual and quality programming into the center.

Like the seniors who reside in nursing homes, the seniors who gather at the senior centers will not be a homogenous group. Their individual abilities will be similar to those residents who live in nursing homes, but they will be self-manageable. Some seniors may come to the center for the low-cost meals that help stretch their budgets, but most of the seniors come to the centers for the camaraderie and the chance to do something "different."

Some public libraries have agreements to provide some type of service to senior centers, much to the pleasure of the seniors who frequent them. The centers appreciate having the ability to give older adults sustenance to both the brain and the body.

Library Services in Senior Housing or Assisted-Living Facilities

Once again, we find that sharing the same mailing address does not necessarily mean sharing the same traits. Some seniors who live in government-subsidized senior housing are faced with similar financial limitations; however, their health and ability to be self-sufficient varies. Generally speaking, seniors who live in senior housing are a snapshot of what life as a senior is like.

The term *assisted-living facility* indicates that the residents who live there need some type of ongoing medical or daily living support, yet this is not always the case. Some residents will have some of the same impairments as those in nursing homes except they can usually be self-sufficient most of the time. Assisted-living arrangements provide residents with both independence and assistance if and when needed.

One common feature of senior housing development and assisted-living facilities is the fact that most support a secure activity room. This opens up the possibility of establishing a minilibrary for the residents, complete with an Internet connection to the library. If this is the case, it might be useful to find volunteer library workers and deputize them to introduce new and longtime residents to the library. A volunteer might also be willing to help form a book discussion group and serve as a facilitator in the event library staff cannot attend a club meeting.

Library Services to the Homebound

Some libraries provide services to the homebound, the majority of whom are seniors. On a predetermined schedule, library staff or volunteers deliver library service materials to those unable to leave their homes because of a physical impairment. Some libraries do not mandate that seniors must be impaired to receive homebound services; a statement of need on the part of the senior usually fulfills their requirements. Some seniors, regardless of their ability or disability, simply do not like going out for any reason but still want to remain alert by reading.

Homebound services are appreciated by patrons and staff alike. Often, home health-care workers and the library's representatives are the only people homebound seniors see and talk with. The service is so appreciated that although staff and volunteers never set out to solicit library donations, patrons' gratitude is often demonstrated monetarily.

How Three Libraries Provide Home Delivery of Books

The Kokomo-Howard County Library (Indiana), the Monroe County Public Library (Bloomington, Indiana), and the Medina County District Library (Ohio) graciously shared the details of how they provide home delivery of books.[12] The communities vary in size, but all serve populations under 170,000. Basically, the libraries ensure that homebound patrons receive the same types of materials that are available at the library.

When Kokomo-Howard initiates service for a homebound patron, a patron file is developed to enable the library staff to select materials for the patron. Favorite authors, subjects, and reading preferences are added to the file, as are such special needs as large-print materials, book holders, magnifiers, audiobooks, or page turners (these are also loaned). The staff attempt to adhere to the reader's profile and encourage requests. The Kokomo-Howard County Library has a well-defined volunteer program and issues a handbook of rules and regulations for the volunteers to follow.

The Monroe County Public Library has been delivering books to patrons since 1972, serving approximately sixty-five people. The service requires a delivery person who works about five hours a week and staff to help select books for patrons. The library visits the patrons once every four weeks and renews materials once, if there are no reserves waiting for the items. Patrons are charged for lost materials. Staff members feel that their homebound patrons are part of their extended family and even send them greeting cards.

The Medina County District Library delivers books to homebound patrons. Volunteers, who have been given a short orientation of the service, help staff make the deliveries and become "book buddies." The personalized service is a boon for isolated, rural residents. The staff have learned to laugh and cry with these residents, and very often they make a last visit to funeral parlors to say good-bye.

These libraries, in addition to others, stated that they do not reimburse volunteers for mileage nor carry liability insurance for them. Some libraries, like Medina, have started following the same hiring process for volunteers as they do for staff, which includes background checks and fingerprinting.

In general, libraries with home delivery state the volunteers are a must. They do remind their colleagues, however, that it is important to advertise for volunteers on a regular basis, interview all potential volunteers, monitor their work, and reward them for a job well done. This includes both hosting an appreciation luncheon and remembering to pass on notes thanking the library for their extra services.

Library Service to Seniors Using Mobile Services

Although bookmobiles never went out of style in rural areas, they did become rather unpopular in urban areas. They are, however, making a comeback in large metropolitan areas around the world, having the mission to serve underserved populations such as seniors.

For example, the Cleveland Public Library put the "People's University on Wheels" on the road in November 2001, with the express purpose of serving seniors and people with disabilities. The bookmobile visits senior housing developments and community centers whose residents indicated that they want to select their own books, magazines, videos, and DVDs. Additionally, the mobile unit maintains a Closed

Circuit Television Video display (CCTV), which can be used by seniors to read letters and bills as well as to help introduce them to adaptive technology. The mobile unit visits each site on a three-week rotation, and feedback from the community has been positive.

Keep these considerations in mind when using a mobile unit to deliver services to seniors.[13] There should be an easy and safe way for seniors to enter the bookmobile. Some bookmobiles have wider steps (twelve inches as opposed to nine inches), which give seniors more confidence as well as a secure spot to place a cane or walker. The steps should be solid, with nonskid surfaces. If the service is limited to older adults, libraries should consider purchasing a low-floored vehicle with only ramp access, not steps.[14] Other features to be included are a comfortable place to sit on the bookmobile, good lighting, software programs for people with disabilities, and readable print media shelved at eye level.[15]

Staff of mobile units that make senior stops say they get more out of the stops than the seniors they serve, but the seniors would be quick to argue the point. As one senior patron stated while checking out an armful of books, "There's nothing like making your own selections even if some of them turn out bad. . . . My daughter means well, but she only brought me those silly little romances. . . . I want something with a little kick to it!"

Bringing Programming into the Senior Environment

In the nursing home setting, as well as in assisted-living facilities and senior centers, the library's programming efforts may serve to broaden a planned activities schedule, but in others it may be one of a few stimulating continuing-education-type programs. The keys to planning and presenting effective programs off-site are to remember that you "are bringing the library with you" and that "many of the people at these sites were once regular library users; they are interested in what's going on at the library and what's new and of broad interest."[16]

Whatever type of program is to be presented, a few general guidelines should be observed:

Select programs that library staff enjoy and can get enthusiastic about when presenting the program.

Always be sure that everyone can hear the presentation. If necessary, use a microphone.

Promote the library's program. Ask staff at the facilities to post flyers announcing the title and type of the program, date, and time of the program. Be sure to state that all are welcome to attend. At each session, hand participants a few flyers and encourage them to invite their friends and family to join them the next time the library visits.

Always set an upbeat tone. Never force a staff member to present a program reluctantly. Their reticence will be picked up by the patrons.

Present programs that will appeal to all the senses. This is useful because some seniors may only have functional use of one or two senses.

Present programs that will appeal to a diverse audience.

Try to involve all who attend the program. This may be as simple as asking seniors' names and saying "We're glad you came."

Prepare to be patient. Some participants might be confused or hard-of-hearing and need to have questions or statements repeated.[17]

Following these guidelines will help any type of program have a greater chance for success. Remember to not be discouraged if the numbers of attendees are few or if some fall asleep during the program (they may be on medication).

Music

Programs that feature music are to be encouraged. Studies have found that music can reach parts of the brain connected to memories and can ignite a reminiscence process.[18] Some prepackaged programming kits, such as those by BiFolkal, include musical tapes. Another company, ElderSong, has as its mission to compile tapes that evoke memories of other times and places.[19]

Musical selections can be woven into almost any type of program. Librarians who are currently providing older adult programming report that they often play music appropriate to the program as patrons drift in. For example, if staff were doing a reminiscence program on World War II, some Glen

Miller or Andrews Sisters music would be appropriate. The possibilities of using music are endless and even help some Alzheimer's patients find a link from the past to the present.

Reading Aloud

Unfortunately, many of us tend to think reading aloud is a programming genre limited to children. In reality, reading aloud is great programming technique to use with adults, and it works well in nursing homes. In fact, staff of the New York Public Library have been successfully using Reading Aloud Programs with Older Adults in their outreach efforts for several years and generously share their experiences and offer useful tips:

The initial visit should include a variety of materials such as poetry, myths, short stories, essays, and biographical sketches. Use this visit to assess the setting and audience before doing long-range planning.

Choose readings that are appropriate for the group. For instance, if presenting a program for an adult day-care group of Alzheimer's patients, short vignettes or memoirs by a local author may be appropriate. If presenting a program at a home whose residents are primarily Jewish, Yiddish folktales might be appropriate.

Unless specifically requested, materials should not be too grim, gloomy, or juvenile.

Attempt to include essays about holidays or traditions.

Prepare for the presentation by reading the material several times. This will allow the presenter to make eye contact with the audience. If a book with reading material in it is too awkward to handle easily or the print is too small, make photocopies of passages and display the book.

Be friendly and open. Introduce yourself and try to find out something about the audience.

Introduce each reading.

Encourage audience participation, but do not demand it.

Be prepared to adapt to the audience. Residents may be having a bad day and respond inappropriately or fall asleep. It may be necessary to stop and explain something or repeat some

lines if the audience becomes disengaged. Some audiences may decide to turn the read-aloud program into a two-way discussion group. If the presenter is all right with this happening, and the audience is enjoying the interplay, then the program is successful.

Enjoy yourself![20]

Staff may use a variety of resources to locate suitable readings. Figure 6-3 provides guidance and a starting point. Variety in the resources that are read aloud is important because those in the audience have personal likes and dislikes. Finding material to read aloud is not hard. Many newspapers have columnists who on occasion will write about their memories, or the op-ed page may have several essays from older adults that could be shared. Additionally, magazines like *Reader's Digest, Good Old Days,* and *Reminisce* are filled with humorous and poignant stories that make excellent read-aloud materials.

Storytelling

Although those of us who are North Americans share a nationalistic commonality, most of us know where our ancestors originally came from, be it England, France, China, Germany, Russia, Spain, or Ethiopia. The immigrants brought tales with them that have been handed down from generation to generation. These stories when retold can bring a flood of memories back for some seniors. Stories can be those found in collections, among friends and families, and among the senior population. Cathy Spagnoli, a master storyteller, offers the following suggestions when telling stories to seniors:

A general selection of stories works well, including historical, humorous, and ghost tales.

When planning programs, remember to include stories from the various ethnic backgrounds of your listeners. Spagnoli's website, available at <http://www.cathyspagnoli.com>, has many rich links to tall tales, fairy tales, mythology, and folklore (indexed by countries and ethnic origin) that may be used by storytelling staff.

Help the seniors to remember true family stories, which recall special events, challenges, joys, and sorrows. It helps for seniors to sketch

FIGURE 6-3
Adult Read-Aloud Resources

Abrahams, Roger, ed. *Afro-American Folktales: Stories from Black Traditions in the New World.*

Burns, George. *100 Years, 100 Stories.*

Canfield, Jack, et al. *Chicken Soup for the Baseball Fan's Soul: From the World of Baseball.*

———. *Chicken Soup for the Cat and Dog Lover's Soul: Celebrating Pets as Family with Stories about Cats, Dogs, and Other Critters.* Or choose any other general titles in the Chicken Soup for the Soul series.

Carter, Jimmy. *Always a Reckoning, and Other Poems.*

———. *An Hour before Daylight: Memories of a Rural Boyhood.*

Erickson, John R. *Hank The Cowdog.* This children's series is full of innuendo, which makes it a lot of fun for adults.

Felleman, Hazel, ed. *The Best Loved Poems of the American People.*

Grizzard, Lewis. *Don't Bend Over in the Garden, Granny, You Know Them Taters Got Eyes.*

———. *Gettin' It On: A Down-Home Treasury.* Or choose any other Lewis Grizzard stories.

Herriot, James. *James Herriot's Cat Stories.*

———. *James Herriot's Dog Stories.*

———. *Selections: The Best of James Herriot: Favorite Memories of a Country Vet.*

Keillor, Garrison. *The Book of Guys: Stories.*

———. *Lake Wobegon Summer 1956.*

Krull, Kathleen. *Lives of Extraordinary Women: Rulers, Rebels (and What the Neighbors Thought).*

———. *Lives of the Artists: Masterpieces, Messes (and What the Neighbors Thought).*

———. *Lives of the Presidents: Fame, Shame (and What the Neighbors Thought).*

Lobb, Nancy. *Sixteen Extraordinary African Americans.*

———. *Sixteen Extraordinary Asian Americans.*

———. *Sixteen Extraordinary Hispanic Americans.*

———. *Sixteen Extraordinary Native Americans.*

Palgrave, Francis Turner, ed. *The Golden Treasury of the Best Songs and Lyrical Poems in the English Language Updated by John Press.*

Reiff, Tana. *Folktales.*

Rizzo, Janis, and Carolyn Banks, eds. *A Loving Voice: A Caregiver's Book of Read-Aloud Stories for the Elderly.*

———. *A Loving Voice II: A Caregiver's Book of More Read-Aloud Stories for the Elderly.*

Rubin, Robert Alden, ed. *Poetry Out Loud, with an Introduction by James Earl Jones.*

Spagnoli, Cathy. *Asian Tales.*

———. *Jasmine and Coconuts: South Indian Tales.* Also hosts a wonderful website, with links to a multitude of resources for storytelling, at http://cathyspagnoli.com.

White, Bailey. *Mama Makes Up Her Mind: And Other Dangers of Southern Living.*

———. *Sleeping at the Starlite Motel: And Other Adventures on the Way Back Home.* Or choose any other title by Bailey White.

---

maps of the houses and neighborhoods they lived in, adding pictures of family and friends.

Use language that paints a picture and captures a character or setting.

Encouraging seniors to add music, such as a melody, a sound, a chant, or a beat, can draw the participants into the story.

Ensure that the beginning is strong and that the ending of the tale works well, helping the listener feel satisfied.[21]

Spagnoli astutely adds that storytelling can be extended beyond the session. If seniors are up to the task, Spagnoli suggests having the seniors craft family story cards, which can be given as gifts to their relatives.

In libraries where staffing does not allow for off-site visiting, creating a storytelling video for nursing homes may be an option. Staff can consider taping stories they know, family stories, and stories from seniors who visit the library. These stories may help nursing home staff reach alienated seniors.

Reminiscing

Reminiscing (covered at length in chapter 4) is an excellent road program and can be taken to nursing homes, senior centers, and even patrons' homes. It can be done with formalized kits, a few props, or with some musical selections.

On the surface, reminiscing appears to be an excuse for people to chat about yesterday and things that don't really matter; however, in reality, oral and folk histories are an important part of society. If we do not try to encourage and collect memories of our seniors, they will be lost forever.

Book Talks and Book Discussions

Book talks and book discussions are programming genres that can successfully be taken on the road and into assisted-living facilities, senior centers, and nursing homes. Many times, the folks who reside in assisted-living facilities or nursing homes or attend programs at senior centers are still eager to hear about best-sellers today (good or bad) as well as to be reminded about best-sellers from yesteryear (very often these books are considered contemporary classics) even if they have no desire to read the book. They want to know enough to carry on conversations with their relatives and friends who might be avid readers. This is where book talks play a key role. Staff who share a book's essence with seniors will help them be aware of its existence and stay attuned with today's pop culture.

Residents of nursing homes or assisted-living facilities should also be given the opportunity of having any of the books discussed delivered to them in a timely fashion.

Extending the Senior Book Club to the Community and Vice Versa

Many communities across the country are focusing on the enjoyment of shared reading by reading the same title. This gives people waiting for transportation or eating at a restaurant "something to talk about" besides the weather. Recently, CAMLS (a library consortium in northeast Ohio) launched a program entitled "Northcoast Neighbors Share a Book," the first book being *To Kill a Mockingbird*. CAMLS cam-

paigned for community involvement. In spite of the complexity of the book, several nursing homes, assisted-living facilities, and a group of seniors who were visually impaired signed up to be official supporters of the reading endeavor and agreed to read and discuss the book. The discussions went on for several sessions and were filled with insightful observations as well as personal anecdotes, both pleasant and disturbing. Positive comments on the diversity of the readership were heard throughout the campaign. Seniors in the assisted-living facilities and nursing homes stressed the fact that they truly felt like part of the community.

Computer Training

Off-site computer training by library staff is possible and, in fact, is being done by several libraries in North America. Among them are the Collier County Public Library (Naples, Florida) and the James V. Brown Library (Williamsport, Pennsylvania). Libraries report that the enthusiasm and success of the residents make the venture worthwhile.

Library staff will need to work closely with activity directors and grant makers to make this happen. A lot of time and effort will have to be devoted to the project, but seniors who are particularly cogent will be able to travel the world, make new friends, and find old ones. Consider the following when establishing computer connections outside the library:

The nursing home, assisted-living facility, or senior center should agree upon a secure location for the computer, install communication lines, and retain an Internet provider.

Facilities should also agree that the computer is for residents, not staff, and that staff usage will be discouraged.

Facilities should apply for a grant to pay for the new, accessible computer, equipment, and furniture and a short-term trainer.[22] Although it may seem logical to place gently used but older equipment off-site, remember, the equipment is older, slower, and more susceptible to incompatibility problems. It is important to have a trainer who can work with residents, volunteers, and staff at the facilities on a fairly regular schedule.

Once a computer is in place, training can begin using the same methods offered to in-house patrons.

The trainer should take note of resident seniors who are quick to catch on to the new technology and suggest that they be deputized to be troubleshooters when library staff are unavailable.

There should always be an adequate supply of paper (facility staff may have to be asked to monitor the paper or dole it out when needed), printer ribbons or cartridges, and diskettes.

The trainer should also make a one- or two-page "Averting a Crisis" guide, which can be laminated and mounted in the work area. This sheet will tell users how to log off the computer, how to turn off the computer in case logging off doesn't work, and how to proceed when a hard boot was done. Information on how to contact the library should also be provided in large, clear type.

The facility should provide a phone adjacent to the workstation.

The library and the facility should not venture into setting up a computer station if either party is not prepared to support it on a long-range basis. The worst thing to do would be to get a patron interested in computers and e-mail and then take it away. This form of outreach is one that takes a lot of commitment and should not depend on one particular individual's enthusiasm.

Conclusion

Outreach service to seniors is time-consuming and not necessarily cost efficient in the minds of many fiscal agents. However, those who use the services cannot adequately express their gratitude for the service existing. One senior who takes advantage of the homebound service commented, "Exceptionally good service. My volunteer manages to get me any book I request, and the books are in great condition, and I really appreciate the company." A volunteer with the same library commented, "I enjoy my visits. . . . It does not take up too much time, and the rewards are worthwhile."

NOTES

1. C. H. Cramer, *Open Shelves and Open Minds: A History of the Cleveland Public Library* (Cleveland: Case Western Reserve Univ., 1972), 199. The first librarian to formally head this department was Clara E. Lucioli, a pioneer in the field of outreach services. Approximately four years earlier, the renowned librarian Linda Eastman had started an informal distribution system to shut-ins using Girl Scouts to deliver books.

2. Candice Brown, "Public Library Service to the Homebound," *Colorado Libraries* 16, no. 3 (September 1, 1990), 14–15. Available at <http://www.colib volunteers.org/Articles/artic016.htm>.

3. Ron Staufer, *Show Them That We Care Handbook: A Nine-Step Guide to Visiting Residents in Nursing Homes* (Hilliard, Ohio: Carevideo, 2000). Available at <http://www.carevideo.com>.

4. Senior-site provides tips on Visiting Someone in a Nursing Home, available at <http://seniors-site.com/nursingm/nhvisit.html>.

5. Ibid.

6. Ibid.

7. Ibid.

8. Anne M. Ring, *Read Easy: Large Print Libraries for Older Adults: Planning Guide, Operations Manual, Sample Forms* (Seattle, Wash.: CAREsource Program Development, 1991), 61–64.

9. Jean Bowman, e-mail to author, April 2002.

10. Dagmar Amtmann and Susan Ford, "Increasing Access to Assistive Technology Devices for People with Disabilities through Public Libraries" (paper presented at the March 2000 California State University–Northridge [CSUN] Conference), available at <http://www.csun.edu/cod/conf/2000/proceedings/0223Amtmann.html>. The full catalog of devices available through this program can be viewed at <http://wata. org/catalog/index.htm>.

11. MSCs offer health, fitness, and wellness programs; recreational and educational opportunities; arts programs; volunteer opportunities; employment assistance; intergenerational programs; social and community action opportunities; meals and nutrition programs; information and assistance; and other services, according to the Administration on Aging, available at <http://www.aoa.gov/factsheets/seniorcenters.html>.

12. E-mails to author, February and March 2002.

13. Clarion University maintains a website that addresses bookmobile issues and services. At this site, libraries can pick up some useful tips on how to buy a bookmobile, survey results of bookmobile usage, and find the National Bookmobile Guidelines. The university is also the publisher of the journal *Bookmobiles and*

Outreach Services. The URL for Clarion is <http://eagle.clarion.edu/~grads/csrl/csrlhom.htm>.

14. M. Tower, "Seniors and Mobile Library Services," *Bookmobiles and Outreach Services* 3, no. 2 (November 2000): 37–42. These vehicles are smaller and cannot carry as heavy a load.

15. Ibid. This can be achieved by ribbon shelving (i.e., arranging materials that seniors use most often in a continuous line on one or both sides of the vehicle from front to back).

16. Frances Rabinowitz, "Tips for Reading Aloud to Older Adults outside the Library" (paper presented at the American Library Association Annual Conference, Chicago, June 2000), 1–5.

17. Ring, *Read Easy*, 71.

18. Oliver Sacks, "Music Heals Body and Soul," *Parade Magazine* (March 31, 2002): 4–5. Further information on the connection between music and neurological diseases and injuries may be found at <http://www.musichaspower.org>.

19. BiFolkal may be reached at 609 Williamson St., Madison, WI 53703; 800-568-5357; or <http://www.bifolkal.org>; ElderSong publications may be found at <http://www.eldersong.com>.

20. Unpublished documents from the Outreach Department of New York Public Library program "Words Are Music" were presented at the American Library Association 2000 Annual Conference.

21. Cathy Spagnoli is a master storyteller and has collected stories from around the world. Her generosity of knowledge sharing can be acknowledged by a visit to her website, available at <http://www.cathyspagnoli.com>. This website is great for locating stories from every possible corner of the globe. She also includes tips and themes to use with storytelling. Share this site with your youth services department staff.

22. The grant should cover the cost of a large monitor, top-of-the-line PC, sturdy chair, worktable, and software. The grant should also allow for recruiting and hiring a trainer. The trainer should be able to teach a diverse group of seniors and must be willing to do the training at the facility. The person should be able to work independently and to assess and respond effectively to emergency situations as they arise.

7
Computers and Seniors

*When I was a boy of fourteen, my father was so ignorant I could hardly
stand to have the old man around. But when I got to be twenty-one,
I was astonished at how much the old man had learned.*

—Mark Twain

When it comes to seniors and their approach to computers and the Internet, it is good to once again remember that seniors come from many "cultures, educational backgrounds, financial levels, and life experiences with skills developed over a lifetime."[1] Although seniors are a diverse group, learning computer technologies and accessing the Internet may be more important for them than any other age group. In addition to needed information being posted on websites, many seniors are freed from the "requirements and obligations of their youth and have the opportunity to explore new vistas and discover fresh interests."[2]

In spite of the promise of computers improving one's life, seniors comprise the smallest number of people using the Internet (18 percent compared to 42 percent for the general population).[3] When trying to determine the reason for this disparity, a common misconception is that seniors are stubborn, resistant to change, and hate everything new. However, this is far from true. Jeff Pepper, chief executive officer of ElderVision, states that the reluctance is caused by the facts that the computer is nonintuitive and that seniors have age-related physical factors (e.g., difficulties operating a mouse, seeing the screen) that inhibit use. Additionally, Pepper states the Windows environment is daunting in itself, and websites are overrun with pop-up ads, streaming video, plug-ins, and so forth, which are confusing.[4]

In spite of all the foibles that exist in cyberspace, more seniors are surmounting these obstacles and using computers and the Internet. In fact, the senior population comprises the fastest-growing demographic of computer users.

In a study conducted in 1995 only 29 percent of seniors surveyed reported having a computer, and only 17 percent of them reported using the Internet.[5] Researchers conducting a similar study approximately two years later saw these numbers rise respectively to 40 percent computer ownership with 70 percent using the Internet![6]

Once seniors realize how they can exploit computers and the Internet, they do. In a study conducted by the Pew Institute, researchers found that 84 percent of seniors who owned computers and accessed the Internet did not do so for work or school.[7] Seniors reported that they use the computer to connect with their children and grandchildren, because the miles between them disappeared with a few mouse clicks. In fact, 60 percent of the group surveyed by Pew reported that the Web improved their relations with their families, inasmuch as their relations included them in groups to which they sent interesting news articles or jokes.

Even though the number of seniors using the Internet is growing rapidly, a significant amount of seniors are still not using it. With the wealth of information that can be found on the Internet, these seniors are losing ground in access to information with their computer-literate peers. Librarians can seek to encourage those who are not using computers by introducing seniors to computers in the same manner as they entice new readers to discover the joy of books. Once seniors are introduced to computers and the Internet in an encouraging and nonthreatening manner, they will see how computers can be of help to them.

Profile of Seniors Currently Online

The Pew study indicated that the digital divide that is present within the younger population extends to the older generation as well. Of the seniors online, it was found that they are more educated, more likely to be married, male (even though there are more seniors who are female), and have higher incomes than their peers who are not Internet users.[8]

Knowing the makeup of the library's senior community will help staff decide what type of classes to host and the number of public PCs to install with accommodations for seniors' physical needs. Knowing if there is the potential for the library's seniors to be wired will also help the library determine how the library's website can be used to help seniors easily connect to the resources they need.

Outfitting the Library's Computers for Senior Hands and Eyes

Because a portion of the senior population has some type of physical disability that limits their abilities to effectively and efficiently access a standard PC, the library must offer PCs that can be used by the entire senior population. Remember that although the library is adding hardware and software to standard computers for seniors, this does not make the computer unusable to the younger population or those without disabilities.

In March 1997 the Seniors' Education Centre, University Extension, University of Regina, conducted a study to determine how a new computer laboratory should be designed.[9] The study surveyed people across Canada and the United States who worked with older adults. The data provide the useful workstation guidelines below.

The Monitor

A large monitor is perhaps the most important piece of hardware to place. The monitor should be at least fifteen inches, although a monitor that is seventeen inches or larger is preferred. The larger display area allows the user who needs to use a text enlarger to see more words on the screen, facilitating reading and comprehension of text displayed.

Ensure there is adequate lighting, and allow the user to adjust the brightness and contrast of the display with the touch of a button. Some people with specific eye diseases can actually see lower-contrast displays better than those with high contrast.

Jane Berliss-Vincent, Center for Accessible Technology, suggests that monitors should have a tilt adjustability range of 5 degrees toward the user and 20 degrees away from the user.[10] The adjustability feature helps avoid glare to the users. She also suggests that the refresh rate and the resolution be balanced. A refresh rate of 85 to 90 hertz is optimal, although the refresh rate may be lower if the luminance is adjustable.[11]

The Keyboard—Solutions for Vision Needs

The Regina study respondents indicated that a standard keyboard would suffice, because many older adults learned touch-typing in their youth and still instinctively know where keys are. Respondents indicated that a large return (enter) and arrow keys would be useful, as would a set of raised dots in strategic places to facilitate navigation.

Many trainers who have worked with older adults suggest there are seniors who need to peek at the keyboards, so it is helpful to have large-print key tops. There are three options: the library can use "peel-and-stick" key tops as shown in figure 7-1, replace the actual keys with large-print keys, or buy a large-print keyboard. Unless the library faces regular ongoing vandalism of computer equipment, the "peel-and-stick" key tops, priced at under $20, are a viable solution.

A more expensive but longer-lasting solution to accommodate persons with low vision is to purchase a bold-print keyboard. These keyboards can be purchased for $100 to $175 and have a plug-in IBM PC or Mac compatibility feature.

For those who feel that only the home row keys need to be designated and do not want to purchase a separate keyboard, individual large-print keys can be purchased for about $12 each.

The Keyboard—Solutions for Physical Needs

Although the respondents to the Regina study did not indicate the need for specially designed keyboards, Berliss-Vincent points out that keys that are more easily depressed are more comfortable to use. There are also keyboards that could enable persons with physical disabilities, such as arthritis, to input data with less difficulty.[12]

The Mouse—Is the Most Usable Mouse in the House?

Not being able to move the cursor to the intended target with the mouse can cause some seniors to become easily frustrated and more willing to give up. Although there are mouse-use tutorials, there are also hardware solutions that may help. The Regina respondents indicated that although a standard mouse may work for some seniors, an alternative mouse, with a large track ball, would be beneficial for people with arthritis or Parkinson's disease as well as for those who have coordination problems. One line of track balls allows the hand to rest on the body of the device while the thumb manipulates the ball to move the cursor, the forefinger moves the page up or down, and large buttons are used to perform the left and right click tasks.

FIGURE 7-1
Alternate Key Tops

Researchers have observed that computer users over age forty take more time zeroing in on the target, which translates to older computer users manipulating the mouse for longer periods of time.[13] Reducing the amount of force required to perform mouse tasks can help alleviate strain and prevent injuries.

A Comfortable Work Space for Seniors

Although some have disagreed on the type of equipment seniors would need in Regina's computer lab, all of the respondents stated the need for adequate lighting and a large desk or work area as an important comfort factor.[14] The respondents also addressed the need for adequate space between workstations and a chair that was both comfortable and supportive (chapter 2 discusses furnishings for seniors).

Software for Seniors— Screen Magnification Programs

Perhaps the most important piece of software the library can purchase is screen magnification software, which allows users to dictate how the information will be displayed. This includes the ability to adjust the font size, change the color of the background and foreground of the text, allow text to be read one line at a time, enlarge the cursor, and add extra magnification where needed. Once patrons find their personalized best settings, they can save the profile for future use.

In general, screen magnification programs are easy to use. Seniors who need to use a screen magnification program should learn how to use it before proceeding to Internet training or word-processing programs. It is difficult to learn if one is fixated on trying to see the screen.

There are several popular software packages in the marketplace, and they are all approximately the same price.[15] Staff should seek guidance from their visually impaired community as to which one has the greatest usage. This approach will save library staff valuable training time, plus create a pool of peer counselors.

Software for Seniors— Screen Reading Programs

For seniors with severely limited vision, it will be necessary to purchase screen reading software. It is highly recommended that seniors who need this accommodation learn how to use the software before proceeding to learn how to use the Internet or do word processing. Users need the immediate feedback of knowing what was keyed or found; waiting until the instructor observes them is simply not enough. Screen reading programs actually make on-screen information available as synthesized speech or as a refreshable Braille display.[16] Screen readers can only read text. This is important to remember when designing or recommending websites. Graphics can only be interpreted to the blind user if the graphic is properly tagged with an [ALT-TEXT] description.

Like the screen magnification programs, there are only a few products on the market, and the prices and attributes of each are similar.[17] Again, it is prudent to inquire as to the product that is being used in the library's print-impaired community.[18] It is useful to establish a pool of potential volunteer or paid tutors who can help patrons learn how to use the software.

Learning how to use a screen reader is not difficult, but it does take patience. Although it is possible to change voices (male and female voices are provided) and change speech output attributes such as verbosity, rate, and pitch of speech, the speech is still synthetic. One must become accustomed to the synthetic speech, and this comes with time.

Microsoft Programs

Microsoft's credo concerning access to technology by persons with impairments is simply "Microsoft Accessibility: Technology for Everyone," and, to their credit, the latest releases have attempted to be inclusive. To that end, the company's website has an extensive overview of disabilities, a "how to" for their products, and links to producers of adaptive equipment.[19]

Microsoft's accessibility products include software that will help those with visual disabilities, mobility impairments, hearing impairments, and cognitive and language impairments. Although these products do not have the sophistication of specialized software, they may be usable by patrons. One caveat: to open the programs one must use the Utility Manager to access the programs. In larger library systems, or in systems where staffing is limited, it may not be possible to activate the package when needed, making this option nonviable.

For libraries where staff can activate the accessibility options, such as in computer labs, note that once a patron finds tools that work for him or her, the tools can be saved to a file. This step alleviates the need to set the preferences for patrons each time they visit.

Two examples of Microsoft accessibility products that can help seniors with limited use of their hands to proficiently perform keyboard and mouse tasks are StickKeys and MouseKeys. StickKeys allows users to press one key at a time rather than use a key combination such as [CONTROL-ALT-DELETE] to perform a task. MouseKeys allows the user to control the pointer using the numeric keypad. Other accessibility features that could help seniors with hearing impairments include the SoundSentry and the ShowSounds feature. When programmed sounds are made to indicate something is happening that the user should be aware of, these devices give visual warnings.

Seniors as Learners— Providing the Right Training Tools

Some people are able to sit down, assemble a product, and use it properly without reading the instructions, but most of us are not able to do this and must read the text provided. It is also true that some people are able to teach themselves new tasks, but most of us learn better when we have a teacher. Thus, it is not sufficient to tell a senior, "Well, there's a computer with a large monitor and display; happy surfing!" Most seniors will need instructions they can read and classes designed for them.

Introducing the Computer to Seniors

For seniors who know little about the potential of computers, an introduction is necessary. Staff must sell computer use to seniors by teaching them why using a computer may be good for them. Figure 7-2 lists a variety of ways seniors might enjoy and profit from computer use. In a study designed to determine how to improve older adults' access to the Internet in a public library setting, Kirsty Williamson, associate director of the Telecommunications Research Group (TNRG), demonstrated the Internet to some seniors who had negative attitudes toward computers yet had never seen a computer "in action."[20] After the demonstration, TNRG asked if the seniors who

FIGURE 7-2

Selling the Concept of Computer Use to Seniors

Keeping in touch with family both distant and far. A senior learning how to use e-mail was astounded when an e-mail sent to his son was answered within minutes. It might be useful to point out that although the library cannot allow patrons to use the telephone to make long-distance calls, the Internet can be used to contact anyone who has access to e-mail.

Expanding the opportunities to read about news and current events. Seniors who have relocated may be interested to learn they can read their old hometown newspapers.

Exploring medical websites. Learning what questions to ask a medical provider is important to many seniors, as they do not want to be perceived as "addle brained."

Gathering information on entitlements and retirement funds.

Gathering travel information. Finding low-priced airfares and hotel accommodations is only the start. Many websites offer unique sightseeing tips and money-saving coupons for meals.

Participating in online discussions and chat rooms. Some seniors live alone, and finding someone to listen and talk with them can be a challenge. The Internet never closes, and there is always someone out there willing to listen and exchange ideas,

Banking and investing. Some seniors have only used passbook savings at their local bank or savings and loans as their investing guide and are hesitant to explore options face-to-face or via the phone. The Internet gives one anonymity: no one knows if the person asking a question is twenty-six or sixty-six or if they have a lot of money or very little. Investing tutorials are a big plus.

Shopping and gift buying. When the weather outside is frightful, the Internet is climate controlled. The Internet also offers the opportunity to comparison shop, for example, to determine if the auto dealer really means it when he says, "You remind me of my grandma [or grandpa], so I'm taking an extra $100 off the price of the car!"

Checking the weather. Although the weather channel is always available (on the cable network), some seniors may not have cable or may be interested in weather in specific cities, states, or countries.

Pursuing other educational opportunities. The Internet offers the opportunity to participate in book discussions, pursue distance-learning opportunities, and obtain that elusive degree. The computer is a very patient teacher.

Adapted from earlSpeak at <http://www.earlspeak.com/visitors.htm>.

originally had negative attitudes toward the new technology would like to use the Internet again, and 85 percent replied affirmatively. Some of the comments made by seniors in this group follow:

> "It's mind boggling! Beats TV any day. At over fifty [years of age] it provides a whole new area of interest."

> "I was glad to be in the survey because I didn't know it was available." [respondent in her seventies]

> "I would use the Internet again, because it's something new. It's worthwhile learning."

The comments by survey participants show an overwhelming affirmation of accepting the Internet once seniors learn how it can help them in life. Staff can help spread their enthusiasm for knowledge and continuous education by demonstrating the Internet's potential to a group of people who have only heard about computers, the Internet, and the World Wide Web (WWW).

As staff meet and work with seniors, they will become aware of more selling points. Don't worry if every senior you approach doesn't embrace this technology, as there are also some younger folks who still haven't been convinced.

Instructing Seniors

Caution about the Web's Fallibility

Although it is important for staff to inform seniors of all of the positive reasons why they should learn how to navigate the WWW, it is also important for staff to tell seniors that the Web is not infallible. Before, and often during, training sessions it behooves staff to caution seniors that not everything they will find on the Internet can be accepted as factual. Many of today's older adults grew up in a time when facts were checked and rechecked before they appeared in print. Newspaper writers verified that their sources and the information they reported were reliable. Although print publishers and editors try to maintain the integrity of their publications, many website publishers do not. Even more dangerous is the explosion of individuals who are starting their own websites and filling them with information that has never been verified or is even deliberately misleading. People need to be taught how to determine who the author is and

how to find out background information about the author, beyond that which is provided on the website.

Basic Teaching Techniques

When planning computer classes for seniors, staff should be aware that what will work with one group of seniors may not work with another. Some older adults may have used a computer before they retired, some may have retired because computers were added to the workplace, some may have been led to believe that computers make mistakes, and still others may believe the computer may solve all of their problems. In her work *Teaching the Internet in Libraries*, Rachel Singer Gordon cautions library staff to "avoid prejudging class attendees as either technophobic or technologically inept or lumping all seniors together . . . , assuming that they will be less able than other trainees to assimilate technological knowledge."[21]

When selecting instructors, ensure that the person chosen will be enthusiastic and have a positive attitude. He or she should be willing to encourage participants with words of praise. The instructor should always seek to reduce stress and anxiety by not rushing the students and allowing time for questions and discussions to help seniors better understand techniques. The instructor should avoid rapid movements and speak in distinct, low tones.

Basic Tips for Senior Computer Training

Instructors believe that there are some common methods that work well for older adults. Listed below are some tips to keep in mind when working with seniors.

1. Ensure that the computer classroom is accessible, free from distractions, and the temperature is set at a comfortable level.

2. Ensure that students can see and hear the instructor.

3. If possible, schedule morning or early afternoon classes. Some seniors have a tendency to lose focus as the day wears on.

4. Limit sessions to a maximum of two hours to avoid fatigue.

5. Ensure that the brightness and contrast settings on your monitors are set at reasonable levels, and be familiar with the quirks of the individual computers.

6. Provide rest breaks to allow participants to stretch and use the rest room.

7. Demonstrate mutual respect.

8. Stress to participants that computers do not break easily.

9. Make learning objectives clear and specific to avoid irrelevant information entering the students' working memory.

10. Break instruction into small units. Tell participants what they are trying to accomplish and let them try it. Let the information and the process sink in before moving on to the next unit. Also, allow the seniors to practice what they learned before moving on to the next lesson.

11. Structure tasks to be simple, independent, and sequential.

12. Help students understand the meaning and relevance of what is being taught.

13. Be careful to explain technical terms to older adults. For example, explain what the computer "icon" is or what it means to be "connected."

14. Remind students that all websites on the Internet are not well designed, and that even if the seniors' vision is good, they may not be able to see everything on the website.

15. Provide students with written handouts and "cheat sheets" that they can review at home. Handouts should include screen shots, pictures, and clearly drawn diagrams. The font used to develop the handouts should be at least fourteen points in size and be sans serif. The paper should not be neon colored or have a sheen. Additionally, handouts should be clearly laid out. It is important to use class time to review the handouts. [22]

If at all possible, seek out volunteers who may be able to act as tutors during the class sessions. Many seniors prefer teachers who are of their own age and can speak their language. Resist the temptation to move the mouse for slow learners, and remind others to do the same.

Although some seniors may have access to computers away from the library, many beginners may not. It is important to block some computer lab time off for older adults to come in and practice between classes. Some may find it helpful to bring a friend with them, and others may partner with a classmate to practice new skills. Establishing a Senior Computer Club may be useful, as it stands to bring users together in an informal setting, allowing them to share tips and lessons learned. In addition to learning new tasks, some older adults may find new friends.

What to Teach

Mousing and Scrolling

The TNRG study (mentioned above) also sought to determine what was causing problems for the seniors who were using the Internet. The most common problem observed was mouse usage for pointing, clicking, and scrolling. Other problems included the concepts of hypertext links, waiting for a screen to load, and remembering to place the cursor in the search box before typing.[23] A track ball device would alleviate some of the problems caused by diminished dexterity, but the eye-to-hand-to-click is a skill that is developed only by practicing.

Several public libraries offer online "tutoring" by providing games that help novices learn mouse skills without inducing stress. Participants can log on to the site whenever and wherever they can get computer access.[24] The familiar game of Solitaire is also a good way for seniors to learn "clicking" and "dragging" techniques.

E-mail

Some have misgivings about teaching e-mail before teaching Windows, yet e-mail instructions may be the carrot that grabs hold of the seniors and retains their interest in computers. When Window functions are used in e-mail, the instructor can point out that this is a "Windows" function.

Without a doubt, most seniors enjoy using the Internet for e-mail. Seniors appreciate having the ability to maintain contact with friends and especially with families, as it is "easier, quicker, and cheaper than making long-distance phone calls or paying for postage."[25] Once seniors acquire an e-mail address and begin receiving e-mail, they are more likely to check for e-mail messages than other e-mail account holders.[26]

It is helpful to provide participants with an overview of how e-mail works. For those who cannot grasp the concept, ask them to have faith. Listed below are some steps that can be used to teach e-mail to seniors:

1. Explain what e-mail is and how it is transmitted.

2. Explain the function of the e-mail icons. Provide a large-print diagram that mirrors the screen.

3. Walk the class through the process of setting up a free e-mail account. Explain that this is his or her personal cyberaddress, and it needs to be given to friends, relatives, and others to allow them to exchange e-mail. Take time to be sure that everyone has successfully set up his or her account. Encourage the seniors to choose a password that they can remember, and remind them to keep it confidential.

4. Explain the different components of an e-mail address. Reinforce the need to have a complete e-mail address when sending e-mail.

5. Describe how to launch an e-mail program, and have the class launch it.

6. Step-by-step, prompt seniors to type in their neighbor's e-mail name and a subject on the appropriate lines. When they get to the message box, have them compose a short message that asks a few questions. When everyone is finished, have him or her send the message to his or her neighbor. Pause to stretch a few minutes.

7. Relay steps for retrieving e-mail. Review with the class how participants can look at a piece of e-mail and determine who sent it. Briefly explain e-mail viruses.

8. Have the class respond to the e-mail message they received and send the message back by hitting "Reply."

9. Allow the class to practice sending and receiving mail with each other, and after they have sent about five or six messages, tell them how to delete some of the messages in their mailboxes.

10. Explain how to check for sent messages, sift through "trash," and empty the mailbox.

These are only the very basic steps of e-mail, and library staff may adapt them to suit the class.[27] Remember to send the class a few e-mails during the week to allow them to practice their e-mail skills. Encourage the class to ask their friends and family for e-mail addresses and have them connect with the new addresses they acquired.

Windows

The thought of teaching Windows is daunting, but basic Windows will have to be explained to allow students to navigate the system. The first concept to get across is that Windows is an operating system that allows the user to give it orders. Include the following topics:

- Desktops
- Tool bar or function keys
- Icons
- Drivers such as A: and C:
- Files, folders, and extensions
- Booting up and logging off
- Opening, moving, and resizing a window
- What a menu is
- When all else fails, how to shut the computer down using the commands [CONTROL-ALT-DELETE]

Once the students know Windows, they will be able to complete most tasks. It is good to pass on any tips by providing students with a troubleshooting or "don't panic" guide. One tip to include is, if a "soft boot" won't allow them to exit Windows, they can always turn off the computer.

The Library's Online Catalog and Databases

If the seniors who attend the library's computer classes have not been recent users of the library, they probably remember the library's catalog as a massive wooden fixture with rows and rows of drawers. In this case, instruction on how to use the library's online catalog would be useful. After showing the class how to find the catalog, explain how to enter an author, title, or subject search. Point out how to locate the call number of the item, the location of the item, and whether the item is available for borrowing.

If there are students who are interested in doing extensive research (the type that can be found in subscription databases), individualized database classes could be offered. Because of the complexity of some of the databases, this curriculum should be offered after the users feel very confident.

Internet Lessons

Most seniors will want to know what the Internet is. It can be explained simply as a worldwide network of computers that talk to each other electronically. Seniors would enjoy knowing that it was developed by their peers, in the 1960s by the Advanced Research Projects Agency of the U.S. Department of Defense, as a way for scientists and government officials to communicate in the event of a nuclear war and was originally called ARPANET.[28]

The following topics should be covered and explained:

- What is the World Wide Web? Tell students that not every document that can be retrieved on the Internet is on the Web.
- Briefly explain website idiosyncrasies and nuances. Talk about pop-up boxes and other annoyances.
- Explain URLs and the different domain names: .com, .org, .net, .gov, .edu, and so forth.
- Describe Web browsers.
- Describe search engines.
- Describe a Web page and a website, why http rules are used to access and display the page, and how to retrieve the pages.
- Describe hyperlinks and how they work.

After these basics have been covered and large-print, easy-to-read, and easy-to-follow directions distributed, the class is ready to surf. The class can browse for any subject of interest or the search can be directed by library staff. Students can also be taught how to key in the URL if they know it. Without a doubt, once the seniors find an interesting article, they will want to find another, and then another.

More than likely, students will want to print much of the information that they find useful. It is easier for older adults who are accustomed to reading printed books and paper to assimilate and retain information that is printed.

After basic Internet functions are satisfactorily absorbed by the students, it is useful to offer reinforcement Web lessons. The Flint Public Library (Michigan) offers a wonderfully developed website training sequence entitled "Computers for Living," which invites speakers to discuss topics such as "How can I interact with my local, state, and national government online?" and "How can I find reliable health information online?"[29] Classes such as these help keep the seniors' interest high as well as bringing them into the library.

A Word on Word Processing

Some seniors would rather "write" their own reports, stories, or prose than surf the Web. This means that word-processing instructions will be requested. More than likely, students will need to learn how to use Microsoft Word. Word has many idiosyncrasies, but students can at least grasp the "clean" sheet principle of the start-up process, because it can be directly related to a sheet of paper in a typewriter.

It is useful to start with teaching basics and providing cheat sheets for the basic functions students will have to know to do the following tasks:

- Start a new document.
- Change the size of the display.
- Change fonts.
- Use spell-check and correct and replace options.
- Use the undo button.
- Name and save files to the hard drive and floppy drive.
- Retrieve files.
- Print documents.

Students could then be taught items such as cut, paste, bold, highlight, change colors of text, alternate keyboards, formatting, and so forth. Programs such as patrons writing their memoirs or autobiographies can be an outgrowth of this program. Another exercise for seniors would be to have them write the favorite "childhood memory" they have of the library.

Word processing allows persons with limited vision to print out notes or phone numbers in bold type, which they can see. Word processing allows people who are completely blind to compete in the world of print. They may compose and print letters and send them without anyone knowing (or caring) that they are blind.

Using the Library's Website as an Instructional Resource

If your library is not able to offer computer training on a regular basis, consider using the library's website as a training tool. Seniors would of course have to have access to a computer and be guided to the library's website. This may entail offering informal one-on-one training, which staff can do on an as-needed basis.

The Multnomah County Library (Portland, Oregon) website is an excellent example of how a website can be used as a teaching resource. Staff, realizing that not everyone knows computer technology, patiently use photographs and words to teach visitors computer terminology. The language used is professional and never condescending. Topics covered include the central processing unit (CPU), monitor, keyboard, common keys and key combinations, mouse, disk drive, printer, system software, and so forth.

Figures 7-3 and 7-4 are typical examples of what visitors encounter when visiting the Multnomah County Library's website. Note that the tutorials are self-paced and allow seniors to familiarize themselves and absorb information that will make them comfortable in the cyberworld. Particularly useful are a glossary of computer terms and a test that visitors can take to see if they really understood and learned what was being explained.

Additionally, there is an overview provided about e-mail and links to useful informational sites, including a listing of free e-mail providers.

Library websites can be useful tools for encouraging seniors to explore and learn about computers. Although the older adults may not make the initial visit to the library's "senior" page, their friends or relatives may and might share the library's Web initiatives with them.

Conclusion

Without exception, libraries that offer specialized computer classes for senior citizens find them to be the most satisfying of all classes taught. The seniors demonstrate excitement and enthusiasm throughout the courses. The Collier County Public Library (Florida) staff report that "on class nights, students are lined up and waiting at the door for their instructors to arrive."[30] Teaching seniors to use computers is definitely a win-win situation.

FIGURE 7-3
Multnomah County Library Online Tutorial Main Page

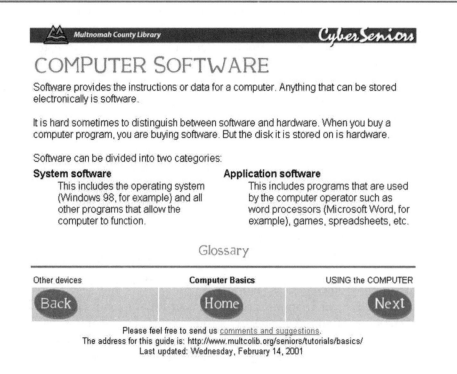

FIGURE 7-4

Multnomah County Library Online Tutorial for the Computer Desktop

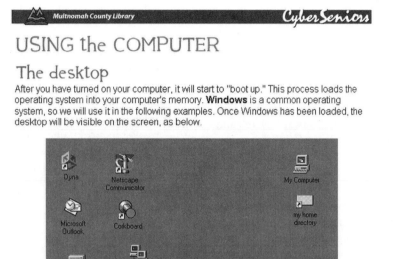

NOTES

1. Al Sommers, *Seniors and Computers in the USA*, speech made at Global LEARN Day III, Benjamin Franklin Institute for Global Education, cached at <http://www.bfranklin.edu/gld3/200/sommers271.html>.

2. Ibid.

3. Administration on Aging, A Profile of Older Americans: 2001: Special Topic: Computer and Internet Access, available at <http://www.aoa.dhhs.gov/aoa/stats/profile/2001/13.html>.

4. Jeff Pepper, Building an Online Ramp for Older Adults, *Senior Journal* (October 19, 2000), available at <http://www.eldervision.net/online.htm>.

5. The November 1995 study was conducted for SeniorNet by Fredrick/Schneiders and was underwritten by the Intel Corporation. The results of this sur-

vey supported a *Wall Street Journal* observation that "One of the last bastions of resistance to technology is crumbling" as more seniors are becoming computer users. *See* Richard P. Adler, Older Adults and Computers: Report of a National Survey, available at <http://www.seniornet.org>.

6. The findings of the 1998 study by Neuwirth Research, Research on Senior's Computer and Internet Usage: Report of a National Survey, 1998, are available at <http://www.seniornet.org>.

7. The Pew Institute survey, *Pew Internet and American Life Project*, polled 26,000 adults between March and December 2000. Available at <http://pewinternet.org/reports/reports.asp?Report=40&Section=ReportLevel 1&Field=Lev>.

8. Ibid.

9. Office of Learning Technologies, Human Resources Development Canada, Older Adults and Learning Technologies: An Assessment of Computer and Multimedia Hardware/Software That Satisfy the Learning Needs of Older Adults, Seniors' Education Centre, University Extension, University of Regina, March 1997. Available at <http://olt-bta.hrdc-drhc.gc.ca/projects/completed/NPLT/69005finalc_e.pdf>.

10. Jane Berliss-Vincent, "The Boomer Effect: Accommodating Both Aging-Related Disabilities and Computer-Related Injuries" (paper presented at the March 2001 California State University–Northridge [CSUN] Conference). Proceedings available at <http://www.csun.edu/cod/conf/2001/proceedings/0194berliss-vincent.htm>.

11. Ibid.

12. Ibid.

13. Ibid.

14. Office of Learning Technologies, Human Resources.

15. The price differentiations are in direct proportion to the products' attributes, and prices generally run from $595 to $795. For instance, if the user desires a voice assist with screen enlarging, expect the package to cost $200 more. The four most popular screen magnification programs in North America are ZoomText (AiSquared), Magic (Freedom Scientific), Window-Eyes, and Panorama Window Bridge. For more information on screen magnification programs, *see* Joseph J. Lazzaro, *Adaptive Technologies for Learning and Work Environments*, 2d ed. (Chicago: American Library Assn., 2001) and Barbara Mates, *Adaptive Technology for the Internet* (Chicago: American Library Assn., 2000).

16. Refreshable Braille displays, priced at approximately $4,000, are the most expensive pieces of adaptive technology. The reason for this is that they are also the most complex pieces of equipment as well as being extremely sensitive devices. As screen information is relayed to the Braille display, actuators raise or lower pins that represent Braille cells. Patrons are able to touch the displayed words.

17. Screen readers are generally priced at approximately $800. The most popular screen reading programs in North America include JAWS and Window-Eyes. Should the library choose not to offer word processing and only offer access to the Internet, staff might consider purchasing IBM's Home Page Reader, as its price comes in at under $200; available at <http://www-3.ibm.com/able/hpr.html>.

18. Screen readers are used by persons who have visual problems as well as those with learning differences. This means software purchased for seniors with visual disabilities may also be used by their grand-children who may have a learning disability such as dyslexia.

19. Microsoft supports an accessibility page, available at <http://www.Microsoft.com/enable/guides>, which has easy-to-follow guides that activate access features. The guides describe exactly what the feature will do for the users as well as the steps to take to activate the feature. Visitors can also sign up to receive a monthly newsletter that alerts users to new features, products, and tips for using products.

20. "Older People and the Internet," reprinted from *Link-Up* (March 1997), available at IFLANET <http://ifla.org/VII/s9/nd1/44pt2.htm>.

21. Rachel Singer Gordon, *Teaching the Internet in Libraries* (Chicago: American Library Assn., 2001), 73.

22. The tips are a compendium of information gleaned from the following resources: Rachel Singer Gordon, Jean Umiker-Sebeck, Stephen Thompson, and Anne Crosby, *Teaching Older Adults to Use Computers*, School of Library and Information Science, Indiana University–Bloomington, July 5, 1999. Available at <http://www.seniorcybernet.org/resource_usecomputer.html>; Shared Results, *The Top Ten Ideas to Remember When Teaching Technology to Seniors*, personal communication provided by Linda Keefe, CEO, January 2002, to author for this publication; Office of Learning Technologies, Human Resources.

23. "Older People and the Internet."

24. Two of the most popular mouse tutorials are New User Tutorial, from the Northville Library, available at <http://northville.lib.mi.us/tech/tutor/welcome.htm>; and Mousercise, available at <http://www.ckls.org/~crippel/computerlab/tutorials/mouse/page1.html>, from Central Kansas Library System, Great Bend, Kansas.

25. Stan Hinden, "Computer Age Brings Wide New World to Golden Age," *Washington Post*, March 19, 2000. Posted on Elderweb, available at <http://www.elderweb.com>.

26. Pew Institute, *Pew Survey*.

27. Gordon's book, *Teaching the Internet in Libraries*, offers excellent suggestions for general teaching methods. Also, Rebecca Sharp Colmer's *Senior's Guide to Easy Computing* (Chelsea, Mich.: Eklektika, 1999) offers bulleted directions for e-mail basics and most simple computer functions.

28. Colmer, *Senior's Guide to Easy Computing*.

29. Further information about the Flint Public Library senior computer training initiative can be found in appendix 3 and on the library's website, available at <http://www.flint.lib.mi.us/seniors>.

30. Linda Fasulo, "Conquering Technophobia . . . a New Lease on Life," *Florida Libraries* (fall 2001): 17.

8
Seniors and Accessible Websites

The most important rule: It's not about age, it's about what you love.
—Jane Scott, world-renowned eighty-two-year-old
rock-and-roll critic upon her retirement

If asked, "Why does the library support a website?" most library administrators would more than likely reply, "This is the information age, and it is the library's obligation to ensure that our community has access to every resource." Some might also add that as patrons add computers and Internet services to their households, the library wants to be able to offer the community remote access to databases and other electronic services. For these same reasons the library's website should be accessible to the entire community.

Unfortunately, some libraries connect with Web designers whose design philosophy is "Click, and move on" rather than "Click and linger." Libraries that wish to encourage seniors to use their websites will have to ensure that they are designed in a manner that invites seniors to linger rather than move on.

Website Considerations for Seniors

Web designers should always keep the end user's needs and concerns in mind when they design any website. If at all possible, they should speak with end users to determine who they are, where they want to go on the Internet, and what equipment they have to take them to their target destination. Web designers would generally find the following commonalities among many of the library's seniors who are currently using computers and accessing the Internet:

Seniors may have older computers and modems. Some seniors are using "hand-me-ups" from their children. In most cases, their children handed the equipment off because they themselves purchased faster systems.

Seniors may have older graphical browsers. Some seniors are reluctant to download new editions of their browsers and often are using the version that came with the computer.

Seniors may have slow Internet connections. Most seniors use a standard modem on an ordinary telephone line. Also, there is a tendency for seniors to use AOL as their carrier, which slows the connection time.

Seniors had childhoods devoid of electronic devices that involved any user interaction. This means that they have had little practice performing tasks that require eye-hand coordination.

Many seniors grew up in the age of radio. As youth they honed listening skills and made use of their imagination and visualization to "see" stories and information unfold.

Many seniors learned early not to play around with electronic devices. Many seniors were taught to "look with their eyes and not with their hands."

Seniors may have some physical limitations that affect their ability to access websites.[1]

Patron education and strategic equipment and browser upgrades will solve some of the access problems, but only good Web design can help seniors overcome access problems caused by physical conditions.

The Model Senior Website

Creating a website that is accessible to seniors means it will be accessible to all visitors. Although seniors as a group share the aforementioned commonalities, such as outdated equipment and inexperience, there are also younger members of the community who have similar limitations. The library's website should always be a reflection of the community's desire to not exclude any of its citizenry.

Reining in the Artist—Color and Font Choice

Special attention should be given to the elements of color and font use. Color choice is subjective, and each of us has a favorite combination that pleases us aesthetically. However, when using colors on a website, designers should choose colors that offer visitors easy access to information.

Web designers should first design the website in black and white and add the color to enhance the site rather than be its focus. When vision is diminished, color attributes can no longer be distinguished. Therefore, avoid using colors that are exceptionally bright, fluorescent, or vibrant, as these attributes can have edges that appear to blur, creating "afterimages" that can be exhausting to senior eyes. Low-vision specialists caution designers to avoid the color combinations of red and green and blue and yellow and state that the safest color choices are black, white, blue, and yellow.

The array of color choice is infinite, and the same can also be said for font choices. Those offered by standard word-processing programs, as well as those offered by Web creation programs, give designers access to virtually every font—good and bad. Avoid the temptation to overdesign, and go with the good (i.e., those that are easy to read).

Generally speaking, easy-to-read fonts are sans serif, of at least eleven-point type, and nonitalicized. Figure 8-1 demonstrates the differences a font makes. All the fonts are eleven points, but all are not as easy to read.

FIGURE 8-1
Font Choice Makes a Difference

The words *Seniors@all_public_libraries.us* are written using an eleven-point font, for which the readability is not the same.

Seniors@all_public_libraries.us using Algerian

Seniors@all_public_libraries.us using Times New Roman

Seniors@all_public_libraries.us using Abadi MT Condensed

Seniors@all_public_libraries.us using Andy

Seniors@all_public_libraries.us using Arial Black

Seniors@all_public_libraries.us using Arial Narrow

Seniors@all_public_libraries.us using Arial

Seniors@all_public_libraries.us using Castellar

Seniors@all_public_libraries.us using Tahoma

Seniors@all_public_libraries.us using Verdana

Seniors@all_public_libraries.us using Greyhound SF

Adhering to Good Design Guidelines

Asking Web designers to rein in their artistic nature when it comes to color and font choices is only one part of creating an accessible website. It is also necessary to ensure that buttons are easy to use and that the user is not required to have superior mouse skills to get to them. Figure 8-2 offers basic, easy-to-adhere-to suggestions for making library websites friendly for the entire community.

If the Web designer adheres to these guidelines, seniors should be able to surf the library's site without peril; however, there is yet another element to be considered. Equally important is the content element of the site. Seniors should never say, "Hmm, I just read that page, but I'm not sure what it said," or "Where is the link I need?"

FIGURE 8-2
Designing Functional and Friendly Senior Library Websites

Colors. When selecting the color elements for your website, such as background and text, remember that some older adults need to view information that is presented using high-contrast elements. The colors that offer the highest contrast are white and black, but designers do not have to limit themselves to this combination; however, don't use colors that are next to each other on the color wheel or complimentary colors. Choices that work the best are light colors on a dark background or dark colors on a light background.[1]

Background and wallpapers. Although patterned wallpapers may be attractive and attention getting, they may also make reading of information difficult. If at all possible, avoid using wallpaper.

Fonts. The font used to display text can increase or decrease the readability of the website. The wrong font choice will cause a senior visitor to move on to another website. Fonts used should be between twelve and fourteen points, be sans serif in design, and be of a medium weight. Designers should avoid condensed typefaces to save space on Web pages.

Use capital and lowercase letters. Website text should be written using uppercase and lowercase letters as it is easier for seniors to determine words, sentences, and paragraphs. The use of all capital letters or italics should be limited to headers.

Physical spacing. Physical spacing refers to the white space between two lines of text or between letters and words. Some seniors lose some of their peripheral vision as they age and need to have the space increased. Older adults prefer text that is double spaced.

Justification. Designers should use left justification when designing pages. Full justification may be confusing to some seniors.

Avoid the use of automatic scrolling text. Because some seniors read screen information at a slower rate, automatic scrolling should be avoided. If it must be used, a static text alternative should be offered.

Keep page length short. This tip applies both to memory requirements of the viewer as well as to what the viewer sees. Pages containing more than one or two screens of information or complex graphics are difficult to read for those using older equipment or those using public access equipment. Longer pages also require users to be agile when using the mouse.

Keep the site clear, logical, and simple. The more complex a library site is, the more difficult it will be for seniors to access and effectively use it. If the designer has used a lot of point and clicks to move through the website, seniors with arthritic hands or seniors just beginning to navigate the Internet may become frustrated and give up.

Use large buttons and icons. Although users can adjust the display of the buttons and icons, some seniors may be new users who are not familiar with the steps that must be followed to adjust them.

Avoid the use of pull-down menus. Pull-down menus often require the user to perform repetitive mouse tasks, which can present difficulty for some senior users.

Pages should be consistently labeled throughout the site. Each page of the library's site should be labeled with the library's site name as well as the name of the page. A consistent tool bar placed near the top of each page could be a great help for new navigators. Site maps help seniors locate where they are in relation to other pages and help them jump to the areas they wish to go to.

Frames. Frames can cause havoc for some new senior surfers, especially those who are using their computers from home or using adaptive technology to access the Internet. Frames load slowly and may cause some users to think that nothing is happening, whereas the information is just taking the slow road. Also, if a user has older equipment, frames may not be properly supported, and information may be lost and screens frozen. Always provide a clearly labeled text version of the frame.

Use adequate spacing for hyperlinks and URLs. When constructing a Web page with hyperlinks, ensure that there is adequate spacing between the links and use icons along with text. This will help seniors with visual impairments that limit their ability to distinguish the text from the underline.

Do not embed hyperlinks in blue or green. It is difficult for seniors to distinguish browser links from the hyperlinks. Instead, use black text to embed hyperlinks.

Offer mouse alternatives. Offer a keystroke alternative to repetitive mouse commands.

Avoid links that require the user to perform meticulous mouse actions. New mouse users may assume their skills are inadequate and become discouraged.[2]

1. AgeLight Institute, Interface Design Guidelines for Users of All Ages, available at <http://www.agelight.org>.
2. These design guidelines include suggestions offered by the following sources: AgeLight, available at <http://www.agelight.org>; Center for Medicare Education, "Creating Senior-Friendly Web Sites," *Issue Brief* 1, no. 4 (2000), available at <http://www.medicareed.org>; GeroTech, Elder Friendly Page Design, available at <http://www.gerotech.com/design/page.htm>; National Institute on Aging and the National Library of Medicine, Making Your Web Site Senior Friendly, available at <http://www.nia.nih.gov> or <http://www.nlm.nih.gov>; SPRY Foundation, Older Adults and the World Wide Web, A Guide for Web Site Creators, available at <http://www.spry.org/pdf/website_creators_guide.pdf>.

Examining the Content of the Library's Website

One of the many things people like about the World Wide Web (WWW) is that they can retrieve the information they are seeking instantaneously. However, dissatisfaction can set in almost as quickly if the site with the information is not laid out in a clear and logical manner. This is especially true for many seniors who are new to the Web or who are experiencing some type of physical or cognitive impairment. It is sometimes difficult for some to simultaneously remember and process new information, to perform complex cognitive tasks, and to comprehend text.[2] Figure 8-3 offers broad concepts for designers to keep in mind when they are scripting texts for the Web.

The guidelines outlined in this work only offer designers broad, basic suggestions. Staff should always ensure that the library's website complies with accessibility guidelines set forth by the federal government and those developed by the World Wide Web Consortium (W3C).[3] The W3C and the National Cancer Institute provide Web designers online tutorials, PowerPoint presentations that can be easily accessed and understood, and, as funding permits, workshops on accessible design.[4]

Testing Your Website

It is always useful to have someone else look at the library's website whenever staff redesign or modify pages. This is especially true when more than one staff member is allowed to add to or modify the site. Everyone who is given the ability to make changes should be cautioned to use the aforementioned guidelines and ensure that the addition he or she makes does not cause access problems.

It is important to have a nonlibrary staff member test the library's website for ease of use by seniors because, much like proofreading one's own text, it is sometimes difficult to see errors because of familiarity with the content. The W3C, in addition to offering guidance and tutorials, will evaluate the library's website and list any infractions of good design rules. Sites that meet all the criteria will be able to post the W3C logo on the website as a sign that the site is accessible.

Another noncommercial site that will evaluate websites and offer simple repair suggestions is A-Prompt, developed by the Adaptive Technology Resource Centre.[5] A-Prompt is easy-to-use and intuitive, as there are help files to guide users through each repair the program suggests. A tutorial is included to help new users effectively access the program.

There are also several commercial sites that will check and validate your pages. Bobby is an online tool developed by the Center for Applied Special Technology (CAST) to analyze Web pages for people with disabilities who may be using some type of assistive technology.[6] The site allows users to have one

FIGURE 8-3
Tips on Formatting Senior-Friendly Web Content

Language should be simple and positive but not demeaning. Phrasing should use the active voice.

Directions should not be open to interpretation. Visitors should never be directed to click on the "red button" or the "green book." Some seniors may be color-blind or unable to interpret the illustrations as needed.

Site organization must be uncomplicated yet detailed. Older adults prefer to finish one task before beginning another. Therefore, it is useful to present material in finite sections. The organization should not presume that the visitor has background information. If the information presented is lengthy, then it should be split into smaller, clearly labeled sections.

Provide a summary of a document if it is long. Summaries at the top of the page will allow persons using adaptive technology and seniors to quickly determine if the information on the page is what he or she is looking for.

Do not use lingo; provide visitors with a glossary. Many older adults who will be visiting the library's website may be relatively new to the computer world and unfamiliar with some of the lingo that has become part of pop culture. A glossary will help them to feel more comfortable with the new language.

Illustrations should be accompanied by text. Illustrations can be very useful when directions are being given and add the human touch to the library's website. Designers should remember to use the [ALT-DESC] tag for each illustration to allow screen reading programs to properly identify them. Otherwise, visitors using adaptive equipment or those with cognitive impairments may not be able to interpret the illustration without assistance. Whenever possible, a text-only option should be offered.

Explain error messages. Many older adults, especially those who are Internet novices, want to know what they are doing wrong and how to fix it. For example, if the library's site offers visitors an opportunity to register online for a program and requires a daytime phone number, including area code, to be accepted, the error message should tell the user who does not include the area code to resubmit using the patron's area code. If the site offers access to a search engine, and the user does not submit a finite subject search, hints on how to improve the results would be helpful.

Redirect archived presentations. If the library maintains an archive of special Web exhibits, be sure that visitors are redirected to the storage location if the exhibits' direct URL is used. The message "The page cannot be found" will discourage a visitor from looking for another way to find the information.

Online help and FAQs are musts. The library's site should feature a help menu with several means of entry. Context-sensitive help aids the visitor in quickly locating the information he or she is seeking both on the Help page and the Frequently Asked Questions (FAQ) page. Be sure to provide a telephone contact listing for the visitor who may still have an unanswered question. If at all possible, use a staff name.

Audio may not be helpful. Currently, the use of audio is to be discouraged. Many seniors have older equipment and may not have enough RAM to handle the operation, or they may not have a sound card or speakers installed. However, if staff feel it is useful, it should be clear, nonrepetitive, and unobtrusive.

---

page of their websites evaluated free of charge. There is a charge for additional pages and for text-only pages. Bobby issues a report that lists any accessibility or browser errors. Bobby is not human, so when problems are not obvious, the user must make some judgment calls. Bobby also ranks the importance of access problems found.

Another commercial site having validation tools is UsableNet, developed by accessibility and usability solutions expert Jakob Nielsen.[7] The advantage of these tools is that they evaluate usability as well as accessibility. Web usability focuses on the axiom that it is not enough to make a web product accessible; it must be easy enough for everyone to use, including those without any knowledge of computers. Usable-Net's products are tailored to specific types of Web-building platforms.

Regardless of which method of website evaluation is used, it is always best that a human look at the suggestions before the design is altered. The best outside eyes to help with this aspect are those that belong to seniors.

Testing the Site with Seniors

One major component of website design for seniors is missing from Bobby, and this is content. Bobby cannot determine, for instance, if the information is easy to find and understand or if the language used is devoid of jargon. This task requires the human interaction of seniors.

Library staff should arrange for a group of seniors to view the site. Ask some seniors who are currently using the library's website and some who are not. If the library is hosting senior computer classes, you have a great test group. If your community has a senior recreation center, request that the activity director solicit input on the site's design and content.

Many times it is useful for the designer and the seniors to sit down and work through some of the problem areas together.

Building a Links Library for Seniors

Once the library's website has been made accessible, library staff must also teach seniors how to determine if websites are providing them with quality information. Any Web user can become frustrated and aggravated trying to surf through the constantly growing sea of information, but it is even worse for the senior novice who may not know how to structure the search command and ends up with thousands of citations. The new Web user does not know how to sift through the vast amount of sites to find those that will be useful.

One way to help seniors gain knowledge on Web surfing is to build a senior links library on the library's website. Basically, you would develop the senior links library as you would develop a print resource collection for seniors, that is, checking for creditability and accessibility of the sites. While doing so, remember that many sites claim they were developed for and by seniors (which may or may not be true), are not easy to navigate, and are embedded with pop-ups and other distractions. After building the library, remember to look for broken link connections on a regular basis.

The SPRY (Setting Priorities for Retirement Years) Foundation, realizing that the Web had the potential to become the source of health information for seniors, developed a website evaluation guide.[8] This guide can be expanded from health sites to serve as the measuring stick for all websites. The guide, included in figure 8-4, should be used by staff when choosing links for the library's links collection. Additionally, its content should be transmitted to seniors to help them judge whether a site should be considered trustworthy.

FIGURE 8-4
Website Evaluation Checklist

---

1. Can you tell who created the content?	○ YES	○ NO
2. Are you given enough information to judge if the author is reliable?	○ YES	○ NO
3. Can you tell if the content is current?	○ YES	○ NO
4. Can you tell if the content is accurate?	○ YES	○ NO
5. Do you have confidence that your privacy is protected?	○ YES	○ NO
6. Is the content copyrighted?	○ YES	○ NO
7. Does the site provide complete contact information?	○ YES	○ NO
8. Is it clear who is funding the site?	○ YES	○ NO
9. Is there a clear disclaimer posted?	○ YES	○ NO
10. Does the site provide references for its content?	○ YES	○ NO
11. Is it clear who is the intended audience?	○ YES	○ NO

Reproduced with the permission of the SPRY Foundation, Washington, D.C.

Focused Forums for Senior Surfers

Most libraries offer staff in-service training when new databases are acquired or share searching strategies with colleagues on a fairly regular basis. Sharing of website and database information with seniors new to the Internet is worthwhile.

Flint Public Library (Michigan), realizing the potential of educating their senior users, instituted a Computers for Living Forum.[9] The forums brought in speakers who were knowledgeable on the topics they were addressing. Some of the topics included "Interacting with Government Online," "Shopping Online," and "Health Information Online." These forums helped to reinforce the reasons why the Internet can be a valuable tool in the lives of older adults.

Conclusion

Library staff should be committed to ensuring access to their virtual library. Seniors who wish to use the library's electronic resources should never be dissuaded from doing so simply because the library's site is not senior-friendly. The library's website has the ability to reach deep into the senior community, as computer usage by older adults is quickly growing. The library should also serve as an example of the right way to do something.

NOTES

1. Sudbury Senior Center Web Site, Design of the Sudbury Senior Center Web Site, available at <http://members.aol.com/sudseniors/design.htm>.
2. F. I. M. Craik and T. A. Salthouse, *The Handbook of Aging and Cognition* (Mahwah, N.J.: Lawrence Erlbaum Associates, 2000).
3. Section 508 is part of the Rehabilitation Act of 1973, which requires federal government agencies to buy and develop information systems that are accessible to persons with disabilities. In 1998 President Clinton amended the act to include websites. Any client who wishes to do business with the federal government must offer their websites as accessible to those using assistive technology. Although the initiative was slow to take effect, many government websites can be the flag bearers for good Web design. The mandates of Section 508 can be found at <http://section508.gov>. The Web Accessibility Initiative is a worldwide effort to ensure that everyone will be able to access the Web regardless of age, race, ability, or economic status. Guidelines and validation tools can be found at <http://www.w3C.org>.
4. Information from the World Wide Web Consortium can be found at <http://www.w3.org/2002/03/tutorials> and from the National Cancer Institute can be found at <http://oc.nci.nih.gov/web508/tutorial>.
5. A-Prompt (Accessibility Prompt) is a collaboration between the Adaptive Resource Centre of Toronto (Canada) and the Trace Center at the University of Wisconsin. The tool kit may be found at <http://www.aprompt.ca>.
6. Bobby is provided by Watchfire Corporation and may be found at <http://bobby.watchfire.com/bobby/html/en/index.jsp>.
7. Demonstration software and an overview of all products from UsableNet may be found at <http://www.usablenet.com>.
8. SPRY Foundation, Evaluating Health Information on the World Wide Web: A Guide for Older Adults and Caregivers, available at <http://www.SPRY.org>.
9. Further information about the Flint Computers for Living Forum is available at <http://www.flint.lib.mi.us/seniors/websites.html>.

9

Preparing and Distributing Marketing and Informational Materials for Senior Programs

It's all that the young can do for the old, to shock them and keep them up to date.

—George Bernard Shaw

When launching senior services and programming, libraries will be trying to reach people who may not have used libraries in a few decades because they are under the assumption that libraries are for the young or they were just too busy. Therefore, libraries will have to be sure that they get the advertising tools and the publicity releases to the media outlets that seniors use. Remember, you have to tell them to get them to come. It is also important that the publicity tools be in a format seniors feel comfortable with and can access independently.

How Is Marketing to Seniors Different?

After formal study of the "mature market," industry leaders are realizing that the senior population cannot be attracted by simply adding glitz, glamour, or seduction to products. Seniors are more attracted to marketing tactics that focus on

- value and good customer service,
- acknowledging abilities rather than disabilities, and
- language that is not condescending or patronizing.[1]

In addition to composing the ideal message, it is necessary to be sure seniors can easily access it. Although print media and the audiovisual outlets have different criteria for presentation, the underlying tenet is the same: keep it simple and easy to process.

Use the Print Media

The most effective media for reaching older adults is the written word. Older adults still rely on normal written communication because it gives them a sense of control over the information.[2] Printed material is portable and can be read when and where the individual desires to learn about the subject being discussed. Unlike the younger population, most older adults have a tendency to look at and read advertisements that are mailed to them, often from beginning to end, which is why the nation's largest providers of senior services use mail campaigns.[3] Therefore, marketing senior services via print is a good route for libraries to take.

Content Should Be Easy to Read

According to the 1992 National Literacy Survey, 44 percent of the people who were sixty-five and older read at about the fifth-grade reading level or less.[4] Although the study was undertaken ten years ago, a good portion of this cohort is still living and comprise the older segment of the senior group. The youngest of the senior population is better educated, but staff should write in a way that will serve all seniors effectively.

Writing easy-to-read materials does not mean writing in a childish way. Rather, it means using an adult format but making the information as easy to understand as possible.[5] Keep these tips in mind for composing senior documents:

Use terms such as *seniors* and *older adults.*

Avoid language that suggests seniors with disabilities are victims or afflicted.

Get to the point as quickly as possible.

If the document is lengthy, provide a summary. For example, if the library is compiling a semiannual calendar of events, provide a bulleted list at the beginning of topics, dates, and times.

Avoid using jargon or abbreviations.

Keep sentences short but not choppy. Average sentence length should be about fifteen words or less.

Avoid paragraphs with more than one idea.

Do not use a complicated word when a simple one will do.

Use the active voice.

Be direct, specific, and concrete.

Use personal pronouns to make readers know how the information applies to them.

Include dialogue or testimonials when possible.

Pose questions or use checklists to encourage interaction with the material.

Be sure to produce printed materials in languages read and understood by seniors in the library's service area.[6]

David Demko, proprietor of AgeVenture and respected professor of gerontology, remarks that advertising must be honest; because "seniors have been around long enough to spot loopholes and gimmicks . . . honesty is the best senior-friendly policy."[7] Demko suggested that creating a bulleted list of pros and cons of products and programs presents the information in a manner seniors like. Figure 9-1 is an example of a flyer designed to encourage seniors to learn about computers.

Consider Translating the Text for Non-English-Speaking Audiences

If the library serves a community whose seniors emigrated from a country where English was not the spoken language, the library should consider translating the documents into this language. These people may speak English but may not be able to read it well enough to fully understand the information being disseminated. As explained in chapter 3, it may not be possible to translate all documents into everyone's native language, but with the help of the community, it can be possible to translate those that have the potential to serve the greatest number of seniors.

When looking to translate literature into others' languages, it is necessary to know the specific target language. For instance, the library may be located in a neighborhood whose seniors are Hispanic, but the library may need to conduct a survey to determine what Hispanic subgroup they are from (e.g., Cuban, Mexican, etc.). If the survey finds that the population is fairly well distributed among the Spanish-speaking countries of origins, then a generic document should be designed.

Online, free translating programs cannot be relied on to render a good translation of text. The library should seek the services of people who are bilingual, bicultural, and interested in libraries and seniors. Marketing staff can seek volunteers from

FIGURE 9-1
A Sample Flyer That Uses Senior-Friendly Design

Senior Computer User Classes @ Combs Public Library

Combs Public Library is pleased to offer computer classes to our senior patrons. Patrons can choose from the following classes:

- **Surfing the Internet**
- **Sending E-mail**
- **Computer Basics**
- **Word Processing**

"You can teach an old dog new tricks!"

For more information on classes or to reserve your seat, please call the CPL Technology Center at 897-4523.

Combs Public Library
290 Main Street
Phone: 897-4500

Designed by Will Reed

community-based groups, ethnic cultural associations, religious organizations whose ceremonies are conducted in a foreign language, graduate students, or instructors from the local college. If the library cannot find free translating services, it can expect to pay $35 to $45 per 100 English words, which would cover the text of most flyers.[8]

Format the Text

Anne FitzGerald, a research manager for Age Wave, a market research firm, stated, "You're not going to make the blind see, but you can compensate for the lack of perfect vision."[9] Various focus groups, when asked "What makes you ignore printed material?" answered "Print that is too small."[10] As shown in chapter 2, although wisdom may increase with age, vision has a tendency to decrease. Formatting documents that are usable for seniors is extremely easy, as the thoughtful and proper choice of fonts, color, paper, and graphics is all that must be done. Figure 9-2 offers formatting suggestions that can be easily accomplished.

Overall, the library's printed promotional and instructional documents should look good and be pleasant and nonintimidating. The documents should convey the library's desire for seniors to be a part of library programming. Figure 9-3 is an example of a flyer designed by staff at the Chicago Public Library to promote senior programs.

FIGURE 9-2
Tips for Formatting Printed Materials for Seniors

- Use dark print on light backgrounds. Black type on white or yellow paper works best, but you do not need to be limited to this combination.

- Be careful with the use of blues, greens, and purples; the yellowing of the eye makes it harder to discriminate between colors.

- Use paper with a matte, nonglossy surface to avoid glare.

- Avoid subtle color contrasts, such as pink on red or light brown on dark brown. It may be useful for designers to look at their potential product through a piece of yellow laminated plastic to simulate the yellowing that takes place in human lenses.

- Use type that is at least thirteen or fourteen points.

- Use a plain, clear typeface. Avoid fonts such as shadow print, outline print, script, italics, or reverse print.

- Use uppercase and lowercase lettering; avoid the use of all capital letters.

- Make important information stand out by putting it in a box or using bold type for the information.

- Increase the font size when introducing new sections, and use bold type.

- Make lists stand out by using bullets or dingbats.

- Include white space. Use generous margins. For example, an 8 1/2-by-11-inch page should have a 2-inch margin on each side, with one column of text. This helps seniors with poor reading skills follow the text from line to line.

- Select comfortable, positive visuals, preferably photographs. Clip art in the public domain, or included in graphics packages, typically helps reinforce ageist tendencies. Be sure to label photographs to enable patrons to know what they are viewing.

- Avoid complicated charts or graphs. If providing a map to the library, also provide a driving narrative.

- Be realistic when choosing images of seniors. Include images of seniors in wheelchairs and using walkers and canes. Depict senior men and women involved in all aspects of life, including nontraditional roles, and include a positive representation of seniors from minority groups.*

---

* These tips were created from the Center for Medicare Education, "Writing Easy-to-Read Materials," *Issue Brief* 1, no. 2 (2000), available at <http://www.medicareed.org/pdfs/papers62.pdf>; Health Canada, Division of Aging and Seniors, Communicating in Print with/about Seniors, available at <http://www.hc-sc.gc.ca/seniors-aines/pubs/communicating/commsen.htm>; Patricia Braus, "Vision in an Aging America," *American Demographics* 17, no. 6 (June 1995): 34; and Carol Bryan, "Help Seniors Respond to Your Printed Message," *Library Imagination Paper* 22, no. 3 (summer 2000): 3–4.

FIGURE 9-3
Chicago Public Library Caregiving Institute Flyer

CHICAGO PUBLIC LIBRARY

Chicago Department on Aging
and
Austin Branch
5615 West Race

CAREGIVING INSTITUTE

"Helping Our Helpers"

SATURDAY   1:00 P.M.

APRIL 20   *How to Care for Yourself as You Care for Others*

MAY 18   *The Family Dynamics of Caregiving and How to Cope*

JUNE 8   *Facing the Financial and Legal Challenges of Caregiving*

AUGUST 10   *In-Home Community Care Options for You and Your Loved Aging Ones*

SEPTEMBER 14   *Education on Aging-Related Diseases*

OCTOBER 12   *Hands-On Care*

 City of Chicago
RICHARD M. DALEY
Mayor

 Chicago Public Library
Jayne Carr Thompson
President, Board of Directors
Mary A. Dempsey
Commissioner

 READ LEARN DISCOVER CHICAGO PUBLIC LIBRARY
www.chicagopubliclibrary.org

 Please call for accommodations:
(312) 747-4252 (Voice)
(312) 747-4066 (TTY)

Test the Documents

It is important to run the documents past the library's senior advisory board (or several seniors whose opinions can be trusted) before they are mass-produced. Once an approved design template has been structured, it is not necessary to test individual program flyers. As long as staff are willing to use a well-designed template, a blanket approval should suffice. The one area where design staff will become bored and tempted to stray is the color combination for flyers. Administrators can prevent this from happening by developing six or eight color combinations that seniors state are usable.

When testing the document with seniors, ask these questions:

- After reading this, what do you think the library wants you to know?
- Is this document easy to read?
- Is any part of the document difficult to read?
- Is the tone friendly?
- Is the information clearly written and understandable?
- Is the information presented in a way that is respectful?
- Do you like the way the document looks?
- Is there anything else you think the library should add to the document?[11]

Be prepared to receive honest and sincere feedback. If the feedback isn't all positive, go back to the drawing board for revisions. It is useless to reproduce materials promoting senior services if the seniors do not want to look at and read them. Readable documents for seniors do not cost more than those that are not readable; they just take thoughtful planning.

Where Do You Distribute Promotional Materials?

The worst thing that can be done with promotional materials is to set them out on a literature distribution table and walk away. This is an acceptable first step, but doing so will only reach the seniors or their relatives and friends who are already coming into the library. The brochures, flyers, handbooks, bookmarks, and such must go where the seniors are. Be aware of those members of the library's community who can help distribute the materials.

Community Partners

All community entities, both commercial and non-profit, stand to heighten their profile and value within the community by working with the library to get the word out about library initiatives for seniors. Agencies and organizations such as the library's local Area Agency on Aging, Medicare office, AARP, senior housing group, United Way, and Kiwanis can help to spread the word. Offer to present a formal program for these groups. This can be a simple slide presentation that will remind the groups that the library exists to serve the entire community and will update them on programs currently offered. The information staff are asking the groups to distribute can be the last slide of the presentation, giving staff an easy segue to the request.

Likewise, hair salons, grocery stores, department stores, pharmacies, and similar commercial enterprises should be willing to assist the library. In most cases, all staff need to do is receive permission to leave the brochures in an appointed location or post the flyer on the bulletin board in an assigned location. If possible, staff should also be willing to pick up and dispose of flyers with dated information. Some potential distribution partners follow:

- Local senior center(s)
- Area Agency on Aging (this group oversees many of the government-sponsored programs for seniors)
- State Agency on Aging
- Local Agency on Aging
- Civic organizations such as the Lion's Club, Jaycees, and so forth
- Membership organizations such as AARP, Gray Panthers, and so forth
- Local hospitals and physicians, specific disease support groups
- Visiting Nurses Association
- Local religious centers and networks
- YMCA and YWCA
- Charitable organizations such as the United Way, Goodwill, Red Cross, Volunteers of America, Easter Seal Society, and so forth

- Local merchants, including pharmacies, grocery stores, department stores, banks, funeral homes, insurance agencies, and real estate agents
- Schools, colleges hosting senior programs[12]

In short, any community entity that has a senior as its member, customer, patient, or patron should be willing to help the library distribute literature. Some of the aforementioned may also be interested in joint-advertising ventures.

Most of us have picked up and read informational brochures on a variety of medical topics while waiting in the doctor's office or for a prescription to be filled. These pamphlets usually are imprinted with the name of the organization paying for the printing. Consider requesting that the doctor's office, hospital, or pharmacy have the printer add the library's name, phone number, and website to those that pertain to senior health, with the tag line "To read more about arthritis, visit the Wonderful Library at 8889 Reading Road or online at www.wonderlib.org or phone them at (999)-999-0000."

An additional tact for libraries with a supportive Friends group or volunteers is to personally distribute the brochures at locations that have a Senior Day or when they are made aware of senior-oriented programs taking place at other agencies.

Community Events

It is helpful to set up a library booth at health fairs and community events designed to attract seniors and their families. These fairs offer staff the opportunity to meet many seniors who aren't aware that the library has materials they want or need and facilitate networking between the staff of the various agencies participating. This is an opportunity to form informal partnerships and share information of value to older adults. Although some of the fees might be out of the range of the library's budget, organizers may be willing to provide a table at a reduced cost in exchange for plastic tote bags for all attendees or a door prize from the library's gift shop.

Community Newsletters and Newspapers

Most communities support newsletters and newspapers. Although many of these newspapers exist purely for the advertising opportunity, they are picked up and read by seniors. Many of the publishers of these newspapers are eager for articles that they do not have to pay for and that will be interesting to the readers. A well-written article about the library's services for seniors would be ideal for such a situation.

If the library's activities are well planned with enough lead time, community partners should be glad to include library information in the newsletters they send out to their staff and clients. The more exposure the programs receive, the greater the chance there will be a response.

Mailing Lists

Mailing lists are useful tools when attempting to reach seniors. The library can create its own, which will take time, or ask community agencies that maintain senior mailing lists to borrow or rent theirs. The latter option may cost money unless the agency is a partner in the senior outreach effort.

Direct Mail Campaigns

Advertising experts who specialize in marketing to seniors vow that direct mail campaigns work because seniors are said to read all mail sent to them. This includes the inserts to utility bills, flyers that are mass mailed to homes in specified zip codes, and coupons that provide discounts to area restaurants and service suppliers. Libraries should consider becoming one of the neighborhood advertisers, perhaps offering a book bag or bookmark for just stopping in to find out what the library has for seniors.

Websites

It is useful to post notices on the library's website as well as those of agencies serving older adults. The library's website can be fully exploited with a notice on the children's page (e.g., "Looking for something to keep Grandma busy?" adding a link to the senior page), the senior information page, the computer lessons page, and the calendar of events page. The more the information is out there, the greater the chance that someone will find the library.

It is also useful to encourage agencies serving seniors that have websites to link to the library's senior information page. People accessing the local hospital's website for information about high blood pressure may not think to look at the library's website for further information and possible programs.

Reach Seniors through Radio and Television

When promoting library services through radio and television venues, it is necessary to apply one of the most important tenets of print advertising. Namely, be honest and straightforward, avoiding the use of modern jargon and images.[13] It is important to use the library's airtime to build rapport and trust, giving seniors reasons to avail themselves of the services the library offers.

When composing the script for the narrative, library staff should be reminded that the senior audience is diverse but unique.[14] This group of people, as a whole, once enjoyed personalized relationships and services from merchants, physicians, and librarians. Unlike the generations that followed them, those who are now age sixty and older are not a product of the mass-produced world. Overall, they will relate to scripts targeting their needs and endorsed by seniors they can trust. Other factors that should be considered when scripting radio or television ads to reach seniors follow:

- Cut background music out of ads, both on radio and television.
- Keep phone numbers and addresses on the screen long enough to be read and copied.
- Avoid jump cuts and fast transitions. These techniques complicate the message and lose the older consumer.
- Consider producing an infomercial about senior library services. Infomercials offer the ability to provide information at a slower pace and in a step-by-step order.
- Use personalized examples rather than statistics.
- Use the idea of exclusivity to market the library's services.
- Tell seniors why availing themselves of the library's services will help them.
- Demonstrate ways in which the library can help them connect with family, friends, and the community.[15]

Media research suggests that radio draws senior audiences during the early morning hours, while the peak time for senior television is early evening. Research indicates that news, documentaries, and game shows are good placements for senior advertising.[16]

News at 11:00!

Free spots on the news are always useful but not easily obtained. The news media are committed to covering what they feel the masses want to hear. Although there always seems to be enough airtime for the dog or cat story, library stories do not often seem to make the cut. Clever planning and unusual themes can often make the difference as to whether a story will or will not be covered.

A library program that includes a mass birthday bash for the community's seniors who will be celebrating their ninetieth or older birthdays during the year may make the news, as might coverage of the local anchor teaching a computer class on how to find reliable news on the Internet. The local radio personality may be willing to teach a senior class on how to find and play old radio programs through the Internet.

Reach Seniors Using Promotional Items

Very few people refuse a free pen or pencil, so consider purchasing small, inexpensive items, imprinted with the library's name and promotional message, for distribution. Pens, for instance, can be purchased and imprinted for as low as thirty-three cents, and magnets can be purchased for as low as twenty-three cents. Other inexpensive items include magnifying glasses, key handles, and jar openers. For special events, distributing items such as lightweight canvas bags, large-print rules, wide-barreled pens, heavily lined paper, notepads, and stress-relieving balls might make for a few new patrons.

Reach Seniors through Word of Mouth

In spite of all that's been said on the value of printed media, direct mailings, and the power of the broadcast word, the best advertising vehicle is still word of mouth. Library patrons, their families, and friends have the potential of filling the computer lab and the meeting rooms simply by talking about senior library initiatives.

It is always good to have flyers for future programs on hand when current programs are in progress. As the program for the day ends, hand each senior a few extra flyers and ask them to share them with friends, family, service providers, and clergy. Tell them they are the library's best advertising agents, which they are.

Conclusion

Although formatting library media and publicity tools and guides is not difficult, marketing does take time. Time spent, however, will pay off. Once the library reaches the senior, he or she will become a loyal library user. Some may only become hooked on using the computer and avail themselves of the library's website from home or another outlet, but they will still be using and supporting the library.

NOTES

1. "Experts Identify Seventy-Seven Truths about Marketing to Seniors," interview with John Migliaccio, NCOA Network Interview, available at <http://www.ncoa.org/news/archives/truths_about_senior_marketing.html>.
2. Douglas Kalajian, "Five New Ways to Think about Aging," *Palm Beach Post*, 21 May 2001. Posted on the LifeExtension Foundation website, available at <http://www.lef.org/newsarchive/aging/>.
3. David Demko, Age-Audit Your Business to Prepare for the Senior Market, AgeVenture News Service, available at <http://www.demko.com/cg000307.htm>.

AgeVenture is a syndicated news service consisting of seven news departments that address aging issues.
4. Center for Medicare Education, "Writing Easy-to-Read Materials," *Issue Brief* 1, no. 2 (2000), available at <http://www.medicareed.org/pdfs/papers62.pdf>.
5. Ibid.
6. This list was created with input from the Center for Medicare Education and Health Canada, Division of Aging and Seniors, Communicating in Print with/about Seniors, available at <http://www.hc-sc.gc.ca/seniors-aines/pubs/communicating/commsen.htm>.
7. Kalajian, "Five New Ways."
8. Center for Medicare Education. "Translating Materials for Non-English-Speaking Audiences," *Issue Brief* 1, no. 3 (2002), available at <http://medicareed.org/pdfs/papers61.pdf>.
9. Patricia Braus, "Vision in an Aging America," *American Demographics* 17, no. 6 (June 1995): 34.
10. Ibid.
11. Center for Medicare Education, "Writing Easy-to-Read Materials."
12. *See* appendix 1 for further ideas for potential advertising partners.
13. Craig Huey, "Twenty Special Insights into Direct Marking to the Mature Market," *Publishers Marketing Association Newsletter* (December 1996): 1.
14. For further information on preparing scripts, *see* Brett Lear, *Adult Programs in the Library* (Chicago: American Library Assn., 2002), 82–83.
15. Tip chart was gleaned from Craig Huey, 1–3; and "Experts Identify Seventy-Seven Truths."
16. Demko, Age-Audit Your Business.

10
Funding Senior Programs

As I approve of a youth that has something of the old man in him,
so I am no less pleased with an old man that has something of the youth.
He that follows this rule be he old in body, but can never be so in mind.

—Cicero

As difficult as it is to admit, sometimes it all comes down to money. Although the amount of money needed to fund senior programs will vary, there will certainly be costs involved. These costs may either be financial or involve the expenditure of staff time. Creative managers can balance both schedules and budgets, but having additional funds will make expansion of services easier on the staff plus ensure other services are not curtailed.

Usually library funds are accumulated from a combination of governmental funds and other sources. According to the National Center for Education Statistics, 77.6 percent of the public library's revenues come from local funds, 12.1 percent from state funds, 0.9 percent from federal funds, and 9.0 percent from other sources, such as user fees and foundation or corporate grants.[1] This funding scheme works well, except during times of economic downturns when tax revenues are down. Although it may not be possible to increase the funding that comes from government programs, it may be possible to increase funding from other sources.

Foundations and grant makers continue to contribute to organizations such as schools, medical facilities, and libraries even through economic downturns. Staff can, by using some creative thinking, astute research, good writing, and a little legwork, locate potential funders who may be willing to underwrite as many of the programs the library wishes to develop.

Aging is becoming a hot topic and a concern within many communities. Grantmakers in Aging (GIA) organizes an annual conference, Building Elder-Friendlier Communities: Opportunities for Creative Grantmaking, to address the needs of older adults that could be solved through funding. Over the last three years, attendance at the conference has risen 300 percent.

The demand for information presented at the conference was so great among philanthropic agencies that GIA developed a tool kit, *Funding across the Ages*, for grant makers.[2] The kit was designed to help foundations determine how they can help communities utilize seniors as resources, help the community respond to the growing needs of older adults, and facilitate intergenerational community problem solving. Throughout the guide, GIA suggests possible grantees within the community, without specifically mentioning libraries.

However, GIA advises agencies to seek out information from the community on aging and politely steers them to the library, where "the librarian can gather aging-related information . . . or develop a road map to locate information or contacts relating to aging."[3] Therefore, library staff need to put themselves on the road map as an organization in need of funding for senior programs. This will require some forethought, planning, and succinct writing.

Foundations: A Good Source for Funding New Programs

Libraries sometimes hesitate to approach foundations to request funds for programs even though their plans are well thought through and would fulfill many of the criteria for a grantee. This hesitation will have to cease if revenues continue to cause budgets to remain flat or decrease. Libraries can start with being proactive in seeking funds for library services for seniors.

One of the first things libraries should do is get to know the funders in the library's geographic area and the library's potential service area. This information is available on the Internet. It is helpful to make a list of the agencies that sound as though they would be able to help the library extend services to seniors. Staff should be careful to read the criteria for the awards. The library must be able to tailor its proposal to match that of the grant maker or the process will be a waste of time, both for the library and the grant

maker. If you are unsure if the library's program meets the criteria of the foundation, it may be helpful to call the foundation and talk about the program.[4]

When the initial list is compiled, learn about each foundation's priorities and concerns. It is also good to know the source of the foundation's money to ensure no one in the community would be offended by the funding source.

Once the foundations or grant makers are decided upon, it is time to do the paperwork. This should be done with care. The library has at its disposal links and resources to ensure that every form is filled out accurately.

The Basics of Successful Grant Proposals

The library will be successful in acquiring grants if it starts with a good idea, locates the right funding source, and translates the idea into a well-crafted written statement. The proposals that are funded in nearly every competition are those that are best written.[5] Take the time to select the exact word or sentence to convey the library's intended vision and mission. Ask someone totally unfamiliar with the inner workings of libraries or library terminology to review the original request for proposal (RFP) and the library's submission to determine if they mesh. The reviewer should not have to ask library staff what words mean or ask for terminology translations.

Be sure that the responsible library administrator signs the proposal. A cover letter should accompany the neatly packaged proposal, which should adhere to the preferences of the foundation. The proposal should be mailed in time to ensure delivery by the deadline.

Answer Questions Before They Are Asked

Although most foundations or grant makers will request specific information from applicants, there are standard questions that will be asked and must be answered satisfactorily to be awarded funds. Staff should think about what they perceive as viable ideas for programs and services and have the answers to the following questions at hand:

1. What kinds of services are the library currently offering seniors?

2. What are the needs of seniors that are not currently being met by the library?

3. How could the library expand its services to meet seniors' needs?

4. What is a reasonable timetable to make the program happen?

5. How many staff or volunteers will be used in this program?

6. Can seniors help to facilitate the program?

7. How does the library collaborate or cooperate with other community agencies to serve seniors?

8. What is the estimated budget?

9. What are the demographic data (e.g., estimate of senior population, potential number of seniors the library hopes to reach, potential growth in the number of seniors using library services)?

10. How will the library evaluate the program's success?

11. How would the library sustain the program or service after the foundation's funding is no longer available?

12. Can the program work with less money?

One of the most important questions to have a solid answer for is question 11. It is essential that the library have concrete plans for the program or services to be self-sustaining. Foundations do not want to spend money on a program that only lasts for the moment; they prefer, instead, to fund projects that have the potential to enrich both the present and the future of the community.

It is also important to have a ready answer to question 12. There are times, typically when the economy is slow, when funders find themselves with less money than anticipated. Staff of the organizations may ask the library if they can make the program work with less money. Library staff must decide to find the shortfall elsewhere, be prepared to make cuts to certain parts of the program, or abandon the project.[6]

Proposal Elements

Proposals follow a certain format, and agencies that submit them are expected to comply with that format. Those who administer the grants look to see that grant seekers have thought the program through completely, are capable of bringing it to fruition, and comply with the foundation's regulations. The Foundation Center, a respected leader in philanthropy, explains that basically there are six key components of any proposal:

1. *The Executive Summary.* This is the most important section of the document because it provides the reader with a *one-page* summation of the proposal. The first few paragraphs should be a statement of the problem and the library's solution. The next paragraph should state and explain the funding requirements. The final paragraph should be a brief statement of the name, history, and purpose of the library, emphasizing its ability and expertise to fulfill the proposal.

2. *Statement of Need.* This section should be succinct and not exceed *two pages.* First, describe with facts and statistics how seniors are being underserved (e.g, statistics can be cited on how seniors are being left behind in this age of digital information). Next, describe how the library can help solve the problem or make the community better for seniors. If the library wishes to be held up as a role model for the project, that can be stated at this point. If the library is trying to solve a senior problem by launching this program, describe what may happen if it is not funded. For example, if the library is seeking to start a computer program for seniors, staff can describe how the digital divide will become greater for the seniors. Next, describe why the library's project is more apt to solve the problem than another agency. Finally, describe a library where a program such as this has worked well.

3. *Project Description and Plan for Continuation of Project.* This *three-page* component should describe how the program will be implemented. The who, the what, and the how should be stated here. Tell how the success of the project will be evaluated and how the program can continue in the future.

4. *Budget.* This *one-page* component should include a financial description of the project, explaining items such as staff salaries and major capital items (e.g., lease cost of a van to deliver library services to homebound citizens or the purchase price of a computer and large-screen monitor).

5. *Organizational Information.* This *one-page* component should give a history and governing struc-

ture of the library, including who the library serves. It should demonstrate how the proposed project will be a natural extension of what the library has been doing.

6. *Conclusion.* This section should only be *two or three paragraphs* in length and summarize the proposal's main objectives.[7]

The Foundation Center cautions that the preceding components and organizational suggestions are not absolute. The center recognizes that each organization seeking money is unique and will have its own specific ideas.

The proposal is one of the most important elements that the grant maker uses to judge who receives a grant, but the organization requesting the funds will also be scrutinized. Libraries still are the pillars of knowledge within the community. They exude trust, leadership, and accomplishment. For the most part, this type of organization is the type foundations ideally want to support.

If the library has good working relationships with agencies that focus on aging, encourage them to write letters of support, which can be included with the proposal. If the library has a history of executing special projects similar to the one for which money is being sought, an "accomplishment page" can also be appended.[8]

Why Grant Makers Give a Thumbs Up

Grant makers say that "grantmaking is an art, not a science."[9] Try as they may, foundation applications and awards may not be uniform, and occasionally missteps will be made. Overall, however, grant makers must decide if the proposal for a grant has the following components:

Clarity of Purpose. Does the grant tell what needs to be done for seniors and how the task will be accomplished?

Sensibility of Process. Does the proposal outline a sensible methodology for accomplishing the task? Also, does the organization demonstrate that a safety net is in place in case plans go awry?

Doability. Does the grant proposal match resources available? Is the overall financial, organiza-

tional, and programmatic situation of the organization healthy without the grant?

Leadership. Are there strong leaders within the organization and capable personnel to oversee the specific project?

Realistic Budget. Do the dollars add up?

Monitoring. Is the organization likely to achieve the results it wants by following the path it laid out? The organization must identify a person to submit reports of activities ensuring the foundation's money is being spent properly.[10]

Keep in Touch and Say Thank You

Should the library receive a grant, it will be necessary to provide an accounting of the funds and report the success of the program to the grantor in relation to the proposal. The grant maker will notify the library about the due dates for this information. These deadlines should be met to maintain future respectability. If possible, include a few photographs of the seniors using the services along with the required narrative.

It doesn't hurt to update the foundation before the accounting is due. For instance, if the library's project was to install a computer connection at the local senior center, encourage seniors to send e-mail messages to the foundation's contact person to thank him or her and explain what having access to and knowledge of computers mean to them.[11]

The library should take every opportunity to credit and thank the funder of particular programs. If a foundation funds a senior computer learning program in which a handbook may be developed for the participants, the manual should have a statement in it similar to "This handbook was made possible through the generous support of the Joy and Irving Hermann Fund." A copy of the handbook should be included with the reporting documents.

Local and Small Foundations

Most professionals in the philanthropic world advise those seeking grants to "think locally." There are foundations in every state that are willing and able to fund projects that will better their communities.

Many small foundations are family trusts and feel the societal obligation to share their wealth with those in the community who are less fortunate. To find those organizations willing to give grants in your area, visit the Foundation Center's website.[12] The center's site allows searching by grant type and location and also provides links to community foundations. Another useful website is GuideStar, which lists non-profit organizations that may give grants.[13] Still another website worth looking at is the Association of Small Foundations, which lists members by state and indicates their geographic donation area.[14]

For those in Canada, NonprofitsCan.org is an initiative of the Canadian Centre for Philanthropy.[15] The site offers links to funding directories as well as links to charitable and nonprofit agencies that may be willing to offer donations of staff expertise and support for library projects.

National Funding Organizations

Corporations and organizations such as Verizon, Bell Atlantic, GTE, IBM, the Robert Wood Johnson Foundation, and the Claude Pepper Foundation are all national organizations that give donations to non-profit organizations. The telecommunications companies often will donate connection fees or provide staff training for libraries that are attempting to create programs to cross the digital divide.

Some of the larger foundations, however, only entertain grant applications from coalitions. Coalitions take time and careful planning to build and require a lot of time to establish and maintain. If the library can support staff specifically assigned to fund-raising, becoming part of a coalition may be plausible.

Government Funds and Assistance

Most federal funding for services for aging and library services is passed on to states and counties for their use and redistribution. So, it is best to start looking for government funds on your state's home page. More than likely, the grant that will be most appropriate to seek is the Library Services and Technology Act (LSTA) grant.

In most states, funds provided under an LSTA grant (recipients must provide local matching funds using in-kind donations or cash equal to one-third the amount requested) are designated for programs to serve persons who cannot readily use library services

but can be assisted to do so with the help of technology. Enabling seniors to use computers, both in-house and off-site, would qualify under LSTA award criteria.

Checking with your state library's grant consultant would be worth the effort. State agencies never want to return federal dollars and are eager and willing to work with libraries in their states to present an acceptable grant proposal.

Also check with the state's agency that oversees aging issues to determine if funds are available for seniors' literacy and information access projects.[16] Libraries are the experts on the topic of information dissemination, and the staff at the state agencies on aging are the experts on aging initiatives.

Libraries located in states that have a Center for the Book may consider talking with staff from the center if they wish to promote senior reading groups. This was successfully done in Arizona. The Arizona Center for the Book supported "The Story-Teller's Story," a statewide reading and discussion series on autobiography for older adults. The project was developed by the National Council on Aging, was funded through the National Endowment for the Humanities, and was hosted by seven libraries throughout the state.[17]

Theme Grants

Do you want to start a storytelling program for seniors but do not have enough staff? A visit to the National Storytelling Network will find that the organization gives grants of up to $1,000 to members who wish to develop a storytelling program for targeted groups.[18] The site can help locate a member in your community or state who is willing to apply for a grant and work with the library to bring stories into nursing homes and to train staff in the art of storytelling.

It also helps to check out broad-themed websites, such as publishers' websites or gardening websites, to see if there are services, money, or goods for the asking. Often, as a goodwill gesture, publishers will donate items such as tote bags or multiple copies of books to small groups. Last year, during National Poetry Month, one publisher gave hardbound books to all poetry groups that requested them. This method of getting assistance takes time but is a better alternative than abandoning the program.

Your Local Wal-Mart

Inasmuch as virtually every library community has a Wal-Mart, there is at least $300 for every library to use for programming. The Wal-Mart Foundation is the funding arm of the national retail chain and offers small grants to groups like libraries who wish to organize a program for senior citizens.[19]

Funding from Friends and Neighbors

The library's friends and neighbors may not have a great deal of money to offer the library for senior programming, but they usually are willing to give whatever they have. In most cases, all that is necessary to receive money is a letter requesting and describing the project and a thank-you when the money is given.

Community service groups, such as the Kiwanis and Jaycees and Scout groups, may be able to provide funds for items such as magnifiers, writing guides, large-print key tops, and dictionaries. This will allow the library to focus its funds on more costly items and demonstrate to other potential funders that the community respects the library's efforts to render improved services to seniors.

Nonfinancial Contributions

Programs for seniors can often use assistance in areas other than finances, so not all contributions need to be cash. Keep in mind such nonfinancial contributions as goods and services, free programs and personnel, and free advertising venues.

Goods and Services

In lieu of cash, the community can contribute goods, services, and even human resources that will enable the library to expand its senior services. The good things about this approach are that applications do not have to be filled out, and everyone in the community can make a difference without having a heavy financial burden placed upon them. Like working with community service groups, accepting contributions from a community commerce member can demonstrate the library's ability to work with others toward a common goal.

Often, all that is necessary is a phone call and a letter outlining the seniors' needs, an explanation of what the library wants to do, and details on how the entity can help the library accomplish the task. Staff can suggest specific contributions, yet they should also state that if the entity cannot extend itself to provide that commodity, it is welcome to suggest alternatives.

A possible scenario is that the library wants to deliver materials to nursing homes and provide programming. The business administrator has found enough money to supplement the materials needs, the human resources manager has managed to find money for a paid staff position, but that's it. There are no library funds available for the van or to pay for a person to assist the paid staff with programming or materials delivery. This is where creativity and cooperation can be a solution. Perhaps a local insurance agent can agree to underwrite the insurance on the senior van, while the local car dealer may be willing to waive the annual lease charges on the van. The local oil and lube station may agree to handle standard maintenance of the van. With the community pitching in what it can, van service can become a reality.

The staffing solutions might be resolved by convincing local business leaders to allow their staff to provide a few hours of community service during workweek lulls. Although library staff would have to work with a variety of people, it will give them extra hands when serving larger nursing homes and bring additional visitors into the nursing homes.

Additionally, local office supply stores may be willing to provide the library with items such as pens, paper, and other miscellaneous supplies. Local grocery stores might be willing to cover the costs of refreshments, and party stores may be willing to donate brightly colored accessories.

Programs and Personnel

Libraries might also wish to look at some of the agencies that are receiving federal funds to determine if they might share in the existing programs of these organizations. For example, federal dollars subsidize the Retired and Senior Volunteer Program (RSVP), which helps seniors find meaningful jobs while learning new skills. RSVP reimburses seniors for expenses such as transportation and food that occur when working out of their homes. RSVP is always looking to place seniors in locations that are safe and have the potential of providing seniors and the organization with a meaningful experience. Frequently RSVP staff look to libraries to provide such places.

RSVP workers can be trained to help novice computer users learn how to use the Internet at a comfortable pace. RSVP workers could also assist staff during children's programs, which could serve to create an intergenerational atmosphere.

There is also the Senior Volunteer Corp, whose members seek volunteer opportunities that involve children and youth. Sometimes all a child who is struggling with reading needs is simply an adult willing to help him or her over the difficult words. The library can serve as a Senior Volunteer Corp resource site, bringing reading and youth together in an intellectually stimulating atmosphere.

Government agencies also offer services that need host sites. One of these is the Internal Revenue Service (IRS) Tax Counseling for the Elderly program. Like RSVP, the IRS reimburses volunteers for out-of-pocket expenses involved with volunteering and looks for safe, centrally located facilities to place the volunteers. Appendix 1 offers additional resources for locating partners for aging projects.

Free Advertising Venues

In most cases, advertising the library's senior services on shopping bags or informational brochures will not cost the business any additional funds. Staff, for instance, can ask the grocery store to help them promote the month of May as Seniors Month. A schedule of events can be printed on one side of shopping bags used from mid-April through May, leaving the grocery store with the other side for their name and their salute to seniors. Chapter 9 discusses ways of advertising the library on informational brochures.

Using the Web for Fund-Raising

Raising money via the World Wide Web (WWW) may seem quite a radical idea, but libraries may wish to consider it. Recently eBay launched an initiative called the Digital Opportunity Program for Seniors to help seniors overcome the digital divide by giving them easy access to technology and education.[20] The Digital Opportunity Program for Seniors is committed to providing $1 million to SeniorNet to set up

training centers across the country and establish online training programs that are available to libraries.

Of particular note to libraries, however, is the fact that along with the money for SeniorNet, eBay created a "Seniors Area" on its website. Here, nonprofit organizations can conduct auctions to raise money for senior programs. Libraries may consider cleaning out their attics and archives and looking for collectibles or antiques they no longer need and asking patrons to do the same, with the goal of placing the items for bid.

Conclusion

This chapter has provided a cursory overview of funding possibilities, but many websites and texts can help libraries be successful in locating and receiving funds.[21] Finding money takes work, but the results mean the funding of programs that will support fellowship, education, and the entertainment needs of the seniors who reside within your community. Although library staff realize that seniors have more to give to the community than the community can possibly give back to the seniors, others may have to be reminded. The grant makers and other members of the community should be reminded that libraries can provide the leadership to capture the wisdom of seniors while enabling the seniors to participate in programs and services that will help them to continue to "live long and prosper."

NOTES

1. Tracey L. Bremer, "Library Funding," *ERIC Digest* (March 2001), available at <http://www.ericit.org/digests/EDO-IR-2001-01.shtml>.
2. GIA is an organization of funders dedicated to promoting and strengthening grant making for an aging society. *Funding across the Ages* and other information and publications are available at <http://giaging.org>.
3. Ibid.
4. John Feather, "The New Face of Aging and the Future of Funding for Senior Programs" (summary of presentation presented at the Comprehensive Health Education Foundation luncheon, Seattle, Wash., June 2000).
5. Donald C. Orlich, *Designing Successful Grant Proposals* (Alexandria, Va.: Association for Supervision and Curriculum Development, 1996). Available at <http://www.ascd.org/readingroom/books/orlich96book.html>.

6. Center for Medicare Education, "Getting Funding from Foundations," *Issue Brief* 1, no. 5 (2000), available at <http://www.medicareed.org/pdfs/papers>.

7. The Foundation Center Learning Lab, Proposal Writing: A Short Guide, available at <http://fdncenter.org/learn/shortcourse/prop1.html>.

8. Orlich, *Designing Successful Grant Proposals.*

9. Edward Skloot, Primer on Grantmaking, Association of Small Foundations, available at <http://smallfoundations.org/why_give_/primer_on_grantmaking>.

10. Ibid.

11. Center for Medicare Education.

12. The Foundation Center, available at <http://fdncenter.org>, annually publishes *Foundation Center's User-Friendly Guide Directory* (New York: The Center). It is worth consulting as there are still foundations that do not have websites or links on the Internet.

13. GuideStar is available at <http://www.guidestar.com>.

14. The Association of Small Foundations is available at <http://www.smallfoundations.org>.

15. NonprofitsCan.org, available at <http://www.nonprofitscan.org>, also offers an online newsletter to which visitors can subscribe.

16. Your state Agency on Aging can be located by consulting the Administration on Aging's website, available at <http://www.aoa.gov/aoa/pages/state.html>.

17. Center for the Book, available at <http://www.loc.gov/loc/lcib/9801/cfb.html>.

18. National Storytelling Network Grants Program, available at <http://www.storynet.org>.

19. Further information is available at <http://www.walmartfoundation.org>. The senior initiative is listed under Grandparent's Day.

20. Chris Connor, eBay Bridges Seniors' Digital Divide, AuctionWatch, September 26, 2000, available at <http://www.auctionwatch.com/awdaily/dailynews/september00/1-092600.html>.

21. There are several senior gateways that can provide visitors with useful links to information. A few are Grantmakers in Aging, available at <http://giaging.org/links.htm>; the National Aging Information Center, available at <http://www.aoa.dhhs.gov/NAIC/Notes/fundingseniors>; the Administration on Aging, available at <http://www.aoa.gov/aoa/pages/grants.html>; and Government Grants Information (note separate doorways for Canadian and U.S. government grants), available at <http://www.governmentgrants.com>.

AFTERWORD
Reaffirming the Need for Senior Services

> *There are queen mothers (and old grandpas) scattered among all of us.*
> *They all have stories to tell. Before they go, they owe us the telling*
> *and we owe them the listening. It's a double blessing, and those are rare.*
>
> —Dick Feagler, "Blessed Are the Old and Their Stories,"
> *Plain Dealer*, April 21, 2002

The world is indeed graying. We are moving toward a world in which there will be more older people than youngsters. By the year 2050 demographers estimate the world as a whole will contain more people aged sixty and older than children under the age of fifteen, and that will be one of the most dramatic shifts in history.[1] It is important for libraries to be part of the process to prepare for the shift.

Ageism is still a major hurdle to clear. Society still is prone to portray seniors as inflexible curmudgeons who vote against school levies while soaking up pension funds. Libraries—by developing and promoting programs for seniors that help them to be enlightened, entertained, and kept current—can serve as the community's standard bearer. The more seniors take advantage of the community's services, the more the community will see that seniors are a diverse group of individuals. It is important that the world start to think of its older people as "less of a burden on society and more as a resource whose experience and knowledge can be tapped, for the benefit of themselves and the societies they live in."[2]

There are libraries throughout the world leading the way. The anecdotal comments from staff that follow hopefully will serve as affirmation that senior programming is both possible and necessary.

> "We believe there are thousands of people who have stories to tell, and they deserve to give these stories a good literary style."
>
> —Hordaland County Library (Norway)

"The senior residents love watching the children participate in the story hour; all who participate feel it is a worthwhile experience."

—Normal Public Library (Illinois)

"Working for Service to the Aging gives me great pleasure; I feel I am doing something for seniors as well as for myself."

—Brooklyn Public Library (New York)

"We take pride to assure that our homebound patrons receive the same services as those who are mobile and are able to visit the library."

—Red Carpet Services, Topeka and Shawnee County Public Library (Kansas)

"READiscover is built on a long-term library commitment to serve older adults, and based on using older adults as volunteers to make the program work. It targets all elements of the senior population, a diverse group with energy, enthusiasm, and a burning need to learn e-mail!"

—James V. Brown Library (Pennsylvania)

"As with all outreach efforts, just coming into the seniors' lives, on-site, makes them feel appreciated and happy."

—Chicago Public Library

"All the programs have been well received. Residents all look forward to the visits by library staff."

—New York Public Library

"It mostly boils down to 'more'—seniors want more classes, more advanced classes, more classes on other computer-oriented topics."

—Davenport Public Library (Iowa)

"The 'Remembering the Depression' program at the Loudoun County Respite Center revived a memorable experience from a frail elderly woman who couldn't remember the lunch she received just a few minutes before the program. During the program, however, she stood up and shared a nostalgic, but joyful event with the group."

—Loudoun Outreach staff (Virginia)

"We are often surprised by seniors' insights and humor!"

—Glenview Public Library (Illinois)

"Not everyone is suited to this type of work, but both Van Delivery library assistants regularly claim to have the best job in the library. Van Delivery staff regularly attends funerals for deceased patrons and frequently comes back with new clients when friends and family of the deceased tell other mourners about how special the library was to their loved one."

—Fairbanks North Star Borough Library, Noel Wien Library (Alaska)

"The seniors are a good group as far as supporting the library in many ways."

—Pickering Public Library (Ontario, Canada)

"The Old Bridge Library has many programs, but the Savvy Seniors is the best attended."

—Old Bridge Library (New Jersey)

"One Thousand Stories refers to our own lives—a mosaic of events that makes up who we are as individuals. All seniors need to get these stories out in a genuine belief that somebody cares."

—One Thousand Stories Project, Kansas City Public Library (Missouri)

"Seniors who embrace this new technology find it enriches their lives and banishes feelings of isolation and disenfranchisement that often plague older adults. E-mail, newsletters, interactive sites, and websites that offer access to relevant information can introduce heightened quality of life for those who find growing older erects barriers and poses challenges of all kinds. We are pleased to contribute to this access."

—Wilton Library Association (Connecticut)

"The audience is appreciative, enthusiastic, and uninhibited about voicing their opinion on certain topics."

—Plano Public Library (Texas)

"Over the past year and a half that the Cyber Seniors program has been in effect, the library has received dozens of thank-you e-mails and letters from senior citizens. Many mention that they are thrilled to be able to e-mail to their children and grandchildren."

—Multnomah County Library (Oregon)

"With the Outreach services actually reaching out into the community, the community's perception of the library is enhanced. Outreach to seniors is one way that the library can maintain contact with our patrons and longtime supporters. By meeting face-to-face with seniors where they reside, staff can better determine their needs."

—Centerville Public Library (Ohio)

"In the short eight months I've been here, I've become a believer in services to seniors and persons with disabilities. The library system seeks to empower all patrons."

—Lee County Library (Florida)

"In the twenty-first century, it is critical that libraries at the local and national level work together to support and nurture the development of reading, lifelong reading, and technology skills among older adults. The library represents an innovative model and should position itself as the primary point of access for seniors seeking information, inspiration, and enrichment."

—Calgary Public Library (Alberta, Canada)

"GAB successfully brings children and older adults together from diverse cultural, ethnic, and socioeconomic backgrounds to share in the love of reading. The library's GAB program helps to personalize the library for the community."

—Los Angeles Public Library

NOTES

1. "The Graying of the Globe," Editorial, *New York Times*, April 12, 2002, A 26.
2. Ibid.

APPENDIX 1
Resources

The following resources may be used by staff to locate possible partners for aging projects and to learn more about aging, including how to work, plan, and interact with older adults. Staff are also encouraged to explore the sites listed in appendix 2, "Suggested Bookmarks for Seniors," for additional information. Commercial entities, which sell products to assist seniors or can be used by staff for senior programming, are provided as a convenience and are not endorsed by the author or the American Library Association.

Agencies Focusing on Older Adult Concerns

AARP (formerly known as the American Association of Retired Persons)
   (800) 434-3410   <http://www.aarp.org>

   Nonprofit, nonpartisan association for people who are fifty years of age or older. Website very useful for research and locating chapters in the library's service area.

Administration on Aging (AoA)
   (202) 619-0724   <http://www.aoa.dhhs.gov>

   The principal federal agency responsible for senior programs authorized under the Older Americans Act of 1965. The website is a treasure trove of information, including printable informational brochures and fact sheets on a wide variety of topics.

Age Exchange
   <http://www.greenwichgateway.com/ageexchange/htm>

   Age Exchange is a leader in all areas of reminiscence. Publications include reminiscing guides. Some subjects are focused on European memories.

Alzheimer's Association (Alz)

(800) 272-3900   <http://www.alz.org>

Organization that focuses on research into the prevention, cure, and treatment of Alzheimer's disease. Also provides education and support to the community in which chapters are located.

American Society on Aging (ASA)

(800) 537-9728   <http://www.asaging.org>

Membership organization that offers continuing education programs and hosts an informative website.

Canada's Association for the Fifty-Plus (CARP)

(416) 363-8748   <http://www.fifty-plus.net>

A nonprofit association that promotes the rights and quality of life of mature Canadians.

Catholic Golden Age

(800) 836-5699

<http://www.catholicgoldenage.org>

Promotes well-being of its members and helps fund programs designed to enhance the well-being of seniors.

Center for Communication and Consumer Services (formerly National Aging Information Center, or NAIC)

(202) 619-7501   <http://www.aoa.gov/naic>

A service of the Administration on Aging, the Center for Communication and Consumer Services maintains aging resources programs, policies, and services that it uses to respond to inquiries. Hosts a very accessible megasite with links to resources on aging.

Corporation for National and Community Service

(202) 606-5000   <http://cns.gov>

Oversees government-supported senior programs. Connecting with any of the supported programs can enrich the library's senior mission.

Department of Veterans Affairs (VA)

(202) 273-5700   <http://www.va.gov>

Oversees all aspects of veterans' entitlements. The website provides links to state agencies as well as social groups.

Experience Works

(800) 901-7965

<http://www.experienceworks.org>

Provides older adults with training, employment, and community service opportunities that will help them reenter the workforce or find a more challenging position.

Families USA Foundation

(202) 628-3030   <http://www.familiesusa.org>

Works with a nationwide network of activist community organizations on problems that challenge families, particularly health care, long-term care, and elderly poverty. Possible partnerships for programming and marketing ventures.

Generations United (GU)

(202) 662-4283   <http://www.gu.org>

Generations United is a coalition of more than 100 national organizations that work to promote an intergenerational approach to advocacy and service. This is accomplished in part through conference and workshop speakers, program ideas, and technical assistance at the state and local levels.

Gray Panthers

(800) 280-5362   <http://www.graypanther.org>

Conducts work on eight national interests: national health care, affordable housing, environmental preservation, peace, ending discrimination, education, economic and tax justice, and social justice. Supports local chapters.

International Federation on Ageing (IFA)

(514) 396-3358   <http://www.ifa-fiv.org>

Headquartered in Montreal, the International Federation on Ageing is a federation of national voluntary organizations from fifty countries. It serves as a clearinghouse for information, practical concerns, and common concerns of the aging world.

Jewish Council for the Aging

(301) 881-8782   <http://www.jcagw.org>

Seeks to assist seniors of all faiths to lead independent lives. Provides transportation, computer training, and information and referral. Presents programs and maintains a speakers bureau.

Literacy Volunteers of America (LVA)
(315) 472-0001
<http://www.literacyvolunteers.org>

Provides training and aid resources for organizations and individuals to tutor adults in English as a second language and in basic literacy.

Meals on Wheels Association of America (MOWAA)
(703) 548-5558   <http://www.givemeals.com>

Membership organization for those agencies that provide home delivery of hot meals to homebound persons and seniors. Volunteers may be willing to deliver library materials to seniors along with the meals.

National Asian Pacific Center on Aging (NAPCA)
(206) 624-1221   <http://www.napca.org>

Supports the health, education, and social services of Pacific Island and Asian American older adults. Operates two federal employment programs for older workers.

National Caucus and Center for the Black Aged (NCBA)
(202) 637-8400   <http://www.ncba-aged.org>

Seeks to improve quality of life for African Americans and other low-income minority Americans. Promotes community awareness of problems and issues affecting low-income aging population. Operates an employment program in fourteen states.

National Center for Health Statistics (NCHS)
(800) 311-3435
<http://www.cdc.gov/nchs/fastats/>

Solid statistics, helpful for grant applications, can be found here.

National Council on the Aging (NCOA)
(800) 424-9046   <http://www.ncoa.org>

Network of professionals and volunteers who support advocacy, education, and model programs, including the arts, for seniors.

National Hispanic Council on Aging (NHCoA)
(202) 745-2521   <http://www.nhcoa.org>

Membership consists of Hispanic and non-Hispanic individuals, organizations, and agencies. Supports demonstration projects, research, train-ing, and development of educational and informational resources.

National Indian Council on Aging (NICOA)
(505) 292-2001   <http://www.nicoa.org>

Seeks to bring about improvement to older Indian and Alaska Natives. Conducts research and disseminates information on the needs of these populations.

National Library Service for the Blind and Physically Handicapped (NLS)
(202) 707-5100   <http://www.loc.gov/nls.>

Catalog and resources of the National Library Service are provided here as are links to network libraries.

National Osteoporosis Foundation (NOF)
(202) 223-2226   <http://www.nof.org>

This organization supports educational research in the field of osteoporosis and promotes public awareness of this disease in part with educational programs.

National Senior Citizens Law Center (NSCLC)
(202) 289-6976   <http://www.nsclc.org>

Provides litigation support services, legal research, and national policy representation for lawyers and paralegals serving the poor older population. Publishes numerous manuals and other informational materials.

Older Women's League (OWL)
(202) 783-6686   <http://www.owlnational.org>

Primary issues include access to health insurance, support for family caregivers, access to jobs, and pensions for older women. Operates a speakers bureau and prepares educational materials.

Senior Community Service Employment Program (SCSEP)
(202) 219-5904   <http://wdsc.doleta.gov/seniors>

Federally funded employment program designed to promote subsidized part-time employment opportunities for unemployed, low-income people age fifty-five and older. Seniors are usually placed in community service activities at nonprofit or public agencies, where they receive training.

Senior Corps

(800) 424-8867 <http://www.seniorcorps.org>

Seeks to involve seniors over the age of fifty-five with their communities in volunteer projects.

Visiting Nurses Association of America (VNAA)

(303) 753-0218 <http://www.vnaa.org>

Works to strengthen business resources and economic programs through contracting, marketing, governmental affairs, and publications.

Volunteers of America

(800) 899-0089 <http://www.voa.org>

The National Retiree Volunteer Coalition of the Volunteers of America is a good resource for forming partnerships between retirees, the community, and employers. The coalition organizes volunteers and offers their skills for civic and business needs.

Books and Journal and Web Articles

Abeles, Norman. "What Practitioners Should Know about Working with Older Adults." *Professional Psychology Research and Practice* [Journal online], 29, no. 5 (1998): 413–27. Available at <http://www.apa.org/pi/aging/practioners/executive.html>.

Overview of ageism and truths about aging.

Cassistre, Debra. *Activity Ideas for the Budget-Minded.* Forest Knolls, Calif.: Elder Books, 1994.

Low-cost program ideas, suited for an older audience, are offered.

Colmer, Rebecca Sharp. *The Senior's Guide to Easy Computing.* Chelsea, Mich.: Eklektika, 1999.

Bulleted presentations in this book will help staff create lesson plans for seniors.

Flynn, Christina, and Kathleen Cameron. Gerontologist Partners in Senior Care. American Society of Consultant Pharmacists website. Available at <http://www.ascp.com/public/pubs/tcp/1999/nov/gerontologists.shtml>.

Written to motivate pharmacists to become involved with senior needs. The article includes an "Aging I.Q." that may be used with staff.

Focus: Library Service to Older Adults, Persons with Disabilities.

Monthly newsletter, currently published by Marilyn Irwin, Indiana University/Indiana Institute on Disability and Community, Center for Disability Information and Referral, 2853 E. Tenth St., Bloomington, IN 47408-2696.

Friedan, Betty. *The Fountain of Age.* New York: Simon & Schuster, 1993.

Friedan's book presents a positive approach to aging and should be mandatory reading for all who have seen their forty-fifth birthdays come and go.

Griebel, Rosemary. "When I'm Sixty-Four: Libraries and the Age Wave." *Feliciter* 44, no. 2 (February, 1998): 14–19.

Kleinman, Allan M. "The Aging Agenda: Redefining Library Services for a Graying Population." *Library Journal* 120 (July 1995): 32–34.

———. "Global Graying: Successful Strategies for Bridging Information Gaps with the Elderly Population." Paper presented at the Sixty-Third IFLA General Conference, Copenhagen, Denmark, August 31 to September 2, 1997. Available at <http://www.ifla.org/IV/ifla63/63klea.htm>.

Lazzaro, Joseph J. *Adaptive Technologies for Learning and Work Environments.* 2d ed. Chicago: American Library Assn., 2001.

In addition to using adaptive technology in a Windows environment, Unix and Macintosh are also covered.

Luey, Beth. Starting a Reading Group. Arizona Center for the Book. Available at <http://aspin.asu.edu/azcb/readgrp.html>.

Mates, Barbara T. "Accessibility Guidelines for Electronic Resources: Making the Internet Accessible for People with Disabilities." *Library Technology Reports* 37 (July–August 2001): 1–84.

———. *Adaptive Technology for the Internet: Making Electronic Resources Accessible to All.* Chicago: American Library Assn., 2000.

McLeod, Beth Witrogen, ed. *And Thou Shalt Honor: The Caregiver's Companion*. Emmaus, Pa.: Rodale, 2002.

This work accompanies the similarly titled PBS video presentation and seeks to give readers advice, support, and direction in caring for older adults. Foreword by Rosalynn Carter.

Ohio Library Council. *Elder-Berries*. 2d ed. Columbus, Ohio: Ohio Library Council, 1998.

———. *Outreach Services to Special Needs Patrons*. Columbus, Ohio: Ohio Library Council, 1997.

Ring, Anne. *Read Easy: Large Print Libraries for Older Adults*. Washington, D.C.: CAREsource Program Development, 1991.

Rubin, Rhea. *Planning for Library Services for People with Disabilities*. Chicago: Assn. of Specialized and Cooperative Library Agencies, 2001.

Rubin, Rhea, and Gail McGovern. *Working with Older Adults: A Handbook for Libraries*. Sacramento: California State Library Foundation, 1990.

Schladwieler, Kief. *The Foundation Center's Guide to Grantseeking on the Web*. New York: The Center, 2001.

Self Help for Hard of Hearing People. Senior Citizen Program Packet. Bethesda, Md.: Self Help for Hard of Hearing People, n.d. Available at <http://www.shhh.org/pubscat/shhhpubs.cfm>.

Information and ideas for anyone working with groups of older adults with hearing loss.

Thorsheim, Howard, and Bruce B. Roberts. *I Remember When: Activity Ideas to Help People Reminisce*. Forest Knolls, Calif.: Elder Books, 2000.

Tower, Mary Jo. "Seniors and Mobile Library Services." *Bookmobile and Outreach Services* 33, no. 2 (2000): 37–42.

Useful information as to how bookmobiles can be used with seniors.

Turock, Betty. "Library Services to Older Adults." *New Jersey Libraries* 21 (winter 1988): 2–25.

Although most of the programs presented in this work are no longer in existence, the principles and ideas are usable and doable.

2000/2001 Older Americans Information Directory: Organizations, Newsletters, Books, Products, Services. Lakeville, Conn.: Grey House, 2000.

A complete guide to every aspect of aging. Organized by national and state affiliations.

The Universal Design File: Designing for People of All Ages and Abilities. Available at <http://www.design.ncsu.edu/cud/pubs/center/books/ud_file/toc3b14.htm>. Online version of Molly Follette Story, James L. Mueller, and Ronald Mace's book, *The Universal Design File: Designing for People of All Ages and Abilities* (Raleigh, N.C.: Center for Universal Design, 1998).

Presents a thorough overview on how buildings, grounds, tools, and so forth should be designed to accommodate all people. Clear photographs of devices are included.

VanFleet, Connie. "A Matter of Focus: Reference Services for Older Adults." *The Reference Librarian* 49/50 (1995): 147–64.

Walling, Linda Lucas, comp. *Library Services to the Sandwich Generation and Serial Caregivers*. ASCLA Changing Horizons Series, no. 4. Chicago: American Library Assn., 2001.

Library Association Guidelines Affecting Seniors

ALA Guidelines for Library Services to Older Adults <http://www.ala.org/rusa/acrobat/older_adults.pdf>

Developed and supported by the members of the American Library Association.

Canadian Guidelines for Library Services to Adults <http://www.cla.ca/resources/olderadults.htm>

Developed and supported by the members of the Canadian Library Association.

Purchasing Resources

Audiovisual Materials

Age Power with Ken Dychtwald
(877) 727-7467   <http://www.pbs.org>

This PBS production addresses the issue of aging baby boomers, exploring topics such as the biological potential to live longer (between 120 and 140 years), the shift from a "work-retire-die pattern" to a more cyclical one, and the growth of a more empowered senior population.

Ageless Heroes
(877) 727-7467   <http://www.pbs.org>

Currently only the script of this hour-long PBS production is available, but it may be used as a sensitizing and educational tool to demonstrate that senior years can be a time of vitality, learning, creativity, community involvement, and new beginnings.

And Thou Shalt Honor
(877) 727-7467
<http://www.thoushalthonor.org>

The documentary examines the aspect of aging and caregiving by profiling actual families who are caring for older adults. The documentary also serves as a "call to arms" for viewers to become activists for reform of the caregiving system.

ElderSong
(800) 397-0553   <http://www.eldersong.com>

Distributor of reasonably priced books, videos, and recordings for those who work with older adults.

Gift of Joy
(713) 376-6186

Services to older adults is the focus of this twenty-seven-minute video produced by the Brooklyn Public Library. Available from the library's Services to the Aging Department.

Good Old Days Audio
(800) 829-5865
<http://goodolddaysonline.com>

The publisher of *Good Old Days* magazine, a good reminiscing tool, also produces audiocassettes of nostalgic themes such as "School Days," "Down on the Farm," "Yuletide," and "Harvest."

Library Media Project
(800) 847-3671
<http://librarymedia.org/aging/age_ distributors.html>

Distributors of videos on aging produced by many small, independent filmmakers.

Terranova
(800) 779-8491   <http://www.terranova.org>

A broad range of videos produced with the intention to move, motivate, and educate viewers on the positive aspects of aging. Includes a number of titles that would be useful to loan to nursing homes. Videos may be purchased or rented.

Computer Software, Adaptive Devices, and Assistive Tools

Ann Morris
(800) 454-3175   <http://www.annmorris.com>

Sells useful everyday items that make life easier and livable for those with impairments.

Assistive Devices for Use with Personal Computers
<http://www.loc.gov/nls>

Provides the sources for purchase of adaptive hardware and software.

Independent Living Aids (ILA)
(800) 537-2118
<http://www.independentliving.com>

Low-priced assistive and adaptive devices such as reachers, grips, magnifiers, book holders, large-print books and games, and computer devices.

LS&S Group
(800) 468-4789   <http://www.lssgroup.com>

A complete line of magnifiers, computer hardware and software, wheelchairs, scooters, and assistive devices for those with physical hearing or visual impairments.

MaxiAids
(800) 522-6294   <http://www.maxiaids.com>

A complete line of magnifiers, computer hardware and software, wheelchairs, scooters, and assistive devices for those with physical hearing or visual impairments.

Sears Health and Wellness Catalog
(800) 326-1750

Although the offerings are not extensive, such items as ramps, scooters, wheelchairs, reachers, and magnifiers can be purchased.

Reminiscing Aids

Betty's Attic
(800) 294-4068   <http://www.bettysattic.com>

This is a good source to locate props for reminiscing programs.

BiFolkal
(800) 568-5357   <http://www.bifolkal.org>

Compiles and sells reminiscing kits. It is possible to purchase pieces of the kits to suit libraries' budgets and needs. Produces informative newsletters and detailed catalogs, which can serve as a guide to create similar reminiscing tools.

Cracker Barrel
(800) 333-9566 <http://www.crackerbarrel.com>

Items that will jog memories and old-fashioned candies (which can supplement refreshments) are sold at reasonable prices.

Cumberland General Store
(800) 334-4640
<http://www.cumberlandgeneral.com>

Simple toys, corncob pipes, and farming and kitchen utensils of yesteryear are only a few of the items that can be purchased for reminiscence programs.

ElderGames
(202) 479-6615
<http://www.unitedseniorshealth.org/html/
pubs_eldergames.htm>

Some ElderGames focus on personal memories, how the world has changed, or remembered stars and heroes of the past. Others provide for group participation or just listening. All are designed to entertain and amuse while awakening and challenging the older mind. All games are priced at under $20.

Vermont Country Store
(802) 362-8460
<http://www.vermontcountrystore.com>

This is a source for old-fashioned candy and other items that can be used to stir memories during reminiscing sessions.

Website Resources

American Music Therapy Association
<http://www.musictherapy.org/factsheets/
olderadults.html>

Offers information on using music when working with seniors and links to other music websites.

Bookbay.com
<http://www.bookbay.com>

Tips on starting or revitalizing book clubs are provided.

Canadianbookclubs.com
<http://www.candianbookclubs.com>

Provides all the necessary information to successfully start and maintain a book club.

Center for the Study of Rural Librarianship
<http://eagle.clarion.edu/~grads/csrl/bib13.htm>

This site provides a nineteen-page bibliography of articles relating to library services for older adults.

Communicating with Seniors
<http://www.hc-sc.gc.ca/seniors-aines/pubs/
communicating/comsen_e.pdf>

The Division of Aging and Seniors, Health Canada, posts this guide as a service for those who interact with seniors. All facets of communication are covered.

Computers Made Easy for Senior Citizens
<http://www.csuchico.edu/~csu/seniors/
computing.html>

Designed to help seniors learn how to use computers and the Internet, this site can serve as a guide for staff to use when designing computer classes for seniors.

Elderhostel

<http://www.elderhostel.org>

Elderhostel promotes educational opportunities for seniors throughout the world via a network of more than 1,900 colleges in seventy countries. The website offers a multitude of suggestions for ideas on senior programming.

Internet School Library Media Center (ISLMC) Ageism Resources

<http://falcon.jmu.edu/~ramseyil/ageism.htm>

This megasite is designed to bring educational sources to one place for use by teachers, librarians, parents, and students. This page provides links to ageism sites.

National Institute on Aging

<http://www.nia.nih.gov>

In addition to posting valuable information on aging, *Making Your Website Senior Friendly: A Checklist*, *Minority Aging Newsletter*, and the *Resource Directory for Older People* (a comprehensive directory of every known service for older adults) are available in portable document file (PDF) format.

Senior Theatre Connections

<http://www.seniortheatre.com>

Information on senior performers. Also publishes and sells books on the subject using drama activities with older adults.

Setting Priorities for Retirement Years (SPRY) Foundation

<http://www.spry.org>

Produces and provides two guides: *Evaluating Health Information on the World Wide Web: A Guide for Older Adults and Caregivers* and *Older Adults and the World Wide Web: A Guide for Website Creators*, both available in portable document file (PDF) format.

U.S. Census Bureau

<http://www.census.gov>

Specialized reports on the older population available. Also offers options of retrieving localized data on aging as related to minority groups, economics, and educational attainment.

Usability.gov

<http://www.usability.gov>

Includes information on accessible website design as well as usability testing and statistics on Internet usage.

Web Accessibility Initiative of the World Wide Web Consortium (W3C)

<http://www.w3.org/wai>

Resources on web accessibility, including guidelines. Information is also provided on workshops to create accessible websites.

APPENDIX 2
Suggested Bookmarks for Seniors

The following websites can be used as a foundation for creating a patron links library for seniors. Staff and patrons no doubt will wish to add to the collection.

Aging "Lite"

AgeVenture
    <http://www.demko.com>

    AgeVenture is a gerontological news resource for print and broadcast journalists. It offers senior-content articles for use in the mainstream media.

Baby Boomer Headquarters
    <http://www.bbhq.com>

    The Baby Boomer Headquarters has information and links to trivia, pictures, books, music, and memories of the 1950s, 1960s, and 1970s.

Baby Boomer Initiative
    <http://www.babyboomers.com>

    The objective of the Baby Boomer Initiative is to unite the boomers. Some interesting and helpful articles are posted on-site as well as a year-by-year "what happened in the year you were born" link.

National Centenarian Awareness Project (NCAP)
    <http://adlercentenarians.com/ncap.html>

    The mission of the National Centenarian Awareness Project (NCAP) is to celebrate centenarians. The NCAP desires to cast a more optimistic, yet realistic, light on the later years for all.

Noted Nonagenarians and Centenarians
    <http://www.tech.org/~cleary/NNC/nncmain.html>

    This website gives examples of people in their nineties or hundreds who are still active and contributing to society.

Too Young to Retire

<http://2young2retire.com/tenways.html>

For those over age fifty-five seeking alternatives to stereotypical retirement. Links to a myriad of innovative volunteer, educational, and health and fitness organizations and opportunities.

Associations and Reference Sources

AARP

<http://www.aarp.org>

Provides visitors with a myriad of information and resources that are not available elsewhere on the Web.

Administration on Aging (AoA) Resource Directory

<http://www.aoa.dhhs.gov/directory/default.htm>

Hosts a broad subject-links library to agencies and organizations.

BenefitsCheckUp

<http://www.benefitscheckup.org>

Created by the National Council on Aging, BenefitsCheckUp is a free, easy-to-use service that identifies federal and state assistance programs for older Americans.

Canada's Association for the Fifty-Plus

<http://www.50plus.com/carp/about/main.cfm>

Canada's Association for the Fifty-Plus (CARP) offers information on health, home, family, and other interests.

Disability Resources Monthly WebWatcher

<http://www.disabilityresources.org/AGING.html>

Provides updated links to information on products and services for seniors who have a disability.

ElderWeb

<http://www.elderweb.com/default.php>

This award-winning site is designed to be a research site for persons seeking information on elder care and includes links to information on legal, financial, medical, and housing issues.

FIRSTGOV for Seniors

<http://www.seniors.gov>

Serves as a megaportal for links to a myriad of federal and local agencies. Site adheres to good senior website design guidelines.

Generations United

<http://www.gu.org>

Generations United serves as a resource to education policymakers and the public about the economic, social, and personal aspects of intergenerational cooperation. Promotes senior service and volunteerism.

Grandparenting Information

<http://seniorliving.about.com/cs/grandparenting>

Links provided on "how to be a grandparent" as well as useful tips on traveling with grandchildren and legal advice for sticky divorce situations.

Resource Directory for Older People

<http://www.aoa.gov/directory/default.htm>

A compete listing (includes contact information) of resource centers, organizations, and programs available to older adults. A portable document file (PDF) format allows users to download and print.

Senior Resource

<http://www.seniorresource.com>

Commercial website offering links to information on retirement, insurance and housing, and long-term care. Posted articles are clearly identified by sponsor, so readers can be aware.

Senior World

<http://www.seniorworld.com>

A well-rounded site with articles on a variety of topics and issues. Seniors may submit their personal stories for the *Senior Story* page of the website.

Seniorcitizens.com

<http://www.seniorcitizens.com>

Site is a portal to a myriad of interesting and useful information. Unique to this site is a "cemetery plots for sale" page that allows visitors to buy and sell plots.

SeniorNet

<http://seniornet.org/php>

One of the original and most accessible "senior-oriented" websites. The site hosts tutoring and online courses, book discussions, and links to topics such as financial planning, travel, and computers.

Seniors-Site.com
<http://seniors-site.com>

Commercial site offering useful information on nursing homes, fraud, and legislation affecting older adults.

60 Plus Association
<http://www.60plus.org>

The 60 Plus Association is a nonpartisan seniors' advocacy group with a free-enterprise, less-government, less-taxes approach to seniors' issues.

Social Security Association
<http://www.ssa.gov>

If a question deals with Social Security, the answer could be found here.

ThirdAge
<http://www.thirdage.com>

Magazine-format site with a lot of confusing drop-down boxes; however, the site may be appealing for baby boomers. Discussion topics are appropriate for a wide range of senior interests and ages.

United Seniors Association
<http://www.unitedseniors.org>

Membership organization of seniors seeking to reform Social Security, Medicare, and taxes.

Consumer Issues

Better Business Bureau (BBB) Shopping Safely Online
<http://www.bbb.org/library/shoponline.asp>

Tips for shopping online are provided and include ways to spot online scams and frauds. Includes a quick checklist of items patrons should be aware of when considering making online purchases.

NADA Appraisal Guides
<http://www2.nadaguides.com>

Learn the buying and selling price of vehicles at this website.

Overstock.com
<http://www.overstock.com>

Just about anything can be found at this website; original prices appear to be accurate.

Health Issues

Aerobic Gardening
<http://ritecode.com/aerobicgardening/index.html>

Ideas for adapting gardening into aerobic activity are shared with visitors. A senior page is provided.

Alzheimer's Association
<http://www.alzheimers.org>

Here you will find information about Alzheimer's disease and related disorders.

American Diabetes Association
<http://www.diabetes.org>

The American Diabetes Association supports diabetes research and provides information and advocacy on diabetes. Tips sheets and articles on healthy living are presented here.

American Heart Association
<http://www.americanheart.org>

Information is presented on heart disease and prevention of heart disease as well as healthy living tips.

Cancer.gov
<http://www.cancer.gov>

The National Cancer Institute's website provides information about every form of cancer, as well as research on the subject, and includes prevention advisories.

Diet Information
<http://diet-i.com>

Presents visitors with information about every possible diet (fad and legitimate) as well as information on nutrition and healthy living.

Fifty Plus Fitness Association
<http://www.50plus.org>

To encourage fitness and a more active lifestyle for those who are age fifty or older.

Gardening for Seniors
<http://www.fbmg.com/references/seniors.htm>

Useful tips for making gardening less stressful.

Hard of Hearing Advocates (HOH)
<http://hohadvocates.org>

Site offers an overview of hearing impairments and older adults. A comparison price guide for hearing aids is given.

Hospice and Palliative Care
<http://www/aoa.gov/NAIC/Notes/Hospice.
      html>

The National Aging Information Center has compiled resources related to end-of-life care. The website offers views on the subject from caregivers, insurance professionals, public officials, and older adults.

Life Expectancy Calculator
<http://www.beeson.org/Livingto100/default.
      htm>

The Living to 100 Life Expectancy Calculator was designed to translate what researchers have learned from studies of centenarians and other longevity research.

Medicare
<http://www.medicare.gov>

Complete resource for Medicare information. Also offers practical tips on choosing a nursing home.

National Osteoporosis Foundation (NOF)
<http://www.nof.org>

Resource information for living with, as well as preventing, osteoporosis, including a referral guide to specialists.

Prescription Drugs
<http://www.aoa.gov/NAIC/Notes/
      prescriptiondrugs.html>

This National Aging Information Center has compiled resources on issues related to the development of new drugs and their safety, the dangerous side effects of multiple prescriptions, the retail cost of proprietary and generic drugs, and various prescription insurance issues.

Self Help for Hard of Hearing People (SHHH)
<http://www.shhh.org>

Organizational website whose goal is to enhance the quality of life for people who are hard-of-hearing. Articles include how to make the decision to get hearing help and how to choose a hearing aid.

Helping Seniors Live

American Association of Homes and Services for the Aging
<http://www.aahsa.org/public/aahsa.htm>

Organization whose mission is advancing the existence of affordable, ethical long-term care for America. The association represents 5,600 mission-driven, not-for-profit agencies. Information provided on government subsidies and entitlements.

American Red Cross
<http://www.redcross.org >

Connects seniors to local Red Cross agencies as well as offers seniors a good overview of precautions and procedures to take if faced with a natural disaster.

Assisted Living Federation of America
<http://www.alfa.org>

Site for professional assisted-living providers and consumers. Tips are given on how to choose a facility, and articles include the rights of individuals and adapting to life in an assisted-living facility.

Caregiver's Handbook
<http://www5.biostat.wustl.edu/alzheimer/
      care.html>

A handbook designed to help both the caregiver and the older care receiver cope with Alzheimer's disease.

Cooking for One or Two
<http://www.gov.mb.ca/health/nutrition/pubs/
      cooking1_2.pdf>

Tips on how to shop and cook for one or two people.

Cooking Solo

<http://www.ext.nodak.edu/extpubs/yf/foods/he5
16w.htm>

Tips on how to shop and cook for one or two
people.

Department of Energy

<http://www.eren.doe.gov/consumerinfo/energy
_savers/intro.html>

Energy-saving tips provided by the U.S. Department of Energy.

Family Caregiving Alliance

<http://www.caregiver.org>

Another California-focused website, this includes
topics such as hiring in-home help, benefits of day
care, and coping with early stage dementia.

Home Improvenet.com

<http://improvenet.com>

A commercial website that provides a home-
improvement-estimator tool that gives the average price home owners would expect to pay for
major improvements such as new roofs or drive-
ways. Also supplies fact sheets on various home-
improvement projects.

National Adult Day Services Association (NADSA)

<http://www.nadsa.org>

The National Adult Day Services Association has
published a printable guide that will help caregivers in their search for quality adult day services.

National Association of Area Agencies on Aging
(N4A)

<http://n4a.org>

The National Association of Area Agencies on
Aging (N4A) is an umbrella organization for the
agencies that provide services making it possible
for older individuals to remain in their homes.

National Resource Center on Supportive Housing
and Home Modification (nrcshhm)

<http://www.homemods.org>

A website providing links and information on
remodeling houses to suit accessibility needs.
Links to resources for architects who design with

accessibility in mind, remodeling resources, and a
safety checklist.

Pets for Seniors

<http://seniorliving.about.com/cs/pets_care/
index.htm>

Links to a variety of information about pets.

Senior Friendly Factsheets

<http://www.dietitians.ca/resources/senior_
friendly_factsheets.htm>

In collaboration with the Senior Friendly Program,
Dietitians of Canada has developed a series of
twelve tip sheets to assist seniors with planning,
shopping for, and preparing healthy meals.

Senior Sites

<http://www.seniorsites.com>

Senior Sites is a comprehensive Web source of
nonprofit housing and services for seniors with
more than 5,000 listed communities.

United Seniors Health Cooperative (USHC)

<http://www.unitedseniorshealth.org/>

Seeks to educate senior citizens about Social
Security, Medicare, and other related issues.

Weather Underground

<http://www.wunderground.com>

Weather conditions and forecasts for the United
States are listed on this site.

Weather.com

<http://www.weather.com>

Site of the Weather Channel.

Learning Experiences

Elderhostel

<http://www.elderhostel.org>

Huge directory of programs inviting older adults'
participation.

Internet Public Library

<http://www.ipl.org>

In addition to the standard library fare, visitors
can peruse newspapers and serials from around
the world as well as many interesting magazines.

Oasis

<http://oasisnet.org>

Offers many opportunities to volunteer in twenty-six communities throughout the United States. One of its focus points is intergenerational tutoring.

Senior Summer School

<http://seniorsummerschool.com>

Senior Summer School offers adventurous senior citizens an affordable opportunity to enhance their summers through education, leisure, and discovery at campus locations across the United States and Canada.

Wannalearn.com

<http://www.wannalearn.com>

Links to free online instructions on how to do anything from academic subjects to financial planning, from making and flying a paper airplane to Cajun dancing.

Legal Issues

AARP Foundation

<http://www.aarp.org/foundation/litigation.html>

The AARP Foundation Litigation Section brings law reform litigation on behalf of older persons and prepares amicus briefs.

American Bar Association Seniors Lawyers Division: National Handbook on Laws and Programs Affecting Senior Citizens

<http://www.abanet.org/srlawyers/handbook.html>

All facets of legal information affecting seniors are spelled out in this handbook.

Estate Planning Center

<http://www.estateplancenter.com>

Commercial website posting useful information on legal topics such as probate, Medicaid, and more.

Guardianship Issues Sponsored by USA Law

<http://guardianship.usalaw.com/guardianperson.html>

A commercial website that offers a very simple overview of legal guardianship issues.

An Older Person's Guide to Finding Legal Help

<http://www.pueblo.gsa.gov/cic_text/misc/funding/leg-hlp.txt>

This manual was developed and published by Legal Counsel for the Elderly (LCE), which is sponsored by AARP.

Libraries with Great Senior Links

Additional suggestions for senior links may be found on the following library websites.

Collier Public Library (Naples, Florida)

<http://public.collier-lib.org/links/senior.html>

Davenport Public Library (Illinois)

<http://www.rbls.lib.il.us/dpl/about_library/services/seniors.htm>

Flint Public Library (Michigan)

<http://www.flint.lib.mi.us/seniors/websites.html>

Hennepin County eLibrary (greater Minneapolis, Minnesota)

<http://www.hclib.org/seniorlinks>

James V. Brown Library (Williamsport, Pennsylvania)

<http://www.jvbrown.edu/senior.html>

Multnomah County Library (greater Portland, Oregon)

<http://www.multcolib.org/seniors/sites.html>

New York Public Library

<http://www2.nypl.org/home/branch/links/dept/older.cfm>

Wilton Library Association (Connecticut)

<http://www.wiltonlibrary.org/senior>

Nostalgia—Finding Yesterday Today

American Memory Page

<http://memory.loc.gov>

American Memory is a gateway to rich primary source materials relating to the history and culture of the United States.

Ellis Island Records

<http://www.ellisislandrecords.org>

If a senior's ancestors came through Ellis Island, a record should be found here.

FamilySearch.com

<http://familysearch.com>

Site describes how to start searching for ancestors and provides access to millions of family records.

Fifties Web

<http://www.fiftiesweb.com>

All the cool things of the 1950s, relived here.

Oldies Music

<http://www.oldiesmusic.com>

Searchable website that allows visitors to look at music charts and locate songs.

Past Times

<http://ptnostalgia.com>

Website devoted to classic movies, vintage music, old-time radio shows, and other popular entertainment of the 1920s, 1930s, 1940s, and early 1950s.

Sixties Project

<http://lists.village.virginia.edu/sixties>

Articles and discussion about the 1960s.

WWII Living Memorial

<http://www.seniornet.org/php/default.php?
    PageID=5801>

An initiative of SeniorNet, the page will invoke memories for many of the seniors who lived through the war years, as pictures, posters, and personal thoughts are shared online.

Recreation

Environmental Alliance for Senior Involvement (EASI)

<http://www.easi.org>

The Environmental Alliance for Senior Involvement's (EASI) mission is to expand senior citizens' involvement in protecting and caring for the environment for present and future generations.

Games

<http://games.yahoo.com>/

A variety of games are presented here, including those that can be played alone.

I Craft Seniors Page

<http://www.i-craft.com/seniors/index.html>

Megasite with a page devoted to crafts that seniors enjoy, according to a survey by the Hobby International Association.

Joseph Luft's Philatelic Resources

<http://my.execpc.com/~joeluft/resource.html>

This website is a good place for stamp collectors.

Play Bridge

<http://playbridge.com>

Tutors visitors in bridge.

Senior Travel

<http://www.smarterliving.com/senior/>

Commercial travel agency focusing on senior travel offers.

Travel Tips for Older Americans

<http://travel.state.gov/olderamericans.html>

U.S. Department of State publication 10337, Bureau of Consular Affairs, offers older adults travel advisories as well as information on items such as insurance and prescription medicines.

Woodworking.org

<http://woodworking.org>

Every facet of woodworking is included on this site.

Retirement Planning

Ballpark Estimate

<http://www.asec.org/ballpark/index.htm>

The American Savings Educational Council has developed a work sheet designed to quickly and simply give visitors a basic idea of the savings they will need when they retire.

Estate Planning

<http://www.legacyalive.com/pages/estate.html>

Lessons on estate planning are presented.

Retirement Planning

<http://retireplan.about.com>

Links to definitions of retirement terminology.

Sports

National Senior Games Association
  <http://www.nsga.com>

  The National Senior Games Association is a not-for-profit organization that is dedicated to promoting healthy lifestyles for seniors through education, fitness, and sports.

Runners' World
  <http://www.runnersworld.com>

  Website presents interesting articles on fitness and nutrition.

Sports for Seniors
  <http://www.seniorjournal.com/sportslinks.htm>

  Links to a wide variety of traditional sports sites for seniors.

Walkers Warehouse
  <http://www.walkerswarehouse.com>

  An affiliate of *Prevention* magazine, this provides exercise and nutrition tips as well as a walkers' log.

APPENDIX 3
Proven Five-Star Senior Programming Initiatives

The following programs and services are offered by libraries and librarians throughout the world. Many of the programs can be easily and economically replicated. Because space constraints prevent many of the programs from being presented in detail here, staff should visit the individual library's website or contact the outreach staff to learn more. Note that these libraries promoted their services for seniors using tools such as flyers, posters, websites, and word of mouth. Some libraries have unique marketing tips, which are shared.

Adventures in Life Long Learning Book Discussion Group

LIBRARY

North Star Borough Public Library and Regional Center, Noel Wien Library, Fairbanks, Alaska, population 114,000

SENIOR PROGRAM WEBSITE

<http://library.fnsb.lib.ak.us>

CONTACT FOR SENIOR PROGRAMMING INFORMATION

Georgine Olson, Outreach Services Manager

PROGRAM DESCRIPTION

The Fairbanks North Star Borough Public Library and Regional Center's Noel Wien Library supports a senior reading club using books bought and distributed by the library's Center for Life Long Learning. The library also supplies books to residential and senior centers by creating a mini–browsing library with the facilities and maintains van delivery services to the homebound. Book discussion groups are held at the Noel Wien Library. The mobile unit delivers books to senior and residential centers, where the minicollections are deposited.

NUMBER OF PARTICIPANTS

Book discussion group—21 registered

Homebound—25 per month

Residential sites and senior center—60

COST

Staff time is the only cost of book discussion groups. Costs for van service to seniors are included in the department's budget ($91,000). Services to seniors account for one-third to one-half of the workload.

FUNDING SOURCE

Budgeted borough funds. Additionally has the help of a volunteer who selects books for delivery.

DURATION

Ongoing program

PREPARATION TIME

Book discussions usually require two hours of preparation time. Van delivery usually requires about one and one-half hours per patron per month.

EXTRA MARKETING

Bookmarks with delivery schedules are used for the van service.

COMMENTS FROM PARTICIPANTS

Van delivery services came into existence on a trial basis in 1995, and each year around budget time, several patrons ask if they are needed to help muster support to maintain the service.

TIPS/COMMENTS

Try it; start small; be open to and solicit suggestions from senior users; keep an eye out for possible cooperative ventures. Be consistent; don't start a program and then let it falter; this will disappoint the seniors.

Aging and Verbal Creativity

LIBRARY

Hordaland County Library, Bergen, Norway, population 458,000

SENIOR PROGRAM WEBSITE

<http://www.hordaland.kulturnett.no/tema/
    edreveven>

**CONTACTS FOR SENIOR PROGRAMMING
INFORMATION**

Odd Saetre or Oddgeir Synnes, Program Directors

PROGRAM DESCRIPTION

Seniors were taught basic writing skills, allowing them to write hundreds of texts including poems, haiku, short stories, essays, articles, and orally told stories. The classes were held at area libraries, a school, and senior institutions.

Many of the poems and narratives are posted in English on the program's website.

NUMBER OF PARTICIPANTS

There were 60 participants in each course.

COST

$2,000 for ten sessions (stipends for the professional instructors)

FUNDING SOURCE

Hordaland County

DURATION

The classes met bimonthly for two hours for a period of six months.

PREPARATION TIME

One hour for each session, plus one monthly meeting to discuss project

COMMENTS FROM PARTICIPANTS

The participants verified the fact that everyone has the ability to create texts that move and enthrall the reader. The seniors reported that the course had a therapeutic effect upon their lives as they felt that their identities were strengthened when producing stories that have had a strong impact on them. Many of the seniors formed groups to continue writing, often with the teacher joining them.

TIPS/COMMENTS

Organizers strongly suggest that librarians have strong literature backgrounds and teaching abilities (or recruit professional teachers).

Beauregard Parish Library's Senior Outreach Services

LIBRARY

Beauregard Parish Library, DeRidder, Louisiana, population 31,000

SENIOR PROGRAM WEBSITE

<http://www.beau.lib.la.us>

CONTACT FOR SENIOR PROGRAMMING INFORMATION

Wanda McWhirter-Heaton, Outreach Services Coordinator

PROGRAM DESCRIPTION

The Beauregard Parish Library program can be described as one that reaches into the soul of every senior in the service area, providing educational and recreational opportunities to all. Books, games, and songs are brought to the places where seniors live and congregate. The library works with other senior organizations to ensure that all that can be done for seniors is being done. Additionally, the library supports computer training for seniors and encourages them to grow along with the community. Some of this is facilitated through a mobile services unit named MEL (Mobile Electronic Library), which brings computer classes to seniors. This includes instructions on how to use the Internet and e-mail.

NUMBER OF PARTICIPANTS

Varies from 5 to 30 participants per program

COST

The cost involves two employees being away from the library about two hours for each program and a small amount for refreshments and other miscellaneous programming needs.

FUNDING SOURCE

General library funds and grants from Wal-Mart and Friends of the Library. Additionally, door prizes are provided by the National Association for the Exchange of Industrial Resources (NAEIR).

DURATION

The program began in 1998 and strives to provide monthly visits to each library.

PREPARATION TIME

Two hours prep time, plus one to two hours at each location

COMMENTS FROM PARTICIPANTS

"Wonderfully stimulating and well received."
—activities director,
Westwood Manor Nursing Home

"The library staff reminded residents that elderly and senior citizens can still use the library and encouraged residents to apply for a library card if they do not have one."

—Melanie Walton, activities director,
DeRidder, LA Housing Authority

TIPS/COMMENTS

Entertain the seniors with poems and music and encourage the activity director to bring the residents to the library. When working with other groups of seniors, tell them not to be afraid of computers and remind them that they can still learn. Highlight celebrations such as Older Americans' Month with a special program.

Calgary Senior Services

LIBRARY

Calgary Public Library, Calgary, Alberta, Canada, population 860,000

SENIOR PROGRAM WEBSITE

<http://calgarypubliclibrary.com/>

CONTACT FOR SENIOR PROGRAMMING INFORMATION

Rosemary Griebel

PROGRAM DESCRIPTION

The library brings its services to senior lodges, continuing-care units, and hospitals as well as having the services available at all branches and the main library. The library launched a very successful PR campaign entitled Rediscover Your Library. The campaign helped to increase the number of senior cardholders from 8,500 to 15,000. The initiative also brought forth a huge senior volunteer force that assists with book deliveries and computer training; members also serve as peer consultants in the library's literacy initiatives. The library maintains a large-print collection, which includes books in foreign languages.

ADDITIONAL INFORMATION

Winner of the W. Kaye Lamb Award for Service to Seniors and 2002 ALA John Cotton Dana Award for the Rediscover Your Calgary Library campaign

NUMBER OF PARTICIPANTS

More than 25,000 homebound seniors and seniors with disabilities

COST

Unavailable

FUNDING SOURCE

Part of general operation costs

DURATION

Ongoing program, which began in 1996

PREPARATION TIME

The strategic three-year plan was developed after a needs assessment study of library services for older adults in Canada indicated that seniors' use of the library was low. The study and the development of the three-year plan took a significant amount of time.

EXTRA MARKETING

Calgary launched an aggressive marketing campaign toward the different generations of seniors, resulting in a 75 percent increase in senior cardholders within the Calgary Public Library. The library placed strategic ads in two major local senior magazines and published a regular column in one. In addition to a television campaign, staff made presentations to 4,600 seniors in the course of a year.

COMMENTS FROM PARTICIPANTS

"The library accommodates my needs—if I can't go to the library, it comes to me." "The Internet for Seniors course was wonderful. It helped me feel confident in my ability to learn new things."

TIPS/COMMENTS

The library must assume a strong advocacy role in addressing the issue of equitable service for seniors. Make presentations at library conferences and also at conferences concerning the health and well-being of seniors to emphasize the power of story in seniors' lives.

Collier County Public Library's Outreach Services and Seniors On-Line

LIBRARY

Collier County Public Library, Collier County, Naples, Florida, population 250,000

SENIOR PROGRAM WEBSITES

<www.collier-lib.org/outreach/> and <public. collier-lib.org/outreach/seniorsonline.html>

CONTACTS FOR SENIOR PROGRAMMING INFORMATION

General Senior Programming, Rand Bass, Outreach Specialist; Seniors On-Line, Ronney Cox, Program Coordinator

PROGRAM DESCRIPTION

The Collier County Public Library (CCPL) supports two strong senior curriculums. The outreach specialist, volunteers, and other library staff deliver outreach special programs in senior facilities and on-site. Reading Hour Volunteers is a program that pairs volunteers who read for an hour a week to residents in assisted-living or health-care settings who have difficulty reading (volunteers work in their immediate neighborhood). Special holiday programs are held at assisted-living facilities and health-care homes (the programs often have a holiday or literary theme and try to include the residents in a group read-aloud segment). The Books to Go program provides book discussions and reviews of selected titles by volunteer discussion leaders and library staff. All titles for book discussion or review must be available in large print and on audio for those who require it and wish to participate and are made available a month ahead of time on-site. Seniors On-Line is a partnership between the CCPL, local health-care facilities, independent living centers, and the Friends of the Library. The program is a community partnership that gives older adults opportunities to learn to use technology and information to enhance their lives. The library uses a well-planned training guide and works with an advisory group and well-trained volunteers.

ADDITIONAL INFORMATION

The library plans to develop a library resource guide for activity directors and county service organizations. Seniors On-Line is willing to share a PowerPoint presentation, which details the steps needed to develop, promote, and maintain this program.

NUMBER OF PARTICIPANTS

2,801 for a year (outreach programs). The number of participating seniors involved with the Seniors On-Line program varies by location, with the more successful sites having approximately 25 seniors online.

COST

Typically $35 for each program; $100 to $500 for special performers for in-house programs. Seniors On-Line cost: $75,000 for the first year; $81,000 for the second year

FUNDING SOURCE

Friends of the Library, CCPL Outreach Services budget, Library Services and Technology Act (LSTA) grant, Gates grant (hardware)

DURATION

Seniors On-Line programs are two-hour programs held in six-week sessions.

PREPARATION TIME

Monthly programs—up to twenty-five hours; major events—sixty hours

EXTRA MARKETING

An outreach letter to activity directors, highlighting library programming news and special services, is mailed to senior activity programs. The program manager attends capacity-building workshops and advisory group meetings of other agencies that target seniors.

COMMENTS FROM PARTICIPANTS

Seniors On-Line: "Almost everyone in my family is sending me e-mail." "One lady burst into tears when she read her first e-mail message, as it was from her grandson at Duke University." "We seniors aren't dead yet; we're just old, and we still like to learn new things and keep up with what is going on."

TIPS/COMMENTS

Programming should speak to the social, physical, spiritual, and emotional needs of senior members of the community and be programs you yourself would want to participate in. Specific requests and interest areas of participants should be directly translated into programming. When seeking volunteer computer tutors, look in cyberspace and use word of mouth. Whenever possible speak to potential volunteers one to one so that you can address their interests and concerns. It is important to have a detailed job description for volunteers.

CyberSeniors

LIBRARY

Multnomah County Library, Multnomah County, Portland, Oregon, population 645,950

SENIOR PROGRAM WEBSITE

<http://www.multcolib.org/seniors/>

CONTACT FOR SENIOR PROGRAMMING INFORMATION

Penny Hummel, Public Relations Coordinator

PROGRAM DESCRIPTION

The computer skills program for older adults is one of the many programs designed by the library for its senior population. Multnomah also offers seniors a great self-paced online tutorial focused on basic computer theory.

ADDITIONAL INFORMATION

The Library Outreach Services team provides bi-monthly van delivery for qualified homebound readers, monthly lobby service at retirement and other care centers, and books by mail for qualified homebound readers.

NUMBER OF PARTICIPANTS

The initial CyberSeniors one-year grant project had 496 participants. The program is currently in several branches and has 8 seniors per branch, per class. Plans exist for all branches to host the class.

COST

Minimal. The only budget items are supplies, printing, and advertising.

FUNDING SOURCE

Originally Qwest and the Library Foundation. Volunteers are also used.

DURATION

Ongoing

PREPARATION TIME

The preparation for the initial outreach project took five months of planning, partnering, and figuring out how to make it work. Staff researched how older adults learn in order to design a curriculum. Recruiting and training the volunteer trainers takes the most time. Each volunteer must take three three-hour training sessions, taught by library staff. They learn to teach the basics of the online catalog, how to search the Internet, how to set up a free e-mail account, basic troubleshooting, and how older adults learn.

COMMENTS FROM PARTICIPANTS

"This is a great service—very helpful and not at all intimidating." "More classes!" "I just hope you [continue] to have time to teach us!" "Keep up the good work. I will return."

TIPS/COMMENTS

Keep the class sizes small (eight maximum) and have enough support at each class session, so that each participant can feel he or she is getting that all-important one-on-one assistance (Multnomah uses one instructor and three assistants, who move around the class, making sure everyone is keeping up). It is also important to sensitize the people teaching the classes to the barriers older adults face as they try to learn new skills (e.g., vision problems, difficulty moving the mouse, hearing loss, and, most important of all, fear of appearing stupid). Older adults feel more comfortable in a situation where they are learning with other older adults, and using instructors who are also older adults puts people at ease. Instructors need to create a supportive environment where questions are encouraged and mistakes are an important part of the learning process.

Glenview Senior Book Group and Read Aloud

LIBRARY

Glenview Public Library, Glenview, Illinois, population 41,847

SENIOR PROGRAM WEBSITE

<http://www.glenview.lib.il.us>

CONTACT FOR SENIOR PROGRAMMING INFORMATION

Kim Comerford, Outreach Librarian

PROGRAM DESCRIPTION

Lively book discussions are facilitated by the library staff at various senior facilities. Discussion groups include the VIP Book Group, the Senior Book Group, and the Patten House Book Group. The library also provides a Nursing Home Read Aloud, delivers books to homebound patrons, maintains a senior Web page, and hosts an annual Senior Fair.

NUMBER OF PARTICIPANTS

VIP Book Group—5 to 7

Senior Book Group—11 to 18

Patten House Book Group—6 to 10

Senior Fair—100 to 200

Nursing Home Read Aloud—15 to 25

COST

The cost for these programs is minimal.

FUNDING SOURCE

Glenview Public Library funds. The Senior Fair is covered by donations from local businesses.

DURATION

The on-site Senior Book Group and Nursing Home Read Aloud are monthly programs; the book discussion groups that are held in senior facilities are bimonthly. The Senior Fair is an annual event.

PREPARATION TIME

Planning for the Senior Fair usually takes a few months, with the outreach librarian and the public information officer working together. Depending on the book and the book group, the preparation time could take two to four hours, not including the time needed to read the book. The Nursing Home Read Aloud usually takes a couple of hours to prepare.

COMMENT FROM PARTICIPANT

The Senior Book Group is noted for being "outspoken and uninhibited."

TIPS/COMMENTS

Planning and programming tips are (1) ask a local senior residence community to sponsor a program for seniors at the library; (2) join all community social service groups; (3) advertise the library's services in church bulletins, local newspapers, and publications targeted for seniors; and (4) work with the library's public information director to sponsor a Senior Fair designed to bring the senior service providers together. Seniors will appreciate having "one-stop" information shopping.

Grandparents and Books (GAB)

LIBRARY

Los Angeles Public Library, Los Angeles, California, population 9.8 million

SENIOR PROGRAM WEBSITE

<http://www.lapl.org/admin/gab.html>

CONTACT FOR SENIOR PROGRAMMING INFORMATION

Maureen Wade

PROGRAM DESCRIPTION

Using the gift of reading, the Grandparents and Books (GAB) program successfully unites older adults with children in an effort to provide literacy enrichment and meaningful volunteer opportunities. GAB recruits older adults who enjoy children and reading to share stories with neighborhood children in branch libraries throughout the system. Although the program is called Grandparents and Books, seniors do not have to be grandparents as they become the "library's grandparent." The ongoing program recognizes non-English proficiency among community members; as a result, some grandparents read (and listen to children read) in Spanish, Chinese, Korean, or other languages in addition to English. Library staff offer training in how to read aloud and share books with children.

ADDITIONAL INFORMATION

The GAB program has been featured in newspapers, various televised news programs, and the nationally syndicated talk show, *Homeshow*. The Los Angeles Unified School District has included GAB in its in-service training for teachers. GAB grandparents were guest readers at the mayor's official residence open house. To help other libraries develop their own GAB programs, the staff of Los Angeles Public have produced a very comprehensive how-to program development and training manual, which is posted on the website.

NUMBER OF PARTICIPANTS

During a seven-year period, 500 volunteers read to more than 200,000 children.

COST

If existing staff are used, the program can be executed for minimal costs (in-house photocopying, identification tags, refreshments, and fingerprinting, if required by human resources). If the library wishes an enhanced program, include costs of coordinator, clerk typists, storytelling materials, and apparel for volunteers.

FUNDING SOURCE

The program was initially funded through a Library Services and Construction Act (LSCA) grant and is now funded through the generosity of the Ahmanson Foundation, the Henry L. Guenther Foundation, the Norris Foundation, the Michael J. Connell Foundation, the Carrie Estelle Doheny Foundation, the Thomas and Dorothy Leavey Foundation, Laurie and Bill Benenson, and the Lon V. Smith Foundation.

PREPARATION TIME

Participants are required to attend two two-hour training sessions and view a GAB demonstration.

COMMENTS FROM PARTICIPANTS

"I get to be a kid again . . . they make me feel young."
"I'm doing something worthwhile and I'm having fun."

TIPS/COMMENTS

Request newspapers to write a special feature article on the program. When releasing public service announcements, include all local television and radio stations (including local-access cable channel), non-English-language stations, city school districts, and college stations. Establish liaisons with organizations that work with seniors such as senior centers, the Department of Aging, and service organizations that promote community services within their retired volunteer ranks (police, fire department).

Lee County Library Assistive Technology Collection

LIBRARY

Lee County Library, Lee County, North Fort Meyers, Florida, population 394,000

SENIOR PROGRAM WEBSITE

<http://www.leecounty.com/library/progserv/ssvcs/ad1.htm>

CONTACT FOR SENIOR PROGRAMMING INFORMATION

Marylou Tuckwiller, Talking Books Librarian

PROGRAM DESCRIPTION

The library system encourages patrons to try out adaptive devices before investing money. By becoming familiar with the devices, individuals are able to formulate appropriate questions for vendors and health-care professionals before they purchase products. Informed consumers have a greater chance of purchasing the best product to serve their individual needs. The collection includes devices for a wide cross section and various degrees of disabilities that are loaned for twenty-eight days.

ADDITIONAL INFORMATION

Winner of the 1997 American Library Association, Association of Specialized and Cooperating Library Agencies, and National Organization on Disability Award, which recognizes libraries that strive to make their libraries and collections available to persons with disabilities. The library has edited a highly detailed and well-illustrated catalog of the devices that they loan.

NUMBER OF PARTICIPANTS

Two hundred eight items were loaned to patrons in 2001; 600 items should be circulated in 2002.

FUNDING SOURCE

Initially started with a $25,000 LSTA grant (used to hire a part-time staff person and purchase devices). The program also received a $30,000 bequest.

DURATION

Ongoing

PREPARATION TIME

Ordering and processing devices take about the same amount of time as other library materials.

EXTRA MARKETING

The library is a stop on the "Lee Grows" tour, an initiative of the county that seeks to highlight county services for residents.

COMMENTS FROM PARTICIPANTS

"It helps to try the devices before you waste money buying them yourself." "We are quite amazed by all this."—Seniors shown the assistive devices for the first time

TIPS/COMMENTS

The entire staff should be aware of the devices. Each department of the library should assign a staff person the task of being knowledgeable about the assistive devices owned by the library. If the library sponsors an in-service day, the products should be highlighted. Ensure that local government agencies are aware of the services and devices provided by the library.

Loudoun Outreach Services

LIBRARY

Loudoun County Public Library, Loudoun County, Leesburgh, Virginia, population 190,000

SENIOR PROGRAM WEBSITE

<http://www.lcpl.lib.va.us>

CONTACTS FOR SENIOR PROGRAMMING INFORMATION

Linda Holtslander, Assistant Director; and Maria McClintock, Outreach Services Manager

PROGRAM DESCRIPTION

The Loudon County Public Library services for seniors cover a wide range of programs. Through these services, hundreds of individuals have easy access to a wealth of library resources that enables them to continue to create, discover, and imagine. Services include bimonthly visits to senior residential facilities, nursing homes, and day programs for older adults, during which seniors may select and request books as well as make reference queries. Outreach programs include Share-A-Read, which encourages individuals at senior residential facilities to talk with library staff about their reading experiences, and Memory programs, which are interactive and multisensory. At the end of each presentation, everyone is left with a heightened level of inspiration and anticipation for the next program. Trained staff and volunteers, many of whom are seniors themselves, conduct the programs.

ADDITIONAL INFORMATION

Every summer, Outreach Services conducts an eight-week Summer Reading Program that offers incentives for seniors to read. The goal of the program is to encourage continued reading among the seniors as they explore new books or topics. Loudoun also promotes a Senior Series, a series of meaningful programs to permit seniors to connect with one another and to their present lives through the sharing of their experiences. These programs are facilitated by a scholar and funded by several foundations. Past programs include "Fast Forward—Science, Technology,

and the Communication Revolution" and "On Our Own Terms: Moyers on Dying in America."

NUMBER OF PARTICIPANTS

Average of 258 seniors served per month

COST

Staff, which includes a level-two librarian and a library assistant. All other programs were underwritten by grants and basic county government.

FUNDING SOURCE

Loudoun County Government, Loudoun Library Foundation, National Science Foundation, Alfred P. Sloan Foundation, the National Endowment for the Humanities, Robert Woods Johnson Foundation

DURATION

Bimonthly senior visits—one hour; Share-A-Read programs—fifteen minutes; Memory programs—thirty minutes

PREPARATION TIME

Varies

COMMENTS FROM PARTICIPANTS

"The Loudoun County Library Outreach program is an invaluable resource for the Arcola Senior Center. We are very remote, and the majority of our seniors do not have transportation to access a library facility. The Outreach Service provides this group with a variety of materials and the ability to make their choices—as a result, seniors that appeared to be 'disconnected' are now avid fans." "Outreach enhances all of our special events, particularly Black History and Heritage Week, by providing an array of related materials for display."

TIPS/COMMENTS

The library purchased digital equipment to enhance the memory program by capturing photographs off the Web and in and around the community.

Medina County District Library's Senior Programming

LIBRARY

Medina County District Library, Medina, Ohio, population 151,000

SENIOR PROGRAM WEBSITE

<http://www.mcdl.info>

CONTACTS FOR SENIOR PROGRAMMING INFORMATION

Barbara Gillespie or Judy Nelson

PROGRAM DESCRIPTION

Staff at Medina totally exploit their resources to bring books and services to older patrons. The Bookmate Volunteer Program pairs volunteers with 125 homebound patrons, making it possible to deliver books to homes and other facilities. Staff have developed their own reminiscence kits and personalized the BiFolkal Kits. A favorite, "My Favorite Books and Characters," encourages the sharing of books and their manufactured characters. For example, Little Lulu spawned the character doll Little Lulu; the book *Little Women* had the dolls Meg, Beth, Jo, and Amy crafted. The dolls help revive memories.

ADDITIONAL INFORMATION

The library delivers books to nursing homes, assisted-living facilities, senior centers, and hospitals. Volunteers assist with delivering the books. Altogether, ninety-four hours a month are used to deliver books to patrons at these locations. Volunteers are given a brief orientation, and background checks are made to ensure no known felons are among the volunteers.

NUMBER OF PARTICIPANTS

Programs presented in skilled-care facilities usually attract about 12 residents. Other groups range from 20 to 50 in number.

COST

Minimal

FUNDING SOURCE

General library funds. An LSTA grant was used to cover the cost of BiFolkal Kits.

DURATION

Ongoing programs are presented year-round.

PREPARATION TIME

New programs take three to four hours to develop.

EXTRA MARKETING

The library newsletter is distributed quarterly with a free edition of the local daily paper.

COMMENT FROM PARTICIPANT

"The Outreach Program means so much, I would like to make a small donation in support of the program" (the check was for $1,000).

TIPS/COMMENTS

Each program will be different depending on the presenter, because that person will bring originality and point of view to the program. Personalize any purchased remembering kit to make it more relevant to the library's service area.

1,000 Stories

LIBRARIES

Mid-Continent Public Library, Independence, Missouri; Johnson County Public Library, Warrensburg, Missouri; and Kansas City Public Library, Missouri; population 1.5 million, combined

SENIOR PROGRAM WEBSITE

<http://www.kcstories.com>

CONTACT FOR SENIOR PROGRAMMING INFORMATION

Michael Humphrey

PROGRAM DESCRIPTION

The program involves teaching older adults writing skills, which they could use to record their memories. The results are part of the "1,000 Stories Collection," posted on the website, and reflect Americana. Several agencies cooperated in the project. These included Shepherd's Center of Kansas City Central, KCMO (an ongoing workshop), and various libraries in the library's service areas.

NUMBER OF PARTICIPANTS

More than 300

COST

$6,000 per year, not including the cost of library staff

FUNDING SOURCE

The Humanities/Education budget for the Missouri Endowment for the Humanities funded the seed project.

DURATION

Long term—broken into six-week sessions

PREPARATION TIME

Twelve to fifteen hours per six-week session (plus class time)

COMMENTS FROM PARTICIPANTS

"I just wanted to thank you very much for the program. I enjoyed it very much and managed to learn the basics of writing. It's too bad this isn't taught in school . . . or maybe it was and I wasn't paying attention . . . hmmm. Anyway, you are a great teacher and I know we all had a fun experience." "I was very impressed with what I saw, and I am impressed that it looks like you have taken this idea of writing it into such a far-reaching program. I imagine this program has meant so much to its participants and to you also, the teacher."—website visitor

TIPS/COMMENTS

The one resource most definitely needed is people willing to do this. Classes range from ten to forty-five participants each, and there is tremendous enthusiasm and plenty of stories to tell. The key is to help them learn to focus their stories by telling them one at a time.

Pickering Public Library Senior Programs

LIBRARY

Pickering Public Library, Pickering, Ontario, Canada, population 80,000

SENIOR PROGRAM WEBSITE

<http://www.picnet.org>

CONTACT FOR SENIOR PROGRAMMING INFORMATION

Colleen Bolin

PROGRAM DESCRIPTION

The Pickering Public Library supports a number of programs, such as computer classes, book clubs, and tax clinics. Additionally, their Visiting Library Service brings service to senior retirement residences and seniors' private homes. The library supports a computer lab at one nursing home.

NUMBER OF PARTICIPANTS

The library serves 64 participants in private homes. More than 350 participants took advantage of the senior computer activities. The book club reaches 15 patrons.

COST

Cost is minimal for the programs (mileage, tea, cookies). The tax program is accomplished with the help of volunteers from Certified General Accountants of Ontario.

FUNDING SOURCE

General operating budget is used. The library received a Community Access Program grant for specialized Internet training at Orchard Villa, a nursing home with library-installed computer stations.

DURATION

Programs are year-round. The tax clinics were established in 2002.

PREPARATION TIME

Approximately three hours per visit to a residence and half an hour (or less) to a home. The initial computer program took about a week to set up, and ongoing preparation time is about two and one-half hours per program (currently four programs). Book clubs require two hours per session plus time spent on publicity and so forth. Tax clinics take half an hour per session plus time spent on publicity.

COMMENTS FROM PARTICIPANTS

"Love the service—books are my friends since I became housebound." "Age does not matter [computer class]; this course was very refreshing. It was more encouraging than I thought. I want to go on." "I still need a lot of practice in all areas, but with a little help was able to grasp and do it all. I will come to use the library computers to practice Internet." "I told my daughter that I couldn't baby-sit on the book club days."

TIPS/COMMENTS

Always call participants to remind them of programs that they have registered for. Make some allowances for disabilities associated with aging—hearing loss, mobility problems, and so forth. If the library decides to place a computer in a nursing home, unless residents are mobile, be prepared for staff to devote a lot of time on-site for one-on-one training.

Reading Aloud to Seniors

LIBRARY

The New York Public Library, Office of Community Outreach Services and Office of Adult Services, New York, population 3.2 million (Manhattan, Staten Island, and the Bronx)

SENIOR PROGRAM WEBSITE

<http://www.nypl.org>

CONTACT FOR SENIOR PROGRAMMING INFORMATION

Susan Gitman

PROGRAM DESCRIPTION

Patrons who are not able to read independently can still enjoy poetry, essays, and anecdotal readings. Staff of the New York Public Library visit nursing homes, hospitals, and senior residences, bringing with them rehearsed scripts that they read aloud to residents at these facilities. The facilities' residents are diverse in their ethnicity. The New York Public Library also maintains an excellent senior Web page.

NUMBER OF PARTICIPANTS

Groups range in size from 4 to 45, depending upon the facility.

COST

Staff time is the only cost incurred.

FUNDING SOURCE

None. This is an activity of branch staff supported by the library's Office of Programs and Services.

DURATION

These monthly programs are scheduled over the course of a year by branch and office staff. The program itself lasts from forty minutes to an hour.

PREPARATION TIME

Readers need from an hour to three hours for the selection, preparation, and rehearsal of material.

TIPS/COMMENTS

Establish an ongoing evaluation of the program with the agency staff. They must be responsive as well to the needs of the program, for example, getting patients moved into day rooms beforehand or setting up a microphone if needed. Formal training for library staff is not necessary; however, if pursued, training should focus on choosing materials and meeting the special needs of a mostly resident senior population. Staff should observe a program before they perform a reading.

READiscover Your Library and SeniorNet Learning Center

LIBRARY

James V. Brown Library, Williamsport, Pennsylvania, population 120,044

SENIOR PROGRAM WEBSITE

<http://www.jvbrown.edu>

CONTACT FOR SENIOR PROGRAMMING INFORMATION

Janice Trapp

PROGRAM DESCRIPTION

The library supports two senior initiatives. The first, READiscover, is comprised of three elements: the READiscover Room in the library, stocked with large-print books, newspapers, and magazines and staffed by older adult volunteers; the READiscover bookmobile, which provides weekly visits to twenty-four retirement centers and nursing homes; and an aggressive marketing campaign to draw older adults back into the library as users, volunteers, and advocates. Additionally, a SeniorNet Learning Center was established (classes fill as soon as they are announced), and eight computers were placed in area retirement homes and senior centers to allow seniors to search the library catalog, request books, or have e-mail questions answered.

ADDITIONAL INFORMATION

Winner of the Bessie Boehm Moore Award, an ALA award for superior senior programming, and an exemplary library services to seniors award from AARP. Program locations include selected senior centers and retirement and nursing homes, the technology branch, and the main library as well as the bookmobile.

NUMBER OF PARTICIPANTS

More than 1,000 people participate in the program.

COST

Approximately $35,000 to $40,000 annually

FUNDING SOURCE

Grant funds initially, local budget ongoing

DURATION

Long term

PREPARATION TIME

The program took about a year to get off the ground.

EXTRA MARKETING

Snazzy purple envelopes with the READiscover logo were stuffed with library information and the READiscovermobile schedule and given to all nursing home residents in the library's service area. Special READiscover promotional library cards were developed as well as brochures, posters, and news articles. Signage was also placed at bus stops. The programs received coverage on talk radio, and the advisory board was a big help in promoting the programs. Seniors who request library cards receive one with the READiscover logo printed on the back, which is good for discounts at participating establishments.

COMMENTS FROM PARTICIPANTS

"Without the READiscovermobile, I wouldn't be able to use the library. You get to see what you want; you get to pick out your own items." "The residents of Roseview Court are thrilled with our new computer. We are so thankful to the James V. Brown Library for this acquisition. I hope you have a chance to read our publication: 'The Rose Review'; our eighty- and ninety-year-olds worked hard on this using the new computer, and they are quite proud of it." "SeniorNet is going bonkers!"—SeniorNet Advisory Council Chair

TIPS/COMMENTS

Establish an advisory council. The library's is comprised of representatives of the local AARP, the Bi-County Office on Aging, the Retired Teachers Association, Friends of the Library, library users, the local health system, and the READiscovermobile librarian.

Red Carpet Services

LIBRARY

Topeka and Shawnee County Public Library, Topeka, Kansas, population 170,000

SENIOR PROGRAM WEBSITE

<http://www.tscpl.org>

CONTACT FOR SENIOR PROGRAMMING INFORMATION

Stephanie Hall, Red Carpet Supervisor

PROGRAM DESCRIPTION

Red Carpet Services assists those with special needs within the confines of the library and has a strong presence in the community. Red Carpet Services owns more than 30,000 large-print books, 350 different magnifiers and assistive-hearing devices, a therapeutic activity collection comprised of games and kits with special adaptations for small-group activities, descriptive videos, and an adaptive computer center. The outreach delivery service provides library materials throughout Topeka and Shawnee Counties, visiting fifty different facilities and about 100 homebound patrons.

NUMBER OF PARTICIPANTS

Red Carpet Services outreach serves approximately 2,000 registered outreach patrons, circulating 105,039 items. Forty-six registered activity directors borrow therapeutic activities materials.

COST

The salaries of ten full-time staff members, a large materials collection budget, and the costs of the service vehicles

FUNDING SOURCE

The library's operating budget covers 100 percent of the daily operations of Red Carpet Services, and it also has tremendous community support; individuals and local civic organizations have worked to assist Red Carpet Services with the purchase of new equipment and supplies as necessary.

DURATION

Red Carpet Services is an ongoing year-round program.

PREPARATION TIME

On average it takes the outreach delivery staff three hours for preparation of deliveries and three hours for deliveries. The homebound program may require eight to twelve hours per week for a group of twenty to thirty homebound patrons. The delivery of the homebound program takes approximately three to four hours.

EXTRA MARKETING

To encourage the use of the Red Carpet Services, special programs are presented throughout the year for activity directors who work with seniors.

COMMENT FROM PARTICIPANT

"You come out in all kinds of weather to bring me what I ask for. . . . Thank you for helping make my life fuller."—Judy (homebound patron)

TIPS/COMMENTS

It is important to ensure that all who are served receive the same quality of care given patrons who use traditional library services.

Reminiscence Resource Group

LIBRARY

Stoke-on-Trent Libraries, Stoke-on-Trent, United Kingdom, population 250,000

SENIOR PROGRAM WEBSITE

<http://www.stoke.gov.uk/council/libraries/services/reminiscence.htm>

CONTACT FOR SENIOR PROGRAMMING INFORMATION

Kath Reynolds

PROGRAM DESCRIPTION

Acknowledging the recreational and therapeutic value of reminiscence, the staff of the library developed reminiscence boxes to be used with older adults. Working along with community partners, the library has developed themed boxes, on a wide variety of topics, that contain books, music, postcards, videos, and museum artifacts relating to the topic. The staff of the library conduct reminiscence workshops throughout the community. The library belongs to the UK Reminiscence Network and has trained community members to successfully use the boxes with seniors.

COST

The price to make a box is minimal, as staff include items found around the house. Staff aim to make all boxes multisensory, but it's not always possible; therefore, some boxes contain only types of materials that appeal to the senses of hearing and sight; others have artifacts, videos, and music and incorporate the sense of touch.

PREPARATION TIME

The time to prepare a box varies. The most recent boxes were assembled to celebrate the Queen's Golden Jubilee and took twenty hours to complete.

FUNDING SOURCE

Local pottery museums have donated items from their handling collections. But the library has also received many donations from library staff and their relatives.

EXTRA MARKETING

Staff have been guests on several radio programs. The local newspaper featured each of the boxes over an eighteen-month period.

COMMENTS FROM PARTICIPANTS

The library seeks to facilitate reminiscence and has received positive comments from users. All who participate love the boxes and the memories they bring.

TIPS/COMMENTS

Encourage staff to join in the treasure hunt for goodies to fill the boxes. An excited staff can help bring items stored in attics or basements, which will cut down on the time needed to create a box. Also, form partnerships that will bring different priorities and contributions to the project.

Senior Appreciation Day and Senior Computer Classes

LIBRARY

LeRoy Collins Leon County Public Library, Tallahassee, Florida, population 285,000

SENIOR PROGRAM WEBSITE

<http://www.co.leon.fl.us/library/pages/seniors/ srapprec_51501.html>

CONTACT FOR SENIOR PROGRAMMING INFORMATION

Mary Jo Peltier, Public Services Manager

PROGRAM DESCRIPTION

The library dedicates the third Tuesday of May, which is officially proclaimed Senior Appreciation Day at the library. Past programs have featured a visit from "Eleanor Roosevelt," musical performances, and visits from politicians. The library regularly offers computer classes, which fill to capacity when announced.

ADDITIONAL INFORMATION

It should be noted that Leon County does not have a large senior population.

NUMBER OF PARTICIPANTS

700 to 800. This does not include seniors served by mobile services.

COST

Undetermined

FUNDING SOURCE

The foundations for this program were laid by Robert "Robie" Visk, whose salary was underwritten by LSTA grants, which were year one: a $21,315 LSTA grant, with a $8,745 match in-kind from the county; year two: a $25,654 LSTA grant, with a $10,256 local contribution.

DURATION

The computer classes are two hours and are held in three-week sessions; the Senior Appreciation Day is annual.

PREPARATION TIME

Time spent to construct the grants: approximately five to ten hours to survey and tabulate to determine needs and twenty hours of grant writing. An additional ten hours of time for midyear and end-of-year grant evaluation reports. Administrative effort was also needed to push the grants through county bureaucracy. Program overseen by a half-time staff member.

EXTRA MARKETING

When marketing your program, try to combine the seniors' activities with ongoing state or local senior initiatives. Tie into their themes with your press releases and marketing. Also, for more media exposure, invite local officials to attend the events and mingle with the seniors.

COMMENTS FROM PARTICIPANTS

"It was wonderful. I will tell others about your program!" Comments about computer classes: "Excellent—patient in answering questions." "Excellent materials—much better than the ones I was given at a commercial class. Thank you for making yours so clear and easy to follow."

TIPS/COMMENTS

Ensure that library management and other staff members securely support these programs as it takes a team effort. Staff need to establish significant partnerships within the senior aging services community and assure the key players in these organizations that they are respected and encourage them to attend some of the library's events. When teaching computer usage, try not to cover too much material in one session. Answer questions as you go so as not to leave people behind.

Senior Book Club Talk

LIBRARY

Plano Public Library System, Plano, Texas, population 231,000

SENIOR PROGRAM WEBSITE

<http://www.planolibrary.org>

CONTACTS FOR SENIOR PROGRAMMING INFORMATION

Cathe Spencer, Senior Public Services Librarian; or Marta Demaree, Public Services Librarian Supervisor

PROGRAM DESCRIPTION

Lively book discussion groups are facilitated by staff at the Plano Senior Center on a monthly basis, January through October. Librarians and volunteers take turns presenting topics that interest them, which makes the discussions realistic.

NUMBER OF PARTICIPANTS

10 to 15 per talk

COST

None

PREPARATION TIME

About five hours per book talk for the presenting librarian

COMMENT FROM PARTICIPANT

"The talks are varied, so they make me aware of 'what's happening.'"

TIPS/COMMENTS

One hour is a good length for the talk. Books that work include all genres, especially mysteries. Nonfiction topics include history, especially local history and World War II. Other topics seniors find interesting include art, gardening, family history and genealogy, and holiday topics. This time is used to promote other library programs such as the summer reading club and story hours. Try to figure out ways to tie fiction to nonfiction; for example, Margaret Atwood's *Alias Grace* had quilt patterns as chapter names, so quilting books were brought along. Door prizes, from donations, are a big hit.

Senior Book Clubs and Caregiving Institute

LIBRARY

Chicago Public Library, Chicago, Illinois, population of more than 3 million

SENIOR PROGRAM WEBSITE

<http://www.chipublib.org/cpl.html>

CONTACT FOR SENIOR PROGRAMMING INFORMATION

Jim Pletz, Director Adult Services

PROGRAM DESCRIPTION

There are two main programs. The Senior Caregiving Institutes are designed to assist those who are nonmobile and to render support and life-sustaining services to seniors. Some of the topics include "The Family Dynamics of Caregiving and How to Cope," "Facing the Financial and Legal Challenges of Caregiving," and "Education on Aging-Related Diseases." Six branch libraries host book clubs as well as Senior Suites of Chicago and Senior Residence Apartments. The library supports two fully ADA-compliant bookmobiles, which make monthly visits to senior facilities. The bookmobiles provide readers with large-print materials, cassettes, and materials in languages such as Spanish, Russian, Korean, Chinese, and more.

NUMBER OF PARTICIPANTS

Caregiving Institutes—45 per site

Senior Book Clubs—approximately 9 per site

COST

Staffing for bookmobile services (four full-time employees) plus book programs and maintenance of vehicles

FUNDING SOURCE

City of Chicago Corporate Budget

DURATION

Programs and institutes are held monthly; the bookmobile delivers on a regular schedule.

PREPARATION TIME

Twelve hours per week (one hour per day Monday through Thursday and all day Friday)

COMMENTS FROM PARTICIPANTS

Senior book club participants love to keep up with the program. Most feel very happy reading titles and authors they might not otherwise have selected.

TIPS/COMMENTS

Remember that the needs of senior caregivers must also be addressed; for example, Saturday afternoons usually work for this program because it is easier for caregivers to locate someone to attend to their loved ones.

Senior Book Discussion Series

LIBRARY

Mary Riley Styles Public Library, Falls Church, Virginia, population 22,000

SENIOR PROGRAM WEBSITE

<http://www.falls-church.lib.va.us>

CONTACT FOR SENIOR PROGRAMMING INFORMATION

Mary W. McMahon, Library Director

PROGRAM DESCRIPTION

The Senior Book Discussion Series offers participants a wide range of titles to discuss in an effort to broaden their range of reading interests. Realizing that all seniors may not be able to get to the library, where the program is held, the library also comes to them at the city's senior center, the Falls Church Community Center Senior Center.

NUMBER OF PARTICIPANTS

The number of participants varies, with an average of 8 at the senior center discussions and between 12 and 20 at the library setting.

COST

The program costs the library around $1,500 a year to purchase multiple copies of the books.

FUNDING SOURCE

City of Falls Church. Money for the multiple copies of books comes from a continuous sale of items donated to the library.

DURATION

The series runs from September through May. The two groups read the same six books during that period. Each discussion group is scheduled to last approximately one to one and one-half hours. Books discussed on Monday at the library are discussed Tuesday at the senior center. Participants are free to go to the discussion that is most convenient to their schedules and locations.

PREPARATION TIME

Two library staff members and a volunteer lead the discussions. The staff members divide the responsibility for the six discussions, and a volunteer participates in all of the meetings. In addition to reading the books, discussion leaders research background information pertinent to the author and subject.

COMMENTS FROM PARTICIPANTS

"Every now and then, I have a doctor's appointment or other engagement on a Monday and can't make the club at the library, but I can meet with the group at the senior center on Tuesday and not miss out." "We retain a youthful attitude by delving into things relevant to the present, inspirational to our mental, emotional, and physical well-being—and we have a darn good laugh."

TIPS/COMMENTS

Large groups are good as they allow those who only want to listen to remain silent without feeling uncomfortable. Allow members to have a voice in what they read, by compiling a list of fifteen titles (write a short synopsis for each) and letting members vote on the next reading series. Be sure to include new authors, books for men, and old masterworks now forgotten while avoiding best-sellers or books dealing with the seamy side of life. Provide snacks and coffee and tea for each meeting. Treat the last meeting of the year as a special event by encouraging members to bring a sandwich so that they can chat informally after the discussion is over.

Senior Day Program

LIBRARY

Hammond Public Library, Hammond, Indiana, population 83,048

SENIOR PROGRAM WEBSITE

<http://www.hammond.lib.in.us>

CONTACT FOR SENIOR PROGRAMMING INFORMATION

Linda Swisher

PROGRAM DESCRIPTION

On a monthly basis, the library provides a diverse program for the seniors of Hammond, Indiana. Programs have included "Law Issues," "Computers," and "Family History." Occasionally, the library organizes bus trips to places such as the Broadcast Museum.

NUMBER OF PARTICIPANTS

The average attendance at the programs ranges from 40 to 50 seniors.

COST

Cost of refreshments and occasionally funds for speakers or bus rental

FUNDING SOURCE

Funding for the extras comes from outside donations. The Greater Hammond Community Services provides rides for seniors who call twenty-four hours in advance.

DURATION

Yearlong monthly program. Each program lasts about two hours.

PREPARATION TIME

About three hours

EXTRA MARKETING

The library works with various members of the community to increase Hammond's visibility and attract new residents, businesses, and institutions. The library's brochures will be in marketing packets and highlighted on the city's website.

COMMENTS FROM PARTICIPANTS

"I appreciate all the nice programs that were given at the library for us senior citizens." "Thank you for the opportunity to visit Border House in Michigan City. The personnel did a wonderful job; I really enjoyed the trip."

TIPS/COMMENTS

It helps to work with your chamber of commerce or growth association to get the word out that the library has programs for seniors.

Seniors' Time Online

LIBRARY

Ann Arbor District Library, Ann Arbor, Michigan, population 135,000

SENIOR PROGRAM WEBSITE

<http://www.aadl.org>

CONTACT FOR SENIOR PROGRAMMING INFORMATION

Madelaine Krolik

PROGRAM DESCRIPTION

Seniors' Time Online is a six-week progressive course that begins by developing seniors' mouse skills and familiarizing seniors with the computer and computer terminology. Word processing is taught, and seniors are encouraged to use some of the tools available in a word-processing package, including formatting and saving their results to disk. The class then moves on to the Internet, with the basics of using a browser and surfing the Web. During the last two weeks of class, the seniors practice using e-mail. The Seniors' Time Online classes are taught at the main library and branches.

ADDITIONAL INFORMATION

The library owns a bookmobile, which makes regularly scheduled stops at ten area senior homes.

NUMBER OF PARTICIPANTS

Over a four-year span, 290 seniors have attended the Seniors' Time Online program.

COST

Staff, printing, and marketing costs

FUNDING SOURCE

General Library Budget, plus a Gates grant

DURATION

Each session is two hours and meets once a week in the morning.

PREPARATION TIME

The Seniors' Time Online was developed over a three-month period. Presently, it takes about an hour before each new six-week session to prepare the handouts and folders for the class.

COMMENTS FROM PARTICIPANTS

The library director regularly receives comment cards from the seniors complimenting the staff on the course. Two of the seniors, who are foster grandparents in the schools, gained the skills to help students who needed extra assistance.

TIPS/COMMENTS

Leave a week or two between the courses as sometimes a senior class needs an extra week depending on the group and the development of their skills. Schedule classes with regard to the weather; it is hard for the seniors to get out in bad weather. The teachers must relay the message that "There is no such thing as a dumb question when asking about computers."

SeniorsConnect@Cleveland Public Library

LIBRARY

Cleveland Public Library, Cuyahoga County, Cleveland, Ohio, population 1.4 million

SENIOR PROGRAM WEBSITE

<http://www.cpl.org>

CONTACTS FOR SENIOR PROGRAMMING INFORMATION

Joan Clark, Head, Main Library; or Jan Ridgeway, Head, Branch and Outreach Services

PROGRAM DESCRIPTION

The entire system participates in senior programming, including the branches, mobile services, and the main library. A wide variety of programs—for example, computer training, recreation, health, exercise, book talks, lectures, and pure entertainment—is offered. A Senior Fair, with a local television personality as guest speaker, is a major highlight. Each of twenty-eight branches, the main library, and the mobile services branch has a Closed Circuit Television Video display (CCTV) for patron use.

ADDITIONAL INFORMATION

The People's University on Wheels offers seniors access to the latest books, CDs, videos, and DVDs. The library was the 2001 winner of the American Library Association, Association of Specialized and Cooperating Library Agencies, and National Organization on Disability Award, which recognizes libraries that strive to make their libraries and collections available to persons with disabilities.

NUMBER OF PARTICIPANTS

More than 5,000

COST

Staff and materials

FUNDING SOURCE

The bulk of the money for the purchase of the People's University on Wheels came from the Judd Foundation. Funding for the CCTVs came from various endowment funds, including the Young and Wickwire Funds. The general operating budget supports the programs.

DURATION

The Senior Fair is an annual program; the computer classes and other programs are ongoing.

PREPARATION TIME

The Seniors' Services Committee spent approximately thirty hours planning the Senior Fair.

COMMENT FROM PARTICIPANT

"After all these years of not asking for any public assistance, I told them that I wanted something from my library, and they delivered, in a big way . . . the library's big blue bus now comes to my apartment complex, and I can choose my own books!"

TIPS/COMMENTS

When the administration buys into a project, it will work. The SeniorsConnect@Cleveland Public Library was administration driven, which translates into added services to the greater-Cleveland-area seniors.

Services to the Aging

LIBRARY

Brooklyn Public Library, New York, population 2.5 million

SENIOR PROGRAM WEBSITE

<http://www.brooklynpubliclibrary.org>

CONTACT FOR SENIOR PROGRAMMING INFORMATION

JoAnn Radioli

PROGRAM DESCRIPTION

A multitude of programs includes book delivery, books by mail, computer classes, and specialized programs like Our Words and Memories and In Other Words. There are also free concerts, informative lectures on a variety of subjects, and book discussions. Additionally, the library supports van service for the Books to Go program, providing deposit collections to 158 senior sites for a combined circulation of 20,000 items per month.

ADDITIONAL INFORMATION

Brooklyn's seniors are ethnically diverse. To respond to the needs of their patrons, the library hosts a series of book discussions and lectures in other languages as well as a book discussion group that uses audiobooks and large-print books.

NUMBER OF PARTICIPANTS

200,000 patrons served annually through this service

COST

Staff time plus other costs, which are not available

FUNDING SOURCE

New York State Coordinated Outreach Services Grant and city and private grants

DURATION

The program has been in existence for twenty-five years; the long-term programs run throughout the year.

PREPARATION TIME

Books by mail requires one part-time worker who spends twenty hours per week to select, pack, and complete the paperwork to get books in the mail and process returns. Books to Go requires forty hours staff time weekly, plus a full-time staff member to ensure that more than 150 senior locations receive a fresh book selection. The Our Words and Memories and Free Events for Older Adults programs vary with the complexity of the programs. Each senior staff assistant spends a minimum of four hours per month per site he or she is responsible for plus two hours on the day of the event per site.

COMMENTS FROM PARTICIPANTS

"Thank you so very much for the marvelous books and videos. Every time I get a pouch, it brightens up my day, my week." "I like the library because it brings many books to our nursing home. I can't wait to make a selection."

TIPS/COMMENTS

Radioli offers several practical tips to ensure success: (1) attract staff who are caring, enjoy working with seniors, and have excellent people skills; (2) be sure marketing material is attractive, informative, and in large print; when appropriate, materials should be translated into other languages; (3) form a senior advisory group that includes seniors as part of the library team; and (4) pool resources of the community organizations that work with seniors.

Stories That Span the Ages

LIBRARY

Normal Public Library, Normal and Bloomington, Illinois, population 100,000

SENIOR PROGRAM WEBSITE

<http://www.normal-library.org>

CONTACTS FOR SENIOR PROGRAMMING INFORMATION

Tori Melican, Children's Services; and Sandy Bush, Adults Services

PROGRAM DESCRIPTION

On an annual basis, the library holds holiday story hours at three area nursing homes. Children and seniors share songs, crafts, and stories.

NUMBER OF PARTICIPANTS

About 40, which includes 20 children and 20 seniors at each nursing home

COST

The program costs about $10 per home.

FUNDING SOURCE

Part of the library budget

DURATION

Each program is thirty to forty-five minutes in length.

PREPARATION TIME

Three to four hours

COMMENTS FROM PARTICIPANTS

The residents love watching the children participate in the story hour, and all who participate feel it is a wonderful experience.

TIPS/COMMENTS

Vivian Carter shares these useful planning and programming tips: (1) learn the stories for the program, and prepare a craft that the children and seniors will make together during the program and leave at the nursing home for the residents to enjoy; (2) call the nursing home's activity director to schedule a date and time. Ten o'clock is a good time, as both residents and children are alert; and (3) call schools and invite them to attend the story hour and explain what the children will be doing. The following programming flow usually works: group song, story (the book should have brightly colored pictures, and all who can see should be shown the pictures), children's group craft, distribution of premade crafts to residents by preschoolers (ensure that each senior has a child interact with him or her), and closing song.

Washington-Centerville Outreach Services

LIBRARY

Washington-Centerville Public Library, city of Centerville and Washington Township, Ohio, population 53,000

SENIOR PROGRAM WEBSITE

<http://www.wcpl.lib.oh.us/adults/seniors.html>

CONTACTS FOR SENIOR PROGRAMMING INFORMATION

Betty K. Pupko or Jane S. Huson

PROGRAM DESCRIPTION

The senior outreach department has a program for everyone. The book clubs (Hithergreen and Page Turners) enable patrons to meet together to discuss plot, theme, characters, their reaction to the book, and more. As an added bonus, residents of the Hithergreen Book Club have become volunteers for the library, selecting and delivering books to home-bound patrons for another library program, the Sunshine Book Delivery service. The Remember When . . . program is a monthly program with guest speakers, focusing on many topics. A relatively new program, WebCat Training, enables staff to train activity directors at facilities with computer access for their residents.

ADDITIONAL INFORMATION

The library also promotes book talks at nursing homes and assisted-living facilities, offering programs at the senior center, Woodbourne Library, Centerville Library, and nine residential senior facilities. The staff member tells the entire story, giving background information as well (e.g., something about the author, historical and regional information relating to the book).

NUMBER OF PARTICIPANTS

Page Turners—25

Remember When . . . —30

Hithergreen Book Club—12

WebCat Training—60 to 90

PREPARATION TIME

Various programs take four to six hours each.

EXTRA MARKETING

Remember When . . . programs are videotaped, and some are shown on a community-access television station.

COSTS

Staff time and refreshments, mileage for off-site programs, and occasionally a speaker's honorarium for the Remember When . . . program

FUNDING SOURCE

Library, senior center book groups, Wal-Mart Seniors Grant

DURATION

All programs are held year-round. Programs held in nursing homes are usually under an hour; in-house programs run slightly longer.

COMMENTS FROM PARTICIPANTS

"It's great to know that the library staff care about me even though I am in the nursing home." "I can't believe I'm still learning about new types of books to read. I'm checking out and reading more books than I did when I was younger."

TIPS/COMMENTS

Choose staff members who are absolutely committed to this program and who genuinely enjoy working with seniors. Staff must realize that, although this target group may be elderly, they are an important, relevant sector in the community. As our fastest-growing demographic group, seniors have much to offer all ages, and they are a resource that should be encouraged into the spotlight.

Web Basics for Seniors

LIBRARY

Davenport Public Library, Davenport, Iowa, population 450,000

SENIOR PROGRAM WEBSITE

<http://www.rbls.lib.il.us/dpl>

CONTACT FOR SENIOR PROGRAMMING INFORMATION

Meg Sarff, Acting Library Director

PROGRAM DESCRIPTION

In addition to supporting a diverse and comprehensive senior Web page, the library promotes computer literacy to their senior patrons through demonstration programs and hands-on computer training. There have been more than fifty classes in the central library, and the library is experimenting with using high schools' media center computer labs. The library supports a bookmobile, which delivers programs and books to Davenport's primary senior activity center. Book talks are done from the bookmobile.

ADDITIONAL INFORMATION

The library's mobile services circulates "Book Club in a Box," a do-it-yourself book discussion group package.

NUMBER OF PARTICIPANTS

Demonstration classes are held for up to 24 participants; hands-on Web training has been for 10 to 24 people, depending on the size of the computer lab.

COST

None. The computer training is provided by grants.

FUNDING SOURCE

Funds for the computer-training lab were provided by grants from Davenport's Riverboat Development Authority and Scott County Regional Authority.

DURATION

The computer classes have been in existence for four years; class length has ranged from one and one-half to two hours each.

PREPARATION TIME

Approximately one hour per week once librarians are trained and have taught the class a couple of times

EXTRA MARKETING

Programs are promoted on the local cable channel.

COMMENT FROM PARTICIPANT

"I feel like I relate better to today's world, because I know what a computer is and am getting better at using it!"

TIPS/COMMENTS

Offer a half-hour tutorial before each class for seniors to come in and practice using a mouse. Demonstration classes require only a teacher, but hands-on classes require helpers. (Davenport uses circulation clerks as helpers.) It's useful to plan classes at least four months (and preferably six months) in advance and publicize them heavily. It helps to call participants a couple of days before the class to remind them of the class.

INDEX

A

A-Prompt, 79
AARP
    and advocacy, 2, 8
    55 Alive program, 41
    handrail guidelines, 24
    lighting recommendations, 18–19
    and marketing, 88
    and programming, 35, 38
    statistics and demographics, 13
accessibility, 5, 17
    to programming sites, 36–37
    to technology, 66–67
    to websites, 76–82
accommodation, 15–16, 17
activity, importance of, 3
adaptive devices, loaning, 54
Adaptive Technology Resource Centre, 79
Advanced Research Projects Agency of
    the U.S. Department of Defense, 71
advertising, free venues, 98
advocacy, 8
Age Wave, 86
ageism, 2–3, 101
AgeVenture, 84
aids, low-vision, 19–21
Albert, Marilyn, 17
Alberta, Canada, 41
alcohol abuse, 17
Alliance for Retired Americans, 8
Almaden Branch Library (San Jose,
    California), 47, 48
Alzheimer's Disease, 4, 40, 58
American Foundation for the Blind
    (AFB), recommendations, 18–19, 22
American Library Association (ALA)
    guidelines for services to older adults,
        4, 28

    lighting recommendations, 18
    White House Conference on Aging
        (1995), 5
American Red Cross, 36
Americans with Disabilities Act (ADA),
    17–18, 22
Arch Assist Palm Support, 24
Area Agency on Aging, 35, 36, 88
ARPANET, 71
assisted-listening devices, 26
assisted-living facilities, 55–56, 60
Association of Small Foundations, 96
audio materials, 21, 44, 56
Aurora Public Library (Colorado), 50

B

baby boomers, 9–10
baskets, "shopping," 25
Beauregard Parish Library (DeRidder,
    Louisiana), 49
"belonging," sense of, 4–5, 60
Berliss-Vincent, Jane, 64–65
Betacom Technologies, 21
BiFolkal, 40, 57
Bobby, 79–80, 81
Book Butler, 25
book discussion groups, 40–41, 43, 45–48,
    56, 60
book holders, 54, 55, 56
book stands, 25, 26
book talks, 40–41, 44–45, 60
bookmobiles, 56–57
books on cassette, 44
Bowman, Jean, 54
Braille, 44
Brooklyn Public Library (New York),
    32
Brown, Candice, 50

Building Elder-Friendlier Communities:
    Opportunities for Creative
    Grantmaking, 93
business community, 36
Butler, Robert, 2

C

CAMLS (library consortium, Ohio),
    60
Canadian Centre for Philanthropy, 96
Canadian Library Association (CLA)
    guidelines for services to older adults,
        4, 28
    lighting recommendations, 18
Canadian National Institute for the Blind
    (CNIB), 21, 44
CARP (Canada's Association for the
    Fifty-Plus), 2, 8, 13
carts, 54–55
Center for Accessible Technology, 64
Center for Applied Special Technology
    (CAST), 79
Center for Technology and Disability
    (University of Washington), 54
Center for the Book, 96
Chicago Public Library, 47, 86
Cleveland Public Library, 34, 43, 47, 49,
    56
Closed Circuit Television Video displays
    (CCTVs), 18, 20–21, 26, 57
coalitions, 96
cognitive changes, 16–17, 31
Collier County Public Library (Naples,
    Florida), 60, 72
colors, 77, 88
community events, 89
community groups, 36, 97
computer skills, 11

computers, 63–73
    and intergenerational programs, 39
    introducing to seniors, 67–68
    and leisure time, 8
    library website as training tool, 71–72
    off-site training, 60–61
    outfitting components for seniors,
        64–66
    training seniors, 40, 68–69
    what to teach, 69–71
Computers for Living Forum, 82
content
    of marketing materials, 84
    of websites, 78, 79, 81
cooperation. *See* partnerships
corporations, 96
cultural needs, 32

D
databases, library, 70
Demko, David, 3, 84
demographics, 7, 12, 13, 64, 101
descriptive videos, 44
desks, 22, 66
dexterity, 16, 24
Digital Opportunity Program for Seniors,
    98
direct mail campaigns, 89
discrimination, 2, 32, 33
diversity
    of audiences (program), 57
    of book club readership, 60
    in computer skills, 63
    ethnic, 8–9, 32
    of nursing home residents, 50–51
    at senior centers, 55
    among seniors, 8–9, 101

E
e-mail, 69–70
E-Z Reacher, 24–25
eBay, 98
educational programming, 38
ElderSong, 40, 57
ElderVision, 63
emotional changes, 31
entertainment programs, 37
ethnic diversity, 8–9, 32
ethnic needs, 32

F
55 Alive program, 41
film series, 37
finances, of seniors, 7–8
FitzGerald, Anne, 86
Flint Public Library (Michigan),
    71, 82
flyers, 36, 91
FM hearing assistance systems, 22
fonts, 77

forums, 82
Foundation Center, 94, 95, 96
foundations, 92–93, 95–96
Fountain of Age, 2
Friedan, Betty, 2
Friedland, Robert, 4
funding, 5, 8, 36
    and community groups, 36, 97
    foundations, 92–93, 95–96
    government funds and assistance, 96
    grants, 92–96
    national funding organizations, 96
    nonfinancial contributions, 97–98
    websites for, 96, 98
Funding across the Ages, 93
furnishings, 22–23

G
glare, 18, 21, 29, 64
goals, 36
Gollop, Claudia, 4–5
Good Old Days, 40, 58
goods and services, 97
Gordon, Rachel Singer, 68
government agencies, 98
government funds and assistance, 96
Grantmakers in Aging (GIA), 93
grants, 92–93
    government, 96
    proposals, 93–95
    successful, 95
    themes, 96
    websites for, 96
Gray Panthers, 2, 8, 35, 88
guidelines
    for services to older adults, 4, 28–32
    for website design, 78
    for workstations, 64–66
GuideStar, 96

H
Hamrick, Sarah, 30
handrails, 24
hearing impairments, 16, 21, 29–30, 46
hobbies, 38
homebound, 49, 56
honesty, 90
Hooked on Books, Ltd., 45
housing, senior, 55–56

I
"Improving Library Services to the Older
    Multicultural Community," 4
institutions and ageism, 2
intergenerational programs, 38–39
Internal Revenue Service (IRS) Tax
    Counseling for the Elderly, 98
International Federation of Library
    Associations and Institutions
    (IFLA), 4

Internet
    fallibility of, 68
    introducing to seniors, 67–68, 70–71
    seniors' use of, 40, 63, 64

J
James V. Brown Library (Williamsport,
    Pennsylvania), 60
jargon, 81, 84, 90
Josey, E. J., 4–5

K
keyboards, 65
keys, 24
King County Library System, 25, 26, 54
Kokomo-Howard County Library
    (Indiana), 56

L
language, 81, 83, 84
language skills, 31–32
large-print materials
    availability of, 21
    for book discussion groups, 44
    keyboards, 65
    for low literacy skills, 32
    for outreach patrons, 54–55, 56
    promotional, 36
Lee County Library System (Florida), 25,
    26
leisure time, 8, 38
lending libraries, 44
lever handles, 24
Library of Congress, 40
Library Services and Technology Act
    (LSTA) grants, 96
lighting, 18–19, 64, 66
links libraries, senior, 81
literacy, 31–32, 84
Live Long and Like It Club, 34
loan programs (for accessibility devices),
    25–26
local organizations, 13
Lynch, Mary Jo, 6

M
magnifiers, 18, 19, 26, 54, 55, 56
mailing lists, 89
manners, 28
marketing, 8, 36, 83, 88
McWhirter-Heaton, Wanda, 49
media, 2, 27
Medina County District Library (Ohio),
    26, 56
mice (computer), 65–66, 69, 78
Microsoft accessibility programs, 66–67
Microsoft Word, 71
minorities, 4–5, 9
mission statements, 28, 36, 49, 93
mobility, 16, 24, 30–31

monitors, 64–65
Monroe County Public Library
    (Bloomington, Indiana), 56
mouse skills. *See* mice (computer)
MouseKeys, 67
Mueller, James, 19
multicultural populations, 4
Multnomah County Library (Portland,
    Oregon), 72–73
music programs, 37, 57–58

N
National Cancer Institute, 79
National Center for Education Statistics,
    92
National Council on Aging, 96
National Endowment for the Humanities,
    96
National Institute on Aging, 2
National Library of Canada, 18
National Library Service for the Blind
    and Physically Handicapped (NLS),
    5, 21, 44, 55
National Literacy Survey, 84
National Storytelling Network, 96
Natke, Nora Jane, 45
needs, basic human, 27–28
New York Public Library, 58
news media, 90
newsletters, 89
newspapers, 89
Nielsen, Jakob, 80
non-English-speakers, 84
nonfinancial contributions, 97
NonprofitsCan.org, 96
"Northcoast Neighbors Share a Book,"
    60
nursing homes, outreach to
    book talks and book discussions, 60
    diversity of residents, 50–51
    initial contact, 51–53
    service contracts, 52–53
    staff preparation, 51
    visiting skills, 54

O
Older Adults Month, 41
Older Women's League (OWL), 8
online catalog, 70
organizations, national funding, 96
Ott, Harold, 5–6
outreach services, 31, 49–61
    to assisted-living facilities, 55–56
    carts, 54–55
    and community partnerships, 50
    community reading, 60
    computer training, off-site, 60–61
    to homebound, 56
    mobile services, 56–57
    to nursing homes, 31, 50–54

planning for, 50
programming, 57, 60
to senior centers, 31, 55
to senior housing, 55–56
vans, 54–55
volunteers for, 50

P
page turners, 25, 56
Palmore, Erdman, 2
Park, Denise, 17
partnerships, 5, 36, 50, 88–89
pens, easy grip, 25, 26
"People's University on Wheels," 56–57
Pepper, Jeff, 63
personal listening devices, 21–22
Pew Institute, 64
physical changes, 15–16
Pik Stik Reacher, 24–25
planning, program, 13, 36–37, 50
Pletz, Jim, 47
policies, 5
prejudices, 2, 33
prescription drug abuse, 17
print media, 84
privacy, 54
programming
    planning, 13, 36–37, 50
    types of, 37–40
promotional materials, 90
Public Broadcasting Service (PBS), 40
public domain literature websites, 44
"Public Library Service to the
    Homebound," 50

R
radio, 90
reachers, 54
Reader's Digest, 58
reading aloud, 58
recorded formats, 44, 55
Regional Library for the Blind and
    Physically Handicapped, 21
relay services, 22, 30
Reminisce, 40, 58
reminiscence, 39–40, 55, 57, 60
Retired and Senior Volunteer Program
    (RSVP), 97–98
Roberts, Bruce, 39
Rostamizadeh, Suzanne, 48

S
safety, 17, 24
scooters, 25
screen magnification programs, 66
screen reading programs, 66
screening of volunteers, 50, 56
scrolling, 69
seating, 22
Secret Life of the Brain, 17

senior advisory boards, 35–36, 88
senior centers, 55, 60
Senior Computer Club, 69
Senior Days, 89
senior services coordinators, 28
Senior Volunteer Corp, 98
SeniorNet, 47, 98
Seniors' Education Centre, University
    Extension, University of Regina,
    64–66
sensitivity, 27
service contracts, 52
sexual orientation, 9
ShowSounds, 67
similarities, among seniors, 4–5, 13
skills, refining, 38
Soas, Amir, 3
social changes, 31
software, 66–67
Solitaire, 69
SoundSentry, 67
Spagnoli, Cathy, 40, 58–59
special media, 44
speech communication impairments, 30
SPRY (Setting Priorities for Retirement
    Years) Foundation, 81
staff
    outreach to nursing homes, 51
    seniors as, 32–33
    training of, 27, 28, 33, 50
stereotypes, 2, 27, 33
StickKeys, 67
Stoke-on-Tent Libraries, 40
"Story-Teller's Story," 96
storytelling, 40, 58
switches, 24

T
Teaching the Internet in Libraries, 68
telecommunication devices for the deaf
    (TDDs), 21, 22, 30
telecommunications industry, 96
Telecommunications Research Group
    (TNRG), 67, 69
teletypewriters (TTYs), 22, 30
television, 90
theme grants, 96
Thorshiem, Howard, 39
touch, 54
training (staff), 27, 28, 33, 50
transportation, 50

U
Universal Design, 17
U.S. Administration on Aging (AoA), 8–9,
    13
U.S. Census, 13
U.S. National Commission on Libraries
    and Information Science, 5
UsableNet, 80

V

Vacaville Public Library (California), 47
vans, 54–55
vision statements, 28, 36, 93
visual impairments, 16
    accommodating, 18, 66, 71
    and print materials, 86
    serving seniors with, 29
    and website design, 77
volunteers
    baby boomers as, 10
    and computer training, 69
    and leisure time, 8
    and outreach, 50, 56
    for programs, 98
    screening, 50, 56
    as translators, 84, 86

W

Wal-Mart Foundation, 97
website, library
    design guidelines, 78
    evaluating, 79–81
    as instructional resource, 71–72
    usability of, 79
websites, Internet
    accessibility of, 76–82
    for book discussion, 47
    for fund-raising, 96, 98
    links to and from other agencies,
        89–90
    for public domain literature, 44
wheelchairs, 25
White House Conference on Aging
    (1995), 5

Williamson, Kirsty, 67
Windows, 70
word of mouth, 90
word processing, 71
Workplace Workbook 2.0, 19
workstations, 22–23, 64–66
World Wide Web Consortium (W3C),
    79
World Wide Web (WWW)
    fallibility of, 68
    guidelines, 79
    online book discussion groups, 45
    teaching, 71

Y

YMCA and YWCA, 36, 88

Barbara T. Mates is head of the Library for the Blind and Physically Handicapped at the Cleveland Public Library. A member of ALA's Association of Specialized and Cooperative Library Agencies (ASCLA), Mates has served on several ASCLA committees and is chair of the Outreach and Special Services Committee of the Ohio Library Council. She is the author of *Adaptive Technology for the Internet: Making Electronic Resources Accessible to All* (ALA, 2000) and "Accessibility Guidelines for Electronic Resources" (*Library Technology Reports*, 2001). She has presented papers at the ALA, Ohio Library Conference, and Computers in Libraries and conducted workshops across North America. Mates was the recipient of the ASCLA Francis Joseph Campbell Award in 2001.